"*Surrender to Christ for Mission* is a masterful guide to the extraordinarily rich, though sometimes underappreciated, French spiritual traditions of the 17th through the 19th centuries. This collection of well-written and reader-friendly essays, authored by a team of distinguished specialists in the field of Christian spirituality, offers a fresh, timely, and judicious introduction to these traditions' major figures and themes that makes this book an essential resource for both the scholar and the general reader."

— Joseph F. Chorpenning, OSFS
    President, International Commission for Salesian Studies (ICSS)

"This helpful collection makes available in straightforward style the many dimensions of traditional French spirituality for today's reader. Through both historical and thematic approaches, and with special attention to mission to the marginalized, it lays out the unity and diversity within the movement."

— Carolyn Osiek, RSCJ
    Archivist, Society of the Sacred Heart
    United States-Canada Province

Surrender to CHRIST for Mission

French Spiritual Traditions

Edited by
Philip Sheldrake

LITURGICAL PRESS
Collegeville, Minnesota

www.litpress.org

1   2   3   4   5   6   7   8   9

Library of Congress Cataloging-in-Publication Data

Names: Sheldrake, Philip, editor.
Title: Surrender to Christ for mission : French spiritual traditions / edited by
    Philip Sheldrake.
Description: Collegeville, Minnesota : Liturgical Press, 2018. | Includes
    bibliographical references.
Identifiers: LCCN 2018010482 (print) | LCCN 2018036201 (ebook) |
    ISBN 9780814687871 (ebook) | ISBN 9780814687864
Subjects: LCSH: Catholic Church—France—History. | Spirituality—Catholic
    Church—History. | Spirituality—France—History. | Spiritual life—Catholic
    Church—History.
Classification: LCC BX1528 (ebook) | LCC BX1528 .S87 2018 (print) |
    DDC 282/.44—dc23
LC record available at https://lccn.loc.gov/2018010482

CONTENTS

CONTRIBUTORS

Thomas A. Donlan currently teaches at Brophy College Prep high school in Phoenix, Arizona. He completed a master's in religious studies at Yale University (2004) and a PhD in history at University of Arizona (2011) within the division of late medieval and Reformation studies. His dissertation examined the religious culture of *douceur* (gentleness) promoted by François de Sales in the midst of the French Wars of Religion. He continues to study violence and nonviolence in the history of French Catholicism.

Mary Frohlich, RSCJ, is professor of spirituality at Catholic Theological Union in Chicago. In addition to teaching, she writes and leads workshops on Carmelite spirituality, spirituality as an academic discipline, and ecospirituality. Her current research interests include mystical dimensions of "conversion to the Earth," the psychology of spiritual transformation, and methodological issues in spirituality. She also enjoys gardening, hiking, and leading outdoor retreats.

Tom McKenna, CM, has been a member of the Congregation of the Mission since 1963. He grew up in Brooklyn, New York, and was ordained in 1970. He spent fifteen years in seminary work and earned a doctorate in systematic theology (1982) from the Catholic University of America. For ten years he taught spirituality as a tenured member of the Department of Theology at St. John's University. Fr. McKenna has published a book on Vincent de Paul as well as articles in various theological journals. He has also been involved in retreat work both nationally and internationally. In 2008 he taught Christology at Tanzaga University, Nairobi, Kenya. After that he taught in the theology department at Niagara University. Since 2012 Fr. McKenna has served as provincial director of the St. Louise Province of the Daughters of Charity and resides in St. Louis, Missouri.

Mary Christine Morkovsky, CDP, is a sister of Divine Providence of San Antonio, Texas. She earned an MA and a PhD in philosophy and has taught for over forty years in universities and seminaries. She is the author of two histories of congregations of women religious and an article on women religious in Texas in the nineteenth century. She has cotranslated the "Directory" of her congregation from French into English and has translated Enrique Dussel's *Filosofía de la Liberación* from Spanish and letters from her uncle (among the first students at the diocesan seminary in San Antonio) from Czech.

Ronald Rolheiser, OMI, is a member of the Missionary Oblates of Mary Immaculate and president of the Oblate School of Theology, San Antonio, Texas. Rolheiser is a theologian, professor, and award-winning author. Apart from his academic knowledge in systematic theology and philosophy, he has become a popular speaker in contemporary spirituality and religion and the secular world. He writes a weekly column that is carried in over seventy newspapers around the world. His latest work is *Sacred Fire: A Vision for a Deeper Human and Christian Maturity.*

Frank Santucci, OMI, was born in South Africa where he ministered as a priest in education, religious formation, and parish ministry for seventeen years. He was subsequently based in Rome and Aix-en-Provence for twenty years and worked extensively as an animator of the Oblate charism and spirituality in countries where the Oblates of Mary Immaculate are based. He holds a BA in English literature from the University of South Africa and a licentiate and doctorate in theology from the Lateran University (Claretianum Institute for Theology of Consecrated Life). Besides teaching spirituality and theology courses, Fr. Santucci is a spiritual director at Oblate School of Theology and Assumption Seminary and a retreat preacher. He has published many articles, is on the editorial board of two OMI publications, and recently became the first Kusenberger Chair of Oblate Studies at Oblate School of Theology.

Raymond Sickinger has been a member of the Providence College faculty since 1974. He has served in a variety of teaching and administrative positions. Dr. Sickinger is currently professor of History and Public and Community Service Studies. He currently serves as chair of the Department of History and Classics. His research interests revolve around the Nazi era in German history, the connection between superstition and folklore in popular culture, and the impact of faith and service in the context of Frédéric Ozanam, founder of the Society of St. Vincent de Paul (SVP), a worldwide Catholic lay organization that serves those in need. Dr. Sickinger has been an active member of the SVP since 1985. He is currently a member of the National Board of Directors and has produced materials and videos for the formation of the society's members and leaders.

Philip Sheldrake is director of the Institute for the Study of Contemporary Spirituality at Oblate School of Theology, San Antonio, Texas. He is also senior research associate of the Von Hügel Institute at St. Edmund's College, University of Cambridge, and senior research fellow at Westcott House in the Cambridge Theological Federation. Philip Sheldrake trained in history and theology at the universities of Oxford and London and was awarded the DD (higher doctorate) by the University of Oxford in 2015. Previously he taught at University of London and subsequently at University of Wales then at Durham University. He has also held visiting professorships in Ireland and the USA. He is the author or editor of fifteen books. He has taught and written extensively on Christian spirituality and on spirituality more generally. He is a past president of the international Society for the Study of Christian Spirituality.

Ronald D. Witherup, PSS, is superior general of the Society of St. Sulpice and lives in Paris. A former academic dean and professor of Sacred Scripture, he previously served as provincial of the United States Sulpician Province. He frequently gives lectures and workshops around the world on biblical and theological themes. He is an active member of the Catholic Biblical Association (CBA), the Society of Biblical Literature (SBL), and the Catholic Theological Society of America (CTSA). He is the author of many publications, most recently *Scripture at Vatican II: Exploring Dei Verbum* and *Paul, Proclaiming Christ Crucified.*

Wendy M. Wright is professor emerita of theology at Creighton University and affiliate faculty at the Institute for the Study of Contemporary Spirituality at Oblate School of Theology in San Antonio, Texas. She earned her PhD in Late Medieval/Early Modern Contemplative Studies in the Program in Interdisciplinary Studies, University of California at

Santa Barbara. In 2000 she received an honorary doctorate from De Sales University for her seminal work in the Salesian spiritual tradition. Professor Wright's areas of expertise include the history of Christian spirituality, family spirituality, and the Catholic devotional tradition. Her scholarship has focused on the Salesian spiritual tradition founded by François de Sales and Jeanne de Chantal. Wright is the author of fifteen books, the most recent of which is *The Lady of the Angels and Her City: A Marian Pilgrimage.* Her interest in the practice of Christian spirituality has led to another eighty articles in pastoral publications. She has cohosted a weekly Creighton University podcast, "Catholic Comments," with her colleague Dr. John O'Keefe.

PREFACE

The purpose of this multiauthor book is partly to celebrate the Bicentenary of the Missionary Oblates of Mary Immaculate (1816–2016), founded by St. Eugène de Mazenod, and an important expression of French spirituality—particularly its emphasis on mission to the poor. The chapters of the book are mainly based on contributions to an international conference on French Spiritual Traditions held at Oblate School of Theology, San Antonio, Texas, in November 2016 to mark this Bicentenary. I had the great honor to be asked to chair this conference.

However, equally importantly, this book also aims to make accessible to the increasing numbers of people interested in Christian spirituality the riches of the important family of French spiritual traditions that appeared between the seventeenth and the nineteenth centuries. This family of spiritual traditions has been significantly underestimated in conventional histories of Christian spirituality and deserves to be better known.

The intended audience for this book is both an intelligent general readership and also students who wish to understand better the wisdom and resources of Christian spirituality.

In particular I wish to express my gratitude to Fr. Ronald Rolheiser, President of Oblate School of Theology, for inviting me to chair the international conference and then to edit the book that arose from this. I am also grateful to the conference speakers for their stimulating presentations and for subsequently turning their spoken presentations into written chapters. I also owe a debt of gratitude to Dr. Wendy Wright, a notable scholar of French spirituality, who advised me extensively on this book and on my introduction to it. Thanks are likewise due to Benjamin PowerGriffin, a current doctoral student in Christian spirituality at Oblate School of Theology, for his assistance with the creation of an Index for this book. Finally, I want to thank Hans Christoffersen of Liturgical Press for agreeing to publish the conference proceedings and then for overseeing the project.

Philip Sheldrake
Director of the Institute for the Study of Contemporary Spirituality
Oblate School of Theology

INTRODUCTION

Philip Sheldrake

The origins of this book lie in an international conference focused on French spiritual traditions held at Oblate School of Theology, San Antonio, Texas, in November 2016. This celebrated the Bicentenary of the Missionary Oblates of Mary Immaculate (OMI) founded in 1816 in the aftermath of the French Revolution by Eugène de Mazenod, French noble, priest, bishop, and ultimately canonized saint. The conference underlined the great variety, significance, and depth of the French spiritual traditions between the seventeenth and nineteenth centuries. However, it was also clear that these rich traditions have been underestimated within the wider history of Christian spirituality.

One of the most striking features of French spiritual traditions is their strong emphasis on mission to the poor. As the French Jesuit scholar of mysticism and spirituality, Michel de Certeau, underlined this was not merely a question of serving the poor or ministering to deprived people but also involved solidarity with them and a process of learning from them. De Certeau suggested that any ambition by the Catholic Church after the Reformation and the Council of Trent to recover its position as the dominant social and cultural force in the Western world ultimately failed. He spoke of how, as a result, "a prophetic faith organized itself into a minority within the secularised state."[1] Christian spiritual and mystical traditions moved prophetically to the margins. One aspect of this was the way that some members of social and religious elites (for example, the circle of Cardinal de Bérulle in seventeenth-century France) actively

---

[1] Michel de Certeau, *The Mystic Fable*, vol. 1, English trans. (Chicago: University of Chicago Press, 1992), 299.

sought to associate themselves with "the little people"—the poor and the illiterate. In de Certeau's words, many people of spiritual and mystical depth sought to leave behind the traditional sources of authority "to turn to the exegesis of 'wild' voices."[2]

It is perhaps partly as a result of this shift of perspective and move away from conventional centers of religious power that the French spiritual traditions placed such an emphasis on the themes of "abandonment," "self-emptying," and "surrender." As the chapters in this book will richly illustrate, in addition to service of the poor and the theme of "surrender," French spiritual traditions also manifested a Christ-centered mysticism, often focused on the theme of "the heart," as well as an increasingly important role for communities of women, an emphasis on the importance of the education of young people, and the development of an active lay spirituality.[3]

Seventeenth-Century Foundations

I wish briefly to try to place French spiritualities in context and to outline significant schools of thought and practice within the tradition. As a foundation, seventeenth-century France witnessed a striking range of Catholic spiritual reform movements. Some of this was influenced by aspects of Ignatian spirituality and Carmelite mysticism. However, French spiritual traditions also had their own particular flavors. It should be emphasised that there was not a single "French School" of spirituality but several distinctive trends. The three best-known traditions were associated with François de Sales (1567–1622) and Jeanne de Chantal (1572–1641), with Pierre de Bérulle (1575–1629), and also with Vincent de Paul (1580–1660) and Louise de Marillac (1591–1660).

François de Sales was partly inspired by the Spiritual Exercises of Ignatius Loyola. In his *Introduction to the Devout Life*, de Sales wrote one of the most popular spiritual classics of all time. Its influence spread beyond the confines of the Roman Catholic Church—for example to the

---

[2] See Michel de Certeau, *Heterologies: Discourse on the Other*, English trans. (Minneapolis: University of Minnesota Press), chap. 6, "Mystic Speech," esp. 86–87.

[3] For summary overviews of the spiritual writers and figures that follow, see Philip Sheldrake, *Spirituality: A Brief History*, 2nd ed. (Oxford/Malden, MA: Wiley-Blackwell, 2013), esp. chap. 5, 137–40; chap. 6, 148–50, 159–61; and chap. 7, 176–77.

seventeenth-century Church of England. A Savoyard aristocrat, François originally trained as a lawyer before becoming a priest. Although he became Bishop of Geneva (1602) he was never able to reside in that resolutely Calvinist city. He encouraged Catholic renewal by means of popular preaching, by reforming the clergy, and by developing a thoughtful lay spirituality. De Sales had a deep friendship with Jeanne de Chantal, a widowed baroness, who went on to found the Order of the Visitation. Together they developed a spiritual vision suited to women and men in every context, not least the everyday world. De Sales encouraged spiritual direction for lay people and, while he appreciated the contemplative tradition, he also taught the service of neighbor, particularly the poor. Salesian spirituality emphasised God in creation and God's love for all humanity and desire to forgive. An important theme was "the heart" where the heart of Christ mediated God to human hearts. The spirituality of François de Sales and Jeanne de Chantal was warm while avoiding sentimentality. Also, despite the focus on humility, the Salesian approach was somewhat different from the austerity of Pierre de Bérulle's notion of "servitude."[4]

In the mid-nineteenth century there was a major revival of Salesian spirituality, expressed in a new family of male and female communities plus lay associates founded by or inspired by the Italian priest Giovanni Bosco, popularly known as Don Bosco. There was a particularly strong concern for work with disadvantaged youth.

On a different note, Pierre de Bérulle founded the French Oratory (inspired by the Italian Philip Neri) which consisted of communities of priests under an overall superior who engaged in preaching, running schools, and reform of the clergy. Bérulle was also a sophisticated theologian who developed a Christ-centered, incarnational spirituality.

While Bérulle was educated by the Jesuits and his spirituality echoed the Christocentrism of Ignatius Loyola, his spiritual teachings need to be distinguished in important ways from the Ignatian tradition. His mixture of Dionysian mysticism and Trinitarian theology led him to teach that Christians are drawn into the glory of God-as-Trinity through the

---

[4] See Francis de Sales, *Introduction to the Devout Life* (New York: Doubleday, 1982); also P-M Thibert, ed., *Francis de Sales & Jane de Chantal: Letters of Spiritual Direction* (New York: Paulist, 1988); and Wendy M. Wright, *Heart Speaks to Heart: The Salesian Tradition* (London: Darton Longman & Todd/Maryknoll: Orbis, 2004).

"servitude" or self-emptying of Christ. By God-in-Christ's "humiliation" in becoming human and then by suffering death, humans were granted access to the life of God. The appropriate human response was self-abasement or an abandonment of self before God's majesty. This developed into a notion of "spiritual servitude" to God's will.[5]

One of the most notable disciples of Bérulle was Jean-Jacques Olier (1608–57) who founded the Society of St. Sulpice (or Sulpicians), a voluntary company of priests who ran seminaries and sought to improve the spiritual formation of diocesan clergy. Less austere than Bérulle, Olier emphasised personal experience of Christ and the role of the Spirit in uniting us to Christ. He encouraged frequent communion, promoted affectivity in prayer, and had mystical sensibilities.

In passing, other important figures in seventeenth-century French spirituality include Jean Eudes, Louis Grignion de Montfort, and Jean-Baptiste de la Salle. De la Salle, another nobleman, was ordained, gained a doctorate in theology and, influenced by aspects of Christian humanism, founded the teaching institute of the Brothers of the Christian Schools (De la Salle Brothers).

The third well-known French spiritual tradition originated with Vincent de Paul (1580–1660) and Louise de Marillac (1591–1660). Unlike de Bérulle and de Sales, Vincent de Paul came from a poor background. However, he was ordained and become a royal chaplain. Eventually, some challenging experiences, not least being captured by pirates and being enslaved for a time, as well as the spirit of François de Sales, led Vincent to identify with the poor and to dedicate his life to them as well as to slaves and victims of war. At the heart of his socially engaged spirituality lay union with God through serving Christ in the poor. The medium for spreading this spirit was a community of priests, the Congregation of the Mission (or Vincentians), and a community of women founded with Louise de Marillac known as the Daughters of Charity. Vincent's vision was also expressed in the development of lay confraternities dedicated to helping the poor in their homes.

These lay confraternities were the forerunners of the famous Society of St. Vincent de Paul (SVP) founded in the nineteenth century by the scholar and Sorbonne professor of Jewish ancestry, Frédéric Ozanam

---

[5] See William M. Thompson, ed., *Bérulle and the French School: Selected Writings* (New York: Paulist, 1989).

(1813–53). The Society continues to flourish today as a large international voluntary organization of women and men dedicated to offering material assistance to the poor and needy. Basically Ozanam was a key figure in the emergence during the nineteenth century of a distinctive lay spirituality of ministry and service. In recent times, the SVP has accepted members from beyond the Roman Catholic Church.[6]

An Eighteenth-Century Expression?
Jean-Pierre de Caussade

In terms of the eighteenth century, while French Catholicism during this period was often influenced by rigorist tendencies, the inspiration of seventeenth-century spiritualities still lingered on. For example, the Jesuit Jean-Pierre de Caussade was assumed for many years to be the author of *L'Abandon à la Providence Divine,* variously translated as *Abandonment to Divine Providence* or *The Sacrament of the Present Moment.* De Caussade was relatively unknown during his lifetime. From 1728 he acted as chaplain to a community of Visitation nuns in Nancy. In 1739 he left Nancy to become a Jesuit superior and ended his life as a spiritual director at the Jesuit house in Toulouse. In recent years a series of scholars have reassessed the attribution of *Abandonment to Divine Providence* to de Caussade. The 2005 critical edition by the French Jesuit Dominique Salin is clear that de Caussade did not write the work. That said, the book has remained a popular spiritual classic. It teaches a kind of mysticism of the everyday based on self-giving ("abandonment") to God in the course of daily life. Prayer is one of simple attentiveness and waiting on God. There are some echoes in the work of Ignatius Loyola, the Carmelite mystics, and François de Sales.[7]

---

[6] See F. Ryan and J. Rybolt, eds., *Vincent de Paul & Louise de Marillac: Rules, Conferences and Writing* (New York: Paulist, 1995).

[7] For an up-to-date review of the debates about authorship see Wendy M. Wright, "Abandonment to Providence and the 'Caussadian Corpus,'" in *A Companion to Jesuit Mysticism,* ed. Robert A. Maryks (Leiden: Brill, 2017). Available English translations still tend to attribute the work to Jean-Pierre de Caussade. See, for example, the translation by Kitty Muggeridge, *The Sacrament of the Present Moment* (San Francisco: Harper, 1982, reissued 2009).

Postrevolutionary French Spirituality

After the upheavals of the French Revolution it was understandable that French Catholicism during the nineteenth century was deeply affected by an emphasis on reconstruction. This placed more value on the restoration of Church institutions than on the development of new forms of spiritual wisdom that engaged with social and cultural realities. However, despite this, there were significant positive developments. Apart from the new Salesian family and the Society of St. Vincent de Paul, already mentioned, there was the restoration of the French Dominicans by Henri Lacordaire and of reformed Benedictines at Solesmes by Prosper Guéranger. A number of new religious communities were also founded dedicated to mission to the poor or to education. One example is the Missionary Oblates of Mary Immaculate (OMI) founded in 1816 by Eugène de Mazenod (1782–1861). Another important example is the women's community known as the Religious of the Sacred Heart (or *Religieuses du Sacré-Cœur de Jésus*: RSCJ) founded by Madeleine-Sophie Barat in 1800. The community continues to play a significant international educational role at high school and university levels. The important role of women in the tradition will be explored in one of the chapters of this book.

Popular piety also increased in prominence and was characterised by an emphasis on miracles and visions. There were several notable reports of apparitions of the Virgin Mary. The ones at Lourdes (1858) to Bernadette Soubirous (1844–79) were the origin of the major center of pilgrimage, especially for sick people. This continues to the present day. As with many visionaries in earlier centuries, the reported apparitions acted as the spiritual empowerment and authorization of someone whose social and religious status was otherwise marginal. Apart from being only fourteen years of age when she reported her visions, Bernadette also came from a poor family. She subsequently worked with the sick at a local hospital and eventually joined a branch of the Sisters of Charity. Her notebooks reveal a deep spirituality of self-donation to God and to neighbor in the spirit of classic French spirituality.

A particularly interesting late nineteenth-century figure in the French spiritual tradition was the Carmelite nun, Thérèse of Lisieux (1873–97). She will be explored in two later chapters in this book. It is worth noting that some commentators believe that after her death her life and spiritual image was "edited" to promote a simplified version of Thérèse. Her spiritual autobiography, *Story of a Soul,* became an international best seller prior to Vatican II. In recent times, a more complex Thérèse has emerged. This reveals a figure of deep spiritual substance.[8] Thérèse entered the Lisieux Carmel at age fifteen and lived there for less than ten years before dying of tuberculosis. Her full writings reveal a close attention to Scripture, particularly the gospels and St. Paul.

Thérèse's spirituality is notable for the concept of "the little way"—a version of the theme of "abandonment" or self-emptying that was characteristic of French spiritualities since the seventeenth century. In Thérèse this is marked by two special features. First, there is a sense of dependence on God in simple trust or "spiritual childhood." Second, there is a spirituality of finding God in the pains and pleasures of each day. This "little way" offered a spirituality of small actions which influenced many people who sought a credible spiritual framework for everyday existence. In addition, Thérèse had a deep sense of sharing in the Church's mission. At one point she sought to volunteer for a foundation in Vietnam and also corresponded with priest missionaries. Thérèse's last period of life was marked not only by illness but by spiritual darkness, a "night of nothingness." There she battled with God's silence and the possibility that her faith was an illusion. However, Thérèse finally broke through to an intensity of mystical engagement with each moment characterized by the desire to love.

As a contrast to Thérèse, a final brief example of the rich theme of "abandonment" in French spirituality is expressed by Charles de Foucauld (1858–1916). Like so many key personalities in the French spiritual traditions, Charles-Eugène de Foucauld was a member of an aristocratic family. During the first part of his life he was nonreligious and something of a hedonist as well as an army officer. After leaving the army he spent time as an explorer in Morocco and then on his return to France in 1886 experienced a religious reconversion under the influence of the eccentric spiritual guide, Abbé Huvelin. He first tried his vocation as a Cistercian monk and then lived as a hermit-gardener for Poor Clare sisters in Nazareth. Returning to France he was ordained and then moved back to North Africa in 1901. Eventually he settled in the desert of southern Algeria

---

[8] For recent revisionist studies of Thérèse, see Jean-François Six, *Light of the Night: The Last Eighteen Months in the Life of Thérèse of Lisieux* (London: SCM, 1996); and by way of contrast also Constance Fitzgerald, "The Mission of Thérèse of Lisieux," *The Way Supplement* 89 (Summer 1997): 74–96.

and led a solitary contemplative life among the Tuareg people seeking to serve their material needs while not seeking to convert them from Islam. His spiritual life was based on eucharistic devotion and meditative scriptural prayer. Tragically, de Foucauld was killed by Bedouins in 1916 during an uprising against French colonial rule. An explicit aspect of de Foucauld's spiritual vision was the theme of "abandonment" to God—very much in the spirit of earlier French spiritual movements. After his death, Frère Charles de Jesus, as he was known, became the inspiration for new semi-monastic movements such as the Little Brothers and Sisters of Jesus who live in small contemplative groups among the poor while supporting themselves by ordinary work.

This Book

As a significant contribution to promoting the French traditions of spirituality this book offers ten illuminating chapters. The book is divided into two sections. Part 1 includes three foundational chapters. First, Wendy Wright, the well-known scholar of French spirituality from Creighton University, opens by offering an overview of the various French traditions. In her "Abandoned for Love: The Gracious Legacy of French Spiritual Traditions," she underlines that the period from the seventeenth to nineteenth centuries was in one sense the most tumultuous of times. The upheavals of the French social and political landscape during this period profoundly shaped Catholic religious life and practice in ways that continue to exercise influence in the present day. However, the era was also, in another sense, the most ecstatic of times. An astonishing outpouring of missionary activity and spiritual energy was released, directed toward creative renewal. From the chaotic conditions emerged some of the most vibrant and innovative religious communities and some of the most enduring Catholic spiritual traditions. The legacy of this ecstasy is very much still with us in the Christian world today.

In the second chapter, Frank Santucci, OMI, the Kusenberger Chair of Oblate Studies, outlines the contribution of St. Eugène de Mazenod (1782–1861) to French spirituality. In "Surrendering to Christ for Mission: The Transformation of a Young Enthusiast," Santucci explains how de Mazenod became the founder of the Missionary Oblates of Mary Immaculate (1816) and later the Bishop of Marseilles. This chapter explores how de Mazenod's years as a seminarian in St. Sulpice deepened his understanding of the theme of "surrender to Christ" and how this was to be expressed in mission during his years as priest, religious founder and bishop. The notion of "surrender to Christ" was the foundation of de Mazenod's sense of mission to the poor and the abandoned in society.

The final chapter of part 1, "A Distant Mirror: Is the French School of Spirituality Still Relevant?" by Ron Witherup, PSS, the Sulpician Superior General, explores the ongoing relevance of the French school of spirituality, a movement that is often overlooked in treatments of major spiritual trends in the history of Christianity. After outlining the parameters of the discussion, five particular themes are identified as particularly relevant because they make contributions to spiritual traditions in the Church today. Using the writings of Jean-Jacques Olier (including texts never before seen in English), the author comments on five areas treated by this founder of the Sulpicians and major figure of the French school. These are context, pastoral orientation, baptism and the relationship with Jesus Christ, Word and sacrament, and the feminine dimension. The conclusion proposes that the French school of spirituality is indeed still relevant, offering modern Christians a kind of "mirror" in which our contemporary spiritual challenges are still evident.

In part 2 of the book, the chapters address specific themes and personalities within the French tradition of spirituality. First, Wendy Wright, in her chapter "Captured Yet Free: The Rich Symbolism of the Heart in French Spirituality," focuses on devotion to the heart of Christ and the heart of Mary. Because these are key themes in several versions of French spirituality, this opening essay also offers an important key to the traditions overall. Wendy Wright seeks to reread this devotional theme of "the heart" beyond the conventional pieties in order to encompass the deeper and central themes of Christ-centered mysticism, the centrality of God's love, and the imitation of Christ.

In the next chapter, "Oasis of Gentleness in a Desert of Militancy: François de Sales's Contribution to French Catholicism," Thomas Donlan from Brophy College Prep uses the examples of St. François de Sales and St. Jeanne-Françoise de Chantal to delve into what may be thought of as an important spiritual "oasis of gentleness" in the midst of what has otherwise been described as a "desert of asceticism" in French traditions of spirituality.

Then Mary Christine Morkovsky, CDP, from the University of Our Lady of the Lake, San Antonio, in "Women and the French School of

Spirituality," focuses her chapter on how, within French spiritualities from the seventeenth century onward, women play an increasingly important and creative role. Their contribution is richly varied as spiritual teachers, writers, founders of communities, and people active in various forms of ministry, not least with a particular emphasis on education.

Next Tom McKenna, CM, a Provincial Director of the Daughters of Charity, writes about "Saint Vincent de Paul: The Practical Mystic." Using the example of Vincent de Paul, this chapter focuses on the radical understanding of "mission" in French spiritualities from the seventeenth century onward.

The chapter by Raymond Sickinger of Providence College, RI, "Sanctification, Solidarity, and Service: The Lay Spirituality of Antoine Frédéric Ozanam," focuses on the development of lay movements, which was one of the outstanding and striking elements of nineteenth-century French spirituality. He focuses on the notable example of the Society of St. Vincent de Paul, founded in 1833 by Frédéric Ozanam who, as I have already noted, was a Catholic of Jewish ancestry. Sickinger outlines how the Society of St. Vincent de Paul became the first international Catholic lay organization dedicated to serving the poor.

Part 2 concludes with two chapters that focus particularly on the position within French spirituality of Thérèse of Lisieux. First, Mary Frohlich, RSCJ, of the Catholic Theological Union in Chicago offers "Abandonment and Apostolic Charity in Thérèse of Lisieux, Daughter of the French School." This chapter initially explores Thérèse of Lisieux's insights into self-giving service to the poor. The chapter then focuses on a number of variations of these concepts in French spirituality such as self-forgetfulness, a correct understanding of "nothingness" before God, waiting on God, the concept of *disponibilité* and "hiddenness."

Finally, Ronald Rolheiser, OMI, the President of Oblate School of Theology, offers his explanation of the continuing popularity of Thérèse. "Our Perennial Fascination with Thérèse of Lisieux" portrays Thérèse of Lisieux (1873–97) as one of the most popular figures in the overall tradition of French spirituality. Few figures in the history of the Catholic Church have so fired the romantic imagination. However, sadly, that over-romanticism has served to falsely encrust her person and spirituality in a naivety and piety that is often alienating to the critical mind. So, who really was Thérèse of Lisieux? And why has she continued to fascinate both the Christian and the secular mind?

The book then ends with an epilogue, also by Ronald Rolheiser, OMI: *Epilogue: Fragments of Our Conversation—Some Poignant Echoes.* Rolheiser uses the gospel image of the loaves and fishes to explore what the 2016 conference left us with. After Jesus had fed the crowd with the five loaves and two fishes, he asked his disciples to gather up the fragments that had fallen to the ground. This filled twelve baskets. In this epilogue, Ronald Rolheiser asks what were the important fragments that "fell to the ground" during the French spirituality conference? What poignant echoes remain? This brief conclusion to the book seeks to be a non-synthetic synthesis.

PART ONE

CHAPTER ONE

Abandoned for Love:
The Gracious Legacy of
French Spiritual Traditions

Wendy M. Wright

Author Charles Dickens famously opened his 1859 best-selling novel *A Tale of Two Cities* with these words:

> It was the best of times, it was the worst of times, it was the age of wisdom, it was the age of foolishness, it was the epoch of belief, it was the epoch of incredulity, it was the season of Light, it was the season of Darkness, it was the spring of hope, it was the winter of despair.

The plot of Dickens's tale is set during the years leading up to the French Revolution and concludes in the Reign of Terror of 1793–94. His characterization of the era might well be extended to include the entire span of the seventeenth century through the long nineteenth century in France. It *was* the best of times, it *was* the worst of times. For the purposes of this overview of the rich and compelling spiritual traditions that emerged from this period, I would like to riff off Dickens a bit and craft my own opening descriptive words: "It was the most tumultuous of times, it was the most ecstatic of times."

Tumultuous: because the upheavals of the French social and political landscape of this prolonged era profoundly shaped Catholic religious life and practice in ways that continue to exercise influence in the present day. Ecstatic: because an astonishing outpouring of missionary activity and spiritual energy directed toward creative renewal was released. From chaotic conditions emerged some of the most vibrant and innovative religious communities and most enduring of Roman Catholic spiritual traditions. The legacy of this ecstasy is very much still with us in the Catholic world today.

But first a brief, if necessarily attenuated and overly simplified, glance at the context in which these ecstatic waves of Catholic renewal came into being. If one were to draw an imaginary graph of the tumult and its corresponding spiritual and missionary ecstasy, one might produce a design that looked like a first volcanic peak followed by something of a steaming valley-shaped lava bed, followed by another volcanic eruption that flowed into another simmering landscape.

The French Wars of Religion

The first vertical visual eruption of the imagined graph represents the vicious late sixteenth-century French Wars of Religion (1562–98) that followed in the wake of the profound upheaval of the sixteenth-century European Reformations. The long-felt need for thorough reform in all aspects of western Christian life, thought, and practice had split coreligionists apart: Roman Catholics versus Lutherans versus Reformed versus Anglicans versus a score of other radical reforming groups. And on and on.

In France the tumult was especially fierce and long lasting as issues of dynastic succession created a situation in which not only were the French Protestant reformers, the Huguenots, pitted against Catholic loyalists but Catholics were viciously aligned against one another, militants accusing their more moderate coreligionists of heresy or apostasy. Physical and spiritual violence was the order of the day, perhaps best represented by the infamous St. Bartholomew's day massacre of 1572 in Paris that set off a mass slaughter of Huguenots across France. The contested heir apparent, Protestant Henri of Navarre (1553–1610) would eventually militarily claim his throne, convert to the Catholic faith, become King Henri IV in 1589, and attempt to quell civil unrest by granting what would become a temporary religious tolerance to the Huguenot minority. Yet from this civil tumult, like a Phoenix from the ashes, emerged what historians have called the "Golden Age of French Mysticism," the "Century of Saints," or the "Great Century of the Soul." It is remembered as the great era of

Catholic reform during which spiritual values were transfused into all aspects of ecclesial, political, social, and cultural life.

For example, at the Paris salon of Madame Barbe Acarie (1566–1618) the leading lights of this Catholic renewal met. Among them were Pierre, later Cardinal, de Bérulle (1575–1629), founder of the French Oratory dedicated to the spiritual formation of the French clergy; English Capuchin Benet of Canfield (1562–1610), author of the influential spiritual manual *The Way of Perfection*, which distilled the essence of the spiritual life into the discerning and doing of God's will; Jesuit Pierre Coton (1564–1626), confessor to the French crown; Vincent de Paul (1581–1660), founder of the Congregation of the Missions, which ministered to the poor, the orphaned, and those on the margins; and Savoyard François de Sales (1567–1622), bishop of Geneva, cofounder of the women's congregation the Visitation of Holy Mary, and author of best selling books designed to encourage spiritual renewal among the laity.

Radiating outward from the circle of this salon, the rays of renewal spread. From their association with Bérulle's Oratory, Jean-Jacque Olier (1608–57) brought into being the Society of the Priests of St. Sulpice (Sulpicians) designed to educate and nurture a renewed priesthood and Jean Eudes (1601–80) forged a network of new religious communities to renew the clerical state, serve the disenfranchised, and reinvigorate French Catholic life. Barbe Acarie, with the aid of her cousin Bérulle, arranged for the reformed Teresan Carmel to be imported onto French soil and herself entered as a lay sister under the name Marie de l'Incarnation. Nor were the laity ignored. Jean-Baptist de la Salle (1651–1719), after a time with the Sulpicians, revolutionized Christian education by starting a community of consecrated laymen to train teachers. Earlier and motivated by a similar concern to educate the populace, especially young girls, Jeanne Chezard de Matel (1596–1670), established the teaching community, Sisters of Charity of the Incarnate Word.

Carried by this same ecstatic spirit, Vincent de Paul founded the Congregation of the Mission and the Confraternities of Charity to share in Christ's labor by serving the poor and encouraging the redistribution of wealth. With him, Louise de Marillac (1591–1660) founded the Daughters of Charity to minister to those in gravest need through direct service. In a similar cross-gender collaboration, François de Sales and widowed baroness Jeanne de Chantal (1572–1641) established a women's congregation, the Visitation of Holy Mary, that received women not eligible for other communities and witnessed to a unique way of "living Jesus" in the world. And as suggested, Bishop de Sales's popular spiritual writing, especially his *Introduction to the Devout Life*, inspired ordinary lay women and men to renew faith and live devout and transformed Christian lives.

The vibrant, ecstatic impulse toward mission expanded beyond France along with the nation's colonial ambitions. Ursuline Marie Guyart (1599–1672), known in religion as Marie of the Incarnation, prompted by her visions and the intrepid witness of Teresa of Avila, pushed the existing boundaries of female religious life and traveled to the colony of New France to educate the native peoples,[1] while laywoman Marguerite Bourgeoys (1620–1700) set out from Troyes to that same North American mission field to educate colonists and found the Congregation of Notre Dame of Montreal. Even farther afield, Pierre Lambert de la Motte (1624–79) patron and supporter of Eudist ministries in Normandy, was sent by the Paris Foreign Missionary Society as Apostolic Bishop to Asia where he planted a unique Vietnamese women's congregation, the Lovers of the Holy Cross.

Each of these figures was fueled by a vigorous adherence to the Catholic faith, a reforming thirst to restore integrity to the church, and a missionary zeal to invigorate the existing church, embrace new insights, explore new mission fields, and create innovative communities to evangelize those left on the margins: the poor, the underserved, the overlooked, the young, women, laity, and those to whom the faith was not yet known.

The Underlying Spiritual Vision

But what of the *deeper spirit* that motivated and sustained these many diverse expressions of the spiritual ecstasy surging in the bosom of the "eldest daughter of the Church"? The term ecstasy is used deliberately here to contrast with the tumult of the social-political and intellectual-theological upheavals of these centuries. Historians recently have suggested that the mysticism that had flowered in the medieval Catholic monastic world underwent a change in the early modern European

---

[1] On this boundary-breaking see Laurene lux-Sterrit, *Redefining Female Religious Life: French Ursulines and English Ladies in Seventeenth Century Catholicism* (Burlington, VT: Ashgate, 2005).

world.[2] In the era of our attention, the mystical impulse became, as it were, democratized and laicized. It moved out of the cloister and into the street, invading the salons of nobles, the households of the married, and the hovels of the poor. It animated women and men, clergy, vowed religious, and laity alike to collaborate together. It also forged a radical Christocentric spirituality, a mysticism really, hidden beneath a life of action and linked to a missionary zeal directed especially toward the least and the overlooked.

To explore the deeper "ecstatic" animating spirit of this French Catholic revival, one might turn to two seminal figures not commonly identified as "mystics": Pierre de Bérulle (1575–1629) and François de Sales (1567–1622). These two men stand at the headwaters of the two major spiritual currents flowing from the era, the Bérullian or French School and the Salesian Spiritual Tradition. The unique ways the two of them articulated and taught this ordinary mysticism of action would profoundly shape the entire sweep of French Catholic spirituality. Both men were trained in the newly flourishing system of Jesuit schools in France which provided them with a fluency in the intellectual, cultural heritage of the past, an understanding of the current issues of their day, and a range of spiritual practices designed to facilitate inner conversion, and moral integrity and to prompt reforming zeal. From there they developed their own unique spiritual visions.

As suggested, Bérulle was an ardent apostolic reformer, but he was not only that. He was a probing thinker compelled by the Pauline dictum, "I no longer live but Christ lives in me." His dense magisterial work, *Discourses on the States and Grandeur of Jesus,* which earned its author the title, "Apostle of the Incarnate Word," posited that when Jesus, the Second person of the Trinity in hypostatic union with the Father became human, the heavens were opened and earth was sanctified. Through the incarnation, humankind entered into unity with God's own self, joined

---

[2] See Edward Howells, "From Late Medieval to Early Modern: Assessing the Mystical Theology of Pierre de Bérulle (1575–1629)," in *Mysticism in the French Tradition: Eruptions from France,* ed. Louise Nelstrop and Bradley B. Onishi (Burlington, VT: Ashgate, 2015), 169–84. The definition of mysticism assumed in the present essay was crafted by Bernard McGinn. It posits that mysticism is that part of Christian belief and practice that concerns the preparation for, consciousness of, and effect of a direct and transformative presence of God. See the first volume of McGinn's *The Presence of God: A History of Western Mysticism* (New York: Crossroad, 1998).

through One Center, Jesus the perfect Adorer of God, who was the Copernican Sun around which all in heaven and earth revolved.

What had occurred, Bérulle averred, was that a series of "states" both external and internal, had been inaugurated. The external states, fully realized in the historic life of Jesus—his infancy, teaching, priesthood, suffering, and death—have passed away but the interior states conforming to those exterior consummated states continue in the Mystical Body of the Church. The Christian enters those states, adheres to them, cleaves to them, just as Jesus does to the Father, in order to adhere to all that God is, to be consumed by God.

This requires an abandonment of oneself to grace, an acknowledgment of one's own powerlessness, and reliance upon God. It implies an interior movement that Bérulle described as *anéantissement* or self-emptying and an acknowledgement of the reality that without the creator, human beings have no existence. Accepting human nothingness restores one to the truth that once one is empty, one becomes pure capacity for God. Jesus, the one who emptied himself and abandoned himself to the will of his Father, is the one into whom believers are incorporated, the one to whom the human person adheres, in order to return to and become one with the Father. A Christian is thus one who is being made one with Christ. No longer is one at the center of his or her own life, having been displaced by God.

Thus adherence to the elevated "states" inaugurated in the Incarnation was in Bérulle's mind the spiritual, indeed mystical, vocation of the Christian. That vision was profoundly ecclesial—for him the sacramental life of the Church initiates and mediates our adherence. Further, his vision was profoundly Marian, the Virgin herself being the one human person most intimately united with Jesus as she carried the Redeemer in the womb, shared his life and agonies on the cross, and was assumed and united with him upon her death. Of Mary, and thus of the vocation of humanity itself, Bérulle would write

> Let us see what the Son of God does in his blessed Mother. For she is the one who is the closest and most united to him by the state of this new mystery [the Incarnation] accomplished in her and through her. . . . The heart of the Virgin is the first altar on which Jesus offered his heart, body and spirit as a host of perpetual praise; and where Jesus offers his first sacrifice, making the first and perpetual

oblation of himself, through which, as we have said, we are all made holy.[3]

The second seminal mystic of this era is François de Sales whose vision, like that of his contemporary Pierre de Bérulle, profoundly shaped the spirituality of his era and the following centuries. The French speaking Savoyard de Sales was at the forefront of the missionary impulse to invite laity and women into serious engagement with the spiritually transformed life. His *Introduction to the Devout Life* was a best seller and he was widely sought out as a preacher and spiritual guide. Like his contemporary Bérulle, de Sales's vision was Christocentric, positing that the vocation of all Christians was to "Live Jesus." But the Savoyard's spirituality was distinctive, being framed in the language of the heart. The medieval mystical trope of the "exchange of hearts" popularized by the lives of saints such as Catherine of Siena became in de Sales's spirituality the goal of *all* Christians. The bishop, known to posterity as the "Doctor of Divine Love," expressed his spiritual vision as a world of intertwined hearts: the heart of God and human hearts together bridged by the crucified heart of Christ. To pursue the Christian vocation, the devout life, was to "live Jesus," to exchange the heart of Jesus for one's own. The quality of the divine heart was for de Sales revealed in the eleventh chapter of Matthew, where the Savior invites all to "come to me and learn from me for I am gentle and humble of heart" (see Matt 11:28).

This exchange of hearts takes place in part through prayer, leaning against the breast of the beloved to glean the secrets of the divine heart, in part through the cultivation of the love of others, especially those who share the love of friendship who together, as John's gospel states, are no longer servants but friends who know the secrets of the Master's heart that Jesus has shown to them (John 15:15). This exchange takes part as well through the alignment of one's will to God's, a will communicated partially through the acts of discernment that prompt human cooperation and partially through the mystery of events that call for a gracious abandonment and surrender. Finally, the exchange of hearts takes place in part through the practice of the little relational virtues such as gentleness and humility so that one can say, "I no longer live but Christ lives in me"

---

[3] *Bérulle and the French School: Selected Writings*, ed. William M. Thompson (Mahwah, NJ: Paulist, 1989), 160–61.

(see Gal 2:20). A 1617 sermon preached for the community of the Visitation of Holy Mary reveals Bishop de Sales's rhetorically vivid depiction of this exchange.

> Certainly, devout souls should not have any heart but God's, no other spirit than his, no other will than his, no other affections or desires than these, in sum they must be totally his. . . . The means with which we purchase this perfection is our own will. Our Lord was on the tree of the cross. . . . His side was opened, they saw he was truly dead from the illness in his heart, that is to say, the love in his heart. Our Lord wished that his side be opened for several reasons. First so that the thoughts of his heart, which are the thoughts of love and dilection for us his beloved children and dear creatures, created in his image and likeness, might be seen and reveal that he desires to bestow grace and blessings upon us and give us his heart itself, just as he gave it to Catherine of Siena. . . . I admire this incomparable grace by which he exchanges his heart for ours.[4]

What is significant in the interiorized, democratized, and laicized mysticism of these two figures is the idea that radical inner transformation must accompany apostolic fervor, that missionary and evangelistic zeal cannot be separated from adherence, or from the exchange of hearts, or from surrender, or from abandonment to divine providence, or from the conforming of one's will to that of the divine Will. All of those to whom we have pointed as part of the ecstatic phoenix-like rising from the ashes of the French Wars of Religion shared this perspective.

At the core of this distinctive French spiritual ethos is thus not merely imitation of Christ but a radical, indeed mystical, participation in the divine energy unleashed in the incarnation, passion, and resurrection. It is a spiritual ethos that for all its majesty, in fact emphasizes hiddenness, littleness, and the least. It finds its deep springs hidden in the depth of the heart. It insists on a profound *interior* conformity to Christ conjoined to lives of apostolic service. Ecstasy flows through the least in the social orders: the laity, especially women—long considered the "weaker sex." It embraces those most marginalized: the poor, the peasant, the uncate-

---

[4] *Oeuvres de Saint François de Sales*, Édition complète d'après les autographs et les éditions originales, par les soins des Religieuses de la Visitation du première monastère de la Visitation d' Annecy (Annecy: 1892--1932) IX, Sermons III, 73–83.

chized, the forgotten, the young, and the lost. It favors the hidden virtues of humility and self-surrender. Ecstasy lodges in the homes of ordinary people: housewives, schoolteachers, and pupils. It speaks in provincial dialects and takes flesh in foreign languages and cultural idioms.

Thus, for example, one finds blended in Jean Eudes the mystical Christocentrism of Bérulle and the Salesian devotional emphasis on the heart as he composed the first liturgical offices for the feast of the Sacred Heart and wrote rapturously of the incomparable heart of Mary. Eudes himself took a vow of martyrdom, an "elevation," to use the Bérullian term, to Jesus in which he offered himself as sacrifice and victim for God's glory, adhering to that sacrificial state inaugurated at the time of the passion.

> (Elevation to Jesus to offer oneself to him as a sacrifice and victim which must be immolated to his glory and his pure love.)
>
> Oh good Jesus, receive and accept this vow of mine and this sacrifice which I make to you of my life and my being in homage to and by the merits of the most divine sacrifice you made of yourself to your Father on the Cross. Look upon me henceforth as an offering and a victim dedicated to be wholly immolated to the glory of your holy name. Grant, through your great mercy, that my whole life may be a perpetual sacrifice of love and praise for you. Let me live a life that may perpetually imitate and honor your own life and that of your Blessed Mother and your holy martyrs. May never a day go by without my suffering something for love of you.[5]

In another but similar vein, Jean-Baptiste de la Salle entreated those he trained to be teachers to act as representing Jesus Christ so that pupils be "convinced that they are the letter Jesus Christ has dictated to you and that you are writing each day in their hearts, not with ink but with the Spirit of the living God."[6]

And in the Vincentian family the ecstatic impulse of conformity to Jesus meant that sight itself, the way one perceived those to whom one ministered, was transformed. Famously, Vincent de Paul understood that the poor are the privileged mediators of salvation. Although they may be

---

[5] Raymond Deville, *The French School of Spirituality: An Introduction and a Reader*, trans. Agnes Cunningham (Pittsburgh: Duquesne University Press, 1987), 135.

[6] *John Baptist de la Salle: The Spirituality of Christian Education*, ed. and trans. Carl Koch, Jeffrey Calligan, and Jeffrey Gros (Mahwah, NJ: Paulist, 2004), 43.

disfigured by deprivation, in the eyes of faith they are children of God, living images of the life and death of Jesus. Thus he encouraged his confreres to "turn the Medal over," to be open to the faces of poverty, to look beyond the external misery and see the faces of the children of God. At the core of Vincentian spirituality is the paradox that in order to live in Jesus one must consent to die in Christ.

The Bérullian or French School tradition marveled at the glory of the Redeemer first hidden in the womb of Mary and from then on perpetually hidden under the eucharistic presence. And François de Sales advocated the practice of the "little virtues" of gentleness and humility for those, he believed, are the virtues of the heart of God. The congregation of the Visitation of Holy Mary that he cofounded with Jeanne de Chantal was characterized as the "hidden violets" in the garden of the church. The Visitation sisters witnessed to the power of transformed hearts realized in a community of widowed, disabled, or frail women. Hiddenness. Littleness. The least. These are enduring themes that characterize the spiritual ethos of the era.

The Legacy Continues

To return to the imaginary graph marking the era's tumult and ecstasy: the flatter simmering lava bed on the graphic, between the late sixteenth-century Wars of Religion, that Century of the Soul, and the end of the eighteenth century was hardly less dramatic for the religious life of France than the earlier tumult. Tolerance for the Protestant minority died with the growing absolutism of the Sun King, Louis XIV. Intraconfessional conflicts ended in the condemnation of the spiritual renewal movements known to posterity as Jansenism and Quietism. A mantle of rigorist practice and suspicion was cast over the landscape of French Catholicism for much of the eighteenth century. Yet the themes crystalized in France in the seventeenth century still resonated.

An example would be the popular book that in English translations is often titled *Abandonment to Divine Providence*. Eighteenth-century Jesuit spiritual guide Jean-Pierre de Caussade (1675–1751) who was confessor and mentor to the Visitation monastery in Nancy, France, is frequently credited with its authorship although some scholars now question this. The guide teaches radical self–surrender as the path to the divine.

There is a time when the soul lives in God and a time when God lives in the soul. . . . When God lives in the soul, it has nothing left of self, but only that which the Spirit imparts to it moment by moment. . . . Let us preach . . . of surrender to God's will to all the pure in heart who fear God and let us make them understand that by this surrender they will attain to whatever particular state has been chosen for them by God's purpose from all eternity. . . . Beloved souls who read this! It will cost you no more than what you are doing, to suffer what you are suffering. It is only your heart that must be changed. When I say heart I mean the will. Holiness then consists in willing all that God wills for us. Yes, holiness of heart is a simple "Let it be," a simple conformity of the will with the will of God. [7]

The French Revolution and Its Aftermath

The second eruption at the end of that century is of course the French Revolution and its lengthy violent and convoluted aftermath: alternating phases of Republican Rule, Empire, Restoration of the Monarchy, and Republican rule reconstituted again and again. Misused concentration of royal power and the emergence of scientific thought and philosophies that challenged the existing order, the *Ancien regime,* eventually brought down the monarchical system and with it the hegemony of the Catholic Church and its institutions. Religious communities that had maintained the spiritual grounding of French life were suppressed. Added to this were the cultural and demographic changes caused by the emerging industrial revolution that would transform an agrarian society into an urban one with all the attendant social upheaval and ills.

Out of this later tumult eventually, and once again phoenix-like, shone a galaxy of new nineteenth-century French Catholic luminaries and communities formed for mission to evangelize, teach, and preach to new

---

[7] Jean Pierre de Caussade, *The Joy of Full Surrender* (Brewster, MA: Paraclete, 2008), 57, 63, 21. Different translations and versions based on variant editions title the book variously: *Abandonment to Divine Providence, The Joy of Full Surrender,* and *The Sacrament of the Present Moment* are the most common. The authorship of *Abandonment* is traditionally ascribed to Jean-Pierre de Caussade. This attribution is disputed. For a fuller exploration of this see Wendy M. Wright, "Jean-Pierre de Caussade and the Caussadian Corpus," in *Companion to Jesuit Mysticism,* ed. Robert Aleksander Maryks (Leiden: Brill, 2017).

generations of the un-catechized, the poor, the marginalized, and those outside the circle of faith both in France and outside it.

In Aix-en-Provence is discovered Eugène de Mazenod (1782–1861), founder of the Missionaries of Mary Immaculate, who, along with a small band of dedicated men open to respond to any call, moved from village to village, preached, instructed in the language of the common people, and shared an intense community life of prayer, study, and fellowship. At the heart of Eugène de Mazenod's vocation was the Lukan passage: "The Spirit of the Lord is upon me" (Luke 4:18). He felt that the Oblates were to share in work of the redemption inaugurated by Christ: like Christ, the Spirit would strip them for the glory of the Lord, they would share in the cross, and their little family—humiliated and despised— would become holy and bear great fruit.

Here too is found the beginnings of what would become the Sisters of the Congregation of Divine Providence, a group of women supported by Jean-Martin Moye (1730–93) bent on catechizing poor girls in the Alsace-Lorraine region while relying only on their faith in divine Providence to supply their needs. In Bordeaux, Guillame-Joseph Chaminade (1781–1850) and his collaborators founded the Marianist family of communities, which embraced the French School's focus on Mary as the exemplar of the human person as they strove to revive the religious spirit in France, animated by the idea that Mary's apostolic mission is to form all persons into the most perfect conformity with the God-Man Christ, her Son.

A native of Joiny, Madeleine Sophie Barat (1779–1865) took part in the postrevolutionary restoration of Catholic life in Paris through the education of young women. The motto of Barat's community, the Religious of the Sacred Heart, "One Heart and One Mind in the Heart of Jesus" attests to her desire to glorify the heart of Jesus by living united with him and conformed to his will, and through service, to extend the love of his heart.

That same heart-focused spirit motivated Barat's sister in religion Philippine Duchesne (a Visitation sister before the Revolution) to extend that love to the Native Americans in the French colony of Louisiana. In Le Mans, Basile-Antoine Marie Moreau (1799–1873), seminary trained by the Sulpicians and a student of the Ignatian *Spiritual Exercises*, established the Congregation of the Holy Cross, dedicated to educating people in the faith. At the Christocentric core of the Holy Cross family of congregations is the cross of Christ. "Hail the cross our only hope" is the motto that Moreau chose for the Congregation in the belief that it is from finding how even the cross can be born as a gift that true educators with hope are born. Finally, in Paris layman Frédéric Ozanam (1813–53) and a band of student friends established the Society of St. Vincent de Paul, aimed at assisting the poor. Inspired by the vision inaugurated by Vincent de Paul, they were to witness to God's love by embracing all the works of charity and justice, but more importantly to provide loving and compassionate interest in any individual who came for aid, discerning the face of Christ in all.

Radiating out from the French capital emerged simultaneously what has become known as the nineteenth-century Salesian Pentecost, a revival of the gentle spirit and teachings of François de Sales. Given the *Introduction to the Devout Life*, de Sales's spiritual manual for laity by his Russian grandmother, the thoroughly secularized young Louis-Gaston de Ségur (1820–81) was drawn back to the faith and later, as a retired bishop in Paris, mobilized Catholics across France by establishing the lay Association of St. Francis de Sales to promote the writings and spirit of the Savoyard. Also in the French capital, parish priest Henri Chaumont (1838–96) in collaboration with wife and mother Caroline Carré de Malberg (1829–91) created a rule inspired by the *Devout Life* to guide the spiritual formation of married women who gathered as a canonical lay association known as the Daughters of St. Francis de Sales. Through their association they would Live Jesus! exchanging the heart of the crucified for their own.

The Salesian Pentecost extended as well to the region of Champagne, where Marie de Sales Chappuis, (1793–1875) Superior of the Visitation Monastery of Troyes, priest-confessor Louis Brisson (1817–1908) and former student-boarder Léonie Aviat (1844–1914) together responded to the upheavals generated by the Revolution and the changing demographics spawned by the Industrial Revolution. A priestly congregation, the Oblates of St. Francis de Sales, dedicated itself to the education of young men while the Oblate Sisters of St. Francis de Sales directed energies toward the plight of young, uneducated and untrained country girls newly arrived in industrialized urban cities seeking work. At the core of the spiritual vision of the latter's foundress, Leonie Aviat, was abandonment and self-forgetfulness, fidelity to the present moment, and confidence in the God of Love. Her confrere Louis Brisson, steeped as he was in the Salesian spirit of humility and gentleness imbibed at the Visitation monastery at Troyes where he was chaplain and confessor, spoke to his Oblate confreres of "reprinting the Gospel," by preaching and by manual labor, which was Brisson's way of contemporizing the idea of Living Jesus.

Apostolic certainly. Bent on mission in the broadest sense of the term, yes. Committed to evangelization, absolutely. But these nineteenth-century figures and communities were also steeped in the language first articulated in the seventeenth century, a language of Christocentric mysticism bent on inner transformation described variously as an exchange of hearts, an adherence, a union, a surrender of the will, an abandonment to divine providence, an annihilation of self, Living Jesus. In all cases a radical apostolic commitment to mission to those on the margins was coupled with a radical interior conformity to Christ.

An Enduring Legacy

Examples of the resonance of these varied communities, schools, and persons are many. They are most obviously found in the aforementioned institutions that still exist and which came into being in the prolonged era of tumult and ecstasy in France that spanned the late sixteenth and long nineteenth centuries. But they also echo further into the dawn of the twentieth century. They are heard in the spirituality of Thérèse of Lisieux (1873–97), the young French Carmelite within whose so called "Little Way" is hidden a profound spiritual maturity. An 1895 poem by this cloistered contemplative, whose sense of zeal for the work of missionaries earned her the official appellation of copatron (with Jesuit Francis Xavier) of the church's missions and copatron (with Joan of Arc) of France, sounds the notes so deeply engrained in the French spiritual legacy.

> On the evening of Love, speaking without parable,
> Jesus said: If anyone wishes to love me
> All his life let him keep my Word.
> My Father and I will come to visit him.
> And we will make his heart our dwelling.
> Coming to him, we shall love him always.
> We want him to remain, filled with peace,
>   In our Love! . . .
>
> Living on Love is living on your life,
> Glorious King, delight of the elect.
> You live for me, hidden in a host.

I want to hide myself for you, O Jesus!
Lovers must have a solitude,
A heart to heart lasting night and day.
Just one glance of yours makes my beatitude.
    I live in Love! . . .

Living on Love is sailing unceasingly,
Sowing peace and joy in every heart.
Beloved pilot, Charity impels me,
For I see you in my sister souls.
Charity is my only star.
In its brightness I sail straight ahead.
I've my motto written on my sail:
    Living on Love! . . .

Dying of Love is truly sweet martyrdom,
And that is the one I wish to suffer.
O Cherubim! Tune your lyre,
For I sense my exile is about to end! . . .
Flame of Love, consume me unceasingly.
Life of an instant, your burden is so heavy to me!
Divine Jesus, make my dream come true:
    To die of Love! . . .[8]

These notes echo as well in the spirit of Charles de Foucauld (1858–1916), the former French military officer, turned Cistercian monk, then hermit who died alone and without the immediate fellowship of others as he attempted to live out in the desert of Algeria the hidden life that Jesus as worker had lived in Nazareth. Br. Charles's vision was one of abandonment grounded in the intimacy of a dual presence: the contemplation of the divine presence hidden the Eucharist and the contemplation of presence in the person of the "other," especially the Muslim neighbors among whom he settled. The sensibilities of Foucauld's well known prayer reflect his spiritual patrimony.

Father I put myself in your hands; Father I abandon myself to you,
I entrust myself to you. Father do with me as it pleases you. Whatever
you do with me, I will thank you for it. Giving thanks for anything,

[8] St. Therese of Lisieux, *Selected Writings*, ed. Mary Frohlich (Maryknoll, NY: Orbis, 2003), 136–40.

I am ready for anything, I accept anything, give thanks for anything. As long as your will, my God, is done in me, as long as your will is done in all your creatures, in all your children, in all those your heart loves, I ask for nothing else O God. I put my soul into your hands. I give it to you, O God, with all the love of my heart, because I love you, and because my love requires me to give myself. I put myself unreservedly in your hands. I put myself in your hands with infinite confidence, because you are my Father.[9]

Out of tumult, ecstasy. Mission on behalf of the outcast, the other, the impoverished, the forgotten, the untaught, and the marginalized. Mission grounded in a deep Christocentric mysticism: an abandonment for Love. This is the gracious legacy the French centuries of tumult have bequeathed to the Church and world.

Selected Bibliography

Aston, Nigel. *Religion and Revolution in France: 1780–1804.* Washington, DC: Catholic University of America Press, 2000.

Beaudoin, Yves, OMI, *Father Louis Brisson (1817–1908): a Documented Biography.* Translated by J. Baraniewicz, J. Bowler, W. Dougherty, D. Gambet, A. Pocetto, J. F. Power. Philadelphia: Oblates of St. Francis de Sales, 2008.

Bergin, Joseph. *Church, Society and Religious Change in France 1580–1730.* New Haven: Yale University Press, 2009.

Bérulle and the French School: Selected Writings. Edited by William M. Thompson. Mahwah, NJ: Paulist, 1989.Curtis, Sarah A. *Civilizing Habits: Women Missionaries and the Revival of French Empire.* Oxford: Oxford University Press, 2010.

Deville, Raymond. *The French School of Spirituality: an Introduction and a Reader.* Translated by. Agnes Cunningham. Pittsburgh: Duquesne University Press, 1987

Francis de Sales, Jane de Chantal. Letters of Spiritual Direction. Edited by Joseph F. Power OSFS and Wendy M. Wright. Translated by Peronne Marie Thibert VHM. Mahwah, NJ: Paulist, 1988.

---

[9] *Spiritual Autobiography of Charles de Foucauld*, ed. Jean-François Six, trans. H. Holland Smith (New York: P.J. Kenedy and Sons, 1964), 95–96.

Francis de Sales. *Introduction to the Devout Life.* Translated by John K. Ryan. New York: Image Classics, 1972.

Gibson, Ralph. *A Social History of French Catholicism 1789–1914.* London/ New York: Routledge, 1989.

Guillon, Clement, CJM. *In All Things the Will of God: Saint John Eudes Through His Letters.* Translated by Louis Levesque, CJM. Buffalo, NY: St, John Eudes Center, 1994.

Hubenig, Alfred, OMI. *Living in the Spirit's Fire: Saint Eugene de Mazenod.* Toronto: Novalis, 1995.

Jean-Baptiste de la Salle: The Spirituality of Christian Education. Edited by Carl Koch, Jeffrey Calligan, and Jeffrey Gros. Mahwah, NJ: Paulist, 2004.

Jeanne Chezard de Matel. *A Hundred Letters from the Correspondence of Jeanne Chezard de Matel.* Edited by. Kathleen McDonagh, IWBS. Corpus Christi TX: Sisters of the Incarnate Word, 1994.

Kilroy, Phil. *Madeleine Sophie Barat: a Life.* Mahwah, NJ: Paulist, 2000.

———. *The Society of the Sacred Heart in Nineteenth Century France, 1800– 1865.* Cork: Cork University Press, 2012.

Koster, Dirk, OSFS. *Louis Brisson.* Noorden: Bert Post, 2007.

Louise de Marillac. *Spiritual Writings of Louise de Marillac: Correspondence and Thoughts.* Translated by Louise Sullivan. Brooklyn, NY: New City Press, 1991.

Rybolt, John, CM. *The Vincentians: Four Centuries of the Congregation of the Missions.* New York: New City Press, 2016.

Sickinger, Raymond L. *Antoine Ozanam.* Notre Dame, IN: University of Notre Dame Press, 2017.

Stopp, Elisabeth. *Madame de Chantal: Portrait of a Saint.* Reprint. Stella Niagara, NY: De Sales Resource Center, 2002.

Vincent de Paul, Louise de Marillac. Rules, Conferences and Writings. Edited by Frances Ryan, DC and John Rybolt, CM. Mahwah, NJ: Paulist, 1995.

Wright, Wendy M. *Francis de Sales and Jane de Chantal.* Boston: Pauline Books and Media, 2017.

———. *Heart Speaks to Heart: the Salesian Tradition.* Maryknoll. NY: Orbis Books, 2004.

CHAPTER TWO

Surrendering to Christ for Mission:
The Transformation of a Young Enthusiast

French Spiritual Traditions,
St. Eugène de Mazenod and the Charism of the
Missionary Oblates of Mary Immaculate

Frank Santucci, OMI

The "Surrendering to Christ for Mission" conference on French spiritual traditions, from which this book arises, was organized as part of the bicentenary celebrations of the foundation of the Missionary Oblates of Mary Immaculate. If it had taken place in another context, Eugène de Mazenod would probably only have had a mention in passing as an important nineteenth-century personality and canonized saint in France who had studied at St. Sulpice and had been influenced by what he learned there. De Mazenod certainly does not stand out as a prominent member of the French School. He was strongly influenced by it, however, because he studied for the diocesan priesthood at the Seminary of St. Sulpice from 1808–12 and was formed for his priestly and missionary ministry by the Sulpicians. It was here that he learned the dynamics of "Surrendering to Christ for Mission" in his formation and it shaped his early ministry as a diocesan priest and was one of the influences in his foundation of the Missionary Oblates.

Who Was Eugène de Mazenod?

Born a nobleman in Aix, de Mazenod was the son of the President of the Court of Finances of Aix, accustomed to the lifestyle of the privileged class of the *Ancien Regime*. Once the Revolution spread to the south of France, the de Mazenod family was forced to flee as émigrés. Eugène de Mazenod was to spend 11 years in exile, moving around from Nice to Turin, to Venice, to Naples and, finally, to Palermo—always one step ahead of the French revolutionary armies set on to destroy the remnants of the ancient regime in Europe. At the age of 20 he was able to return to Aix and lived the aimless existence of a self-centered wealthy young member of the privileged class.

A Directionless Young Man Finds a Compass

Aged twenty-five, while attending the Good Friday liturgy and looking at the Cross, de Mazenod received a life-changing insight. For the first time in his life he understood how unfocused his existence had been. A self-centered young man found himself gazing at Jesus the Savior and understanding the meaning of this self-giving for him and for humanity. His eyes were opened and he understood the direction that his scattered life needed to take. As he later reflected on what had happened he concluded: "I looked for happiness outside of God and for too long with resulting unhappiness."[1] Through the loving look of Christ the Savior his eyes had been opened and he was able to see his life as it had really been. "Could I ever express what I experienced then? Just the memory of it fills my heart with a sweet satisfaction. So I had looked for happiness outside of God, and outside him I found but affliction and chagrin."[2] The image that comes to mind is that of a compass that finally pointed him to the "true north" that would become the pivot of his life and his spirituality: Christ the Savior.

Always Seeking to Point Toward Jesus his Savior

Transformed, de Mazenod's life took on a new meaning with the birth of a passionate love for his Savior:

> Let me at least make up for lost time by redoubling my love for him. May all my actions, thoughts, etc., be directed to that end. What

---

[1] Eugène de Mazenod, "Retreat made in the Aix Seminary, December 1814," *Oblate Writings* I, 15 (Rome: OMI General Archives, 1996), no. 130, 81.
[2] Ibid.

more glorious occupation than to act in everything and for everything only for God, to love him above all else, to love him all the
more as one who has loved him too late.[3]

With this fixed point in the compass of his life, Eugène de Mazenod
became aware of the suffering of others. In a particular way, he saw the
church and the destruction that the Revolution had caused to its members. De Mazenod felt that he could not remain an impassive spectator.
He had to act. Seeking advice from Fr. Duclaux, a Sulpician, and discerning with a Jesuit spiritual director, he understood that God was calling
him to the priesthood as the way of serving the broken Church. De
Mazenod affirmed that he could not "sit back with arms folded, sighing
softly to himself about all these evils, but not raising a finger to awaken
even in the least degree men's hardened hearts."[4]

Eugène de Mazenod arrived at the Seminary of St. Sulpice in 1808 at
the age of twenty-six with this realization and its effects in his heart. Here
was the raw material of a passionate and enthusiastic young man that
was entrusted to the formative hands of the Sulpicians formators in Paris.

Inviting Others to Use the Compass of the Savior

For the sake of the story as background, we need to "fast-forward" to
1812, the year after his priestly ordination when Eugène de Mazenod
returned to Aix-en-Provence. Aware of the precarious state of the faith
of the victims of the Revolution, he had asked not to be sent to a parish,
but to be allowed to dedicate himself to sharing the Good News of salvation with those who were the most abandoned. He dedicated himself to
the domestic servants, menial laborers, and peasants who knew only
Provencal in a French-speaking church that did not cater to their needs.
De Mazenod became aware of the abandonment of the youth, the prisoners, and the inhabitant of the small forgotten villages. In each situation,
he always had the same message: the one that he had received as he had
been embraced by Jesus the Savior on that unforgettable Good Friday.

In 1815 with the restoration of the monarchy, it became possible for
Eugène de Mazenod to invite others to join him in his mission, and the

---

[3] Ibid.
[4] Letter to his mother, 4 April 1809, *Oblate Writings* I, 14, no. 50, 117.

Missionary Oblates came into existence in 1816.[5] Within two years he discerned that God was calling them to become a religious society with vows. In 1826, the Oblates received papal approbation. In 1837 Eugène de Mazenod became Bishop of Marseille and in 1841 he sent the Oblates out as foreign missionaries across the seas. When he died in 1861, there were over four hundred Missionary Oblates in four continents.

With that framework, let us return to the young man who had just arrived at the seminary of St. Sulpice in Paris.

A Plant in the Hands of the Sulpician Formators

We recall how Jean-Jacques Olier (1608–57), as pastor of St. Sulpice parish, had named his group of priest companions Sulpicians after the parish. One of their major concerns for the renewal of the Church was to establish a seminary, whose purpose he had stated in 1641:

> For several years now, a number of persons have come together with us, after having worked in missions and parishes. We recognize the futility of our efforts, if we have not first labored to purify the source from which the holiness of the people comes, that is, priests. As a result, these former missionaries have come to cultivate the new plants placed in their hands, namely, those who seem to be called to the priesthood.[6]

One hundred and sixty-seven years later Eugène de Mazenod came to this same seminary as "a new plant" placed in the hands of the Sulpicians, who were to have a lasting influence on him. Thirty years later, while looking back to those days, he wrote:

> I shall always be grateful to God for the blessing of having lived for several years under the direction and, I may say, in the friendship of men like Father Emery, Father Duclaux, Father Montagne. . . . It seems to me that, through them, were handed down the finest and

---

[5] In 1816, Eugène de Mazenod and his group called themselves "Missionaries of Provence," but in 1826 they took the name "Missionary Oblates of Mary Immaculate." To avoid confusion, I will refer to the group as "Oblates" throughout.

[6] *Divers écrits* 1:67; quoted by Raymond Deville, *The French School of Spirituality* (Pittsburgh: Duquesne University Press, 1994), 84.

holiest traditions of the Church and the most inspiring examples of every priestly virtue. It would indeed be criminal to let the memory of these holy men of God die out with our generation.[7]

De Mazenod grew close to Fr. Emery, the rector, and received much personal attention and individual formation. As a result, he was given an experience of the persecution of the church by Napoleon by being involved with the Roman cardinals in exile in France. He cultivated an ultramontane loyalty to the pope, and the ability to *sentire cum ecclesia* and actively participate in the life of the universal church. Emery's active opposition to Napoleon also trained the young seminarian to fear no power in his struggle to defend the good of the Church. In the last months of Emery's life de Mazenod nursed him and assisted him at his deathbed.

Fr. Duclaux, another influential Sulpician, had been de Mazenod's spiritual director while he discerned his vocation, and then in the seminary itself. Once he was ordained, de Mazenod consulted him before every major step in his life until 1820, including the foundation of the Oblates and the writing of the Rule.

The Compass Is Given a Definite Shape— The Apostolic Spirit

Eugène de Mazenod entrusted himself to be formed by the Seminary of St. Sulpice that had as its purpose in the words of Olier:

> The Seminary of Saint-Sulpice is consecrated and dedicated to Jesus Christ our Lord, in order to honor him not only as Sovereign Priest and the great Apostle of his Father, but also to venerate him living in the College of Apostles.
>
> This seminary daily prays that the apostolic spirit be given to its community and to the entire Church, so that the love of Jesus Christ and the worship of his Father might be renewed in her.[8]

---

[7] Letter to M. Faillon quoted in Jean Leflon, *Eugène de Mazenod, Bishop of Marseilles, Founder of the Oblates of Mary Immaculate, 1782–1861*, vol. I (New York: Fordham University Press, 1961), 314.

[8] *Divers écrits* 1:67; quoted by R. Deville, *The French School*, 86.

The first thing that would have struck him, visually and in practice, was the model of the apostles:

> Adopting the view that the seminary was like the Cenacle where the Spirit of God would descend afresh to form apostolic men who would revitalize the knowledge and love of Jesus Christ, it was M. Olier's desire that all the clerics would take on the sentiments and attitudes of the holy Apostles and that they would become perpetual students of the Apostles' virtues. He had them depicted . . . in the chapel's main painting so that the seminary would have recourse to them as to full flowing channels of apostolic grace whose first fruits they had received for future ages, and so that they should honor them with a special devotion as being, after Jesus Christ, the foundations of the Church[9]

Every time he entered the seminary chapel, he saw the picture of the apostles in the cenacle. It was this model that became his life-long compass as he began to be trained to walk in their footsteps and to focus with them on Jesus Christ the Savior.

Olier had written: "To prepare his apostles, the Son of God . . . kept them in his company for three years. . . ."[10] Similarly, for just over three years, Eugène de Mazenod was trained in this school and it is not surprising that when he founded the Oblates, he used the same model:

> My intention when I devoted myself to the ministry of the missions, working especially to teach and convert the most abandoned souls, had been to imitate the Apostles in their life of dedication and self-denial. I had reached the conviction that to obtain the same results in our preaching we had to walk in their footsteps and practice the same virtues in the measure possible for us.[11]

When reflecting on the identity of his Oblates, he unhesitatingly declared: "What more sublime purpose than that of their Institute? Their founder

---

[9] Faillon, *M. Olier*, III, 1873, pp. 81–82. Quoted by Yvon Beaudoin, "Apostles," in *Dictionary of Oblate Values* (Rome: AOSR, 2000), 19.

[10] Jean Olier, *Maximes sur le Sacerdoce*; quoted by Yvon Beaudoin, "Preface of the Rule," in *Dictionary of Oblate Values* (Rome: AOSR, 2000), 795.

[11] Toussaint Rambert, *Vie de Monseigneur Charles-Joseph-Eugène de Mazenod, évêque de Marseille, fondateur de la Congrégation des Missionnaires Oblats de Marie Immaculée*, vol. I (Tours: Mame, 1883), 187.

is Jesus Christ, the very Son of God; their first fathers are the Apostles. They are called to be the Savior's coworkers, the coredeemers of mankind."[12]

Throughout his writings as founder, as missionary, and as bishop, de Mazenod repeatedly referred to the apostolic model. He had learned his lesson well at St. Sulpice, and this lesson has continued to be transmitted to his followers till this very day—two hundred years later—in the Oblate Constitutions and Rules:

> The community of the Apostles with Jesus is the model of our life. Our Lord grouped the Twelve around him to be his companions and to be sent out as his messengers (cf. Mk 3:14). The call and the presence of the Lord among us today bind us together in charity and obedience to create anew in our own lives the Apostles' unity with him and their common mission in his Spirit. [13]

The ideal of walking in the footsteps of the apostles is the most important heritage given to the Missionary Oblates by St. Sulpice—a compass that has molded our spirit for two centuries and continues to do so.

Guided to Understand That the Compass Always Points to the Savior

Eugène de Mazenod's focus, to which his compass needle always pointed, was his experience of Jesus as Savior. He thus needed to study and understand what this meant theologically and spiritually. The Sulpicians formed him step-by-step using their unmistakable Christocentric theology and spirituality. He learned the theology of the incarnate Word, and explored the mysteries of the life and teaching of the God-made-man. Each mystery, each word spoken by the incarnate Word was a grace-filled moment for the disciple. He was taught how to lovingly contemplate each

---

[12] *Constitutions et Règles de la Société des Missionnaires de Provence* (Rome: OMI General Archives), DM XI, 1818, *Part One, Chapter One, §3. Nota Bene*. The text was published as "Constitutions et Règles de la Société des Missionnaires de Provence," in *Missions* 78 (1951): 1–97.

[13] *Constitutions and Rules of the Congregation of the Missionary Oblates of Mary Immaculate* (Rome: 2012), Constitution 3, 25.

mystery, and to enter into the sentiments and dispositions of the Savior who was totally given to the Father.

Eugène de Mazenod imbibed this and made the method his own as this reflection in one of his class exercise books reveals:

> To make myself like Jesus Crucified. It is like the painter who copies a model. He places the model in the best light, studies him carefully, concentrates on him, tries to engrave his image in his spirit, then he traces some lines on the paper, which he compares with the original, then he makes corrections until he is satisfied that it conforms with the original, then he continues.[14]

The future priest was trained to look at Jesus Christ, the perfect Priest, as the model of how to give perfect worship to the Father. Here he would have been led to understand the meaning of the oblation of Jesus in perfect love and the need to imitate this total faithfulness in his own priestly vocation in the same spirit of oblation. His retreat journals and spiritual notes until the time of his ordination show how influenced he had been by the Sulpician theology and spirituality.[15]

Once he had completed his seminary formation, de Mazenod summarized all this in a pastoral resolution at the service of others in his first retreat as a priest:

> I will meditate on Jesus my love in his incarnation, his hidden life, his mission, his passion and death; but especially in his Sacrament and Sacrifice. My chief occupation will be to love him, my chief concern to make him loved. To this I will bend all my efforts, time, strength, and when after much toil I have succeeded in winning but a single act of love towards so good a Master, I will rightly consider myself very well paid.[16]

As he became more immersed in ministry and in the development of the Oblates, the expressions of his theology moved away from that of the French School and became more strongly influenced by Alphonsus Liguori and Ignatius of Loyola.

---

[14] Unpublished exercise book from the time he was a seminarian, in the Archives of the OMI General House, Rome.

[15] *Oblate Writings* I, 13, 14 and 15.

[16] Retreat notes, December 1812, *Oblate Writings* I, 15, n. 109, 14.

Various Points on the Compass: Learning to Become One with the Savior

Continuing to use the image of the compass and exploring its defining points, it can be said that Eugène de Mazenod was not only taught about Jesus, but also learned how to focus the direction of his life on relating to Christ in prayer. He learned to pray by looking and meditating, contemplating and adoring the incarnate Word and being led into communion. He developed a love for the Scriptures and, for the rest of his life, would spend time reading, studying, and reflecting on the Word each day. As a priest, and then as an Oblate, de Mazenod set aside thirty minutes per day for this.[17] Then as the bishop of a major diocese he aimed at one hour per day.[18] The seriousness with which de Mazenod took this can be seen in the list of penances that he imposed on himself when he failed. Among them: "This penance will be proportionate to the gravity of the point neglected . . . if it is the reading of Holy Scripture, two hours' hair shirt the next day."[19]

He was thus able to make his own the words of St. Paul that were a foundational conviction of every member of the French School from Bérulle onward: "It is no longer I who live but Christ who lives in me" (see Gal 2:20).

Eugène de Mazenod's model for entering into the life of Jesus Christ was Mary. Before his daily meditation he adopted this Sulpician prayer, which has since become part of the tradition of the Missionary Oblates:

> O Mary, . . . faithful adorer of the Father, Mother most admirable of the Son, Spouse of the Holy Spirit, inspire within me the same sentiments that were yours while pondering the revealed mysteries which you treasured in your heart.
>
> Grant that I may ever live in union with your Son, my Savior, together with all who, by meditation, give honor to the most Holy Trinity.[20]

---

[17] Cf. Rule of Life for his return to Aix, August–September 1812, *Oblate Writings* I, 15, n. 107.

[18] Daily Schedule, May 1837, *Oblate Writings* I, 15, n. 186.

[19] Retreat Notes, December 1813, *Oblate Writings* I, 14, n. 121.

[20] Missionary Oblates of Mary Immaculate, *Oblate Prayer* (Rome: General House, 2016), 21.

Learning to Pray

The Sulpicians formed in Eugène de Mazenod the habit of an hour of meditation each day, using a practical three-step method: adoration, communion, and then cooperation after prayer. The Oblate scholar, Yvon Beaudoin, points out the Sulpician influence on the prayer of Eugène, which became part of Oblate tradition until the Second Vatican Council. He lists the morning and evening prayers, part of the midday particular examen, the manner of participating at Mass, the thanksgiving after Communion, the hour of daily meditation, visits to the Blessed Sacrament, the rosary, among many other customs.[21]

The prayer that Eugène de Mazenod learned and practiced was intimate in nature and touched his heart. In a particular way, the practice of *oraison*, usually in the evening, was not a formally structured prayer, but a time of intimacy between Jesus and himself. It was a "tête-à-tête" between friends. It is not surprising then to see that he had a devotion to the Sacred Heart and that he was the one to reintroduce this devotion in Aix-en-Provence after the Revolution.

Learning to Live the Virtues—Establishing the Same Sentiments as Jesus

In his meditation and study, the seminarian was taught to integrate and practice a list of virtues, which were those present in the life of Jesus. Joseph Labelle, OMI, who has made an extensive study of these virtues, describes how in:

> Olier, *Introduction à la vie et aux vertus chrétiennes /pietas seminara,* ch. 1, 8, we find "Our Lord has continued . . . to give (to men) his same Spirit, which is that of GOD, living in him, for establishing in them the same sentiments of his soul, . . ."

> It is interesting to note the list of these virtues found in the table of contents, namely, the virtues of religion, humility, penance, mortification, patience, the French *douceur,* poverty, chastity, obedience,

---

[21] Yvon Beaudoin, "Les Oblats de Marie Immaculée, des Sulpiciens Missionnaires?," *Vie Oblate Life* 51 (1992): 286–87.

and charity towards the neighbor. Eugene had some acquaintance with this list; a personal copy of Olier's book, given to him and signed by his mentor Fr. Emery, is displayed in the Museum of the Postulation of the Missionary Oblate General House.[22]

When Eugène de Mazenod wrote the *Preface* of his Rule, that fiery document that defines the Oblate vocation, he asked himself: "And how should men who want to follow in the footsteps of their divine Master Jesus Christ conduct themselves if they, in their turn, are to win back the many souls who have thrown off his yoke?" He responds, "They must constantly renew themselves in the spirit of their vocation, living in a state of habitual self-denial and seeking at all times to reach the very summit of perfection." Then follows the list that he has taken from Olier and the Sulpicians:

> They must work unremittingly to become humble, meek, obedient, lovers of poverty and penance, mortified, free from inordinate attachment to the world or to family, men filled with zeal, ready to sacrifice goods, talents, ease, self, even their life, for the love of Jesus Christ, the service of the Church, and the sanctification of their brethren.
>
> And thus, filled with unbounded confidence in God, they are ready to enter the combat, to fight, even unto death, for the greater glory of his most holy and sublime Name.[23]

The daily midday particular examen invited them to take one of these virtues over a period of time and to review how it was being lived.

Learning from Mary Immaculate

The focus on the incarnation at St. Sulpice gave Eugène de Mazenod an understanding of Mary's privileged role as co-operator. She was seen as the first disciple, and just as Jesus came to live in Mary, so did this become the goal of all Christian life. He was taught that Marian devotion

---

[22] Joseph T. LaBelle, *Truly Apostolic Men: Apostolic Life in the Early Ministry of Saint Eugène de Mazenod*, Oblatio Studia 3 (Rome: Missionarii OMI, 2014), 95.

[23] *Constitutions and Rules*, Preface, 19–20.

flowed naturally from contemplation of Jesus, as the beautiful prayer that he made his own and gave to the Oblates as part of our heritage, shows:

> O Jesus, living in Mary, come and live in your servants:
> in the spirit of your holiness,
> in the fullness of your power,
> in the reality of your virtues,
> in the perfection of your ways,
> in the communion of your mysteries; have dominion over every
> adverse power, in your own Spirit, to the glory of God the Father.
> Amen[24]

Eugène de Mazenod's focus was on the Cross and he was enabled to express Mary's role in that light:

> And what a Mother! She has given us him who is the world's life and salvation, she has engendered all of us spiritually at the foot of the Cross through the pangs of the passion and death of the God-Man, the blessed fruit of her womb; she is rightly called the new Eve and the coredemptrix of the human race[25]

Years later de Mazenod was able to apply this to the mission of the Oblates as being the same as Mary's: "the glory of her divine Son and the conversion of the souls he has redeemed with his precious blood."[26] It is not difficult to understand why his religious family came to be dedicated to Mary Immaculate.

Becoming a Worthy Priest, Conscious of the Majesty of Ministry

Eugène de Mazenod emerged from St. Sulpice with a lofty idea of the priesthood. The priest was the "mystery" of Jesus Christ, just as Jesus Christ himself was the "mystery" of God on earth. The priest was the

---

[24] *Oblate Prayer*, 21.

[25] *Mandement de Monseigneur l'Evêque de Marseille, qui prescrit les Prières demandées par N.S.P. le Pape, au sujet de l'Immaculée Conception de la Très-Sainte-Vierge* (Marius Olive, Marseille, 1849), 4.

[26] Actes de visite, N.D. de l'Osier, July 16, 1835. Copy Post. DM IX 4.

visible expression of Jesus Christ on earth. This was an understanding of priesthood that has been described as "a worthy priesthood, conscious of the majesty of its ministry and utterly dedicated."[27]

On the day of his priestly ordination, Eugène de Mazenod had written to his mother: "Dear, darling mother, the miracle has happened: your Eugène is a priest of Jesus Christ. That one word says everything; it contains everything. It really is with a sense of deepest lowliness, prostrate in the dust, that I announce such a huge miracle worked in such a great sinner as myself."[28] He repeated the same sentiments to his spiritual director: "Very dear and beloved Father, I am writing this on my knees, prostrate, overwhelmed, stunned, to share with you what the Lord, in his immense, incomprehensible mercy, has just accomplished in me. I am a priest of Jesus Christ."[29] While maintaining the highest respect for the priesthood throughout his life, in the practical demands of the ministry his focus grew increasingly in favor of service.[30]

From Bérulle and Vincent de Paul, Eugène de Mazenod picked up an abhorrence for priests who were not faithful to their vocation and imitated Vincent de Paul's strong words against bad priests.

> The Church has no worse enemies than her priests. Heresies have come from them . . . and it is through them that heresies have prevailed, that vice has reigned, and that ignorance has established its throne among the "poor" people; and this has happened because of their undisciplined way of life and refusal to oppose those three torrents now inundating the earth with all their might.[31]

---

[27] Yves Krumenacker, "The French School of Spirituality & John Baptist de La Salle," trans. Allen Geppert, *AXIS: Journal of Lasallian Higher Education* 7, no. 1 (Institute for Lasallian Studies at Saint Mary's University of Minnesota, 2016).

[28] Letter to his mother after his priestly ordination, 21 December 1811, *Oblate Writings* I, 14, n. 97, 227.

[29] Letter to his spiritual director, Fr. Duclaux, 21 December 1811, *Oblate Writings* I, 14, n. 98, 228.

[30] Cf. Frank Santucci, "All for God: Eugene de Mazenod's Priesthood," in *Oblatio*, n. 2 (2012), accessed February 1, 2017, http://archive.omiworld.org/en/oblatio/oblatio -review/2-22-38/all-for-god-eugene-de-mazenod-s-priesthood/.

[31] André Dodin, ed., *Entretiens spirituels aux missionaires* (Paris: Seuil, 1960), 502. Quoted by W.M. Thompson, *Bérulle and the French School: Selected Writings* (New York: Paulist, 1989), 11.

In the first Rule of the Oblates, Eugène consequently prescribed:

> Article 1. A no less important end of their Institute, an end they will as zealously strive to achieve as they do the main end, is that of clergy reform and of repairing to the full extent possible to them the evil caused in the past and still being caused by unworthy priests who ravage the Church by their lack of care, their avarice, their impurity, their sacrileges, their felonies and heinous crimes of every description.[32]

Through the example of their lives and through direct ministry to priests Oblates were to "make a frontal attack on all these horrible vices. They will apply the probe, iron and fire to this shameful festering sore which is consuming everything in the Church of Jesus Christ."[33] Their approach was that:

> Article 3. Consequently, they will preach retreats to priests and the Mission House will always be a welcoming refuge for them, like a health-giving pool where these putrid and festering sick persons will come to cleanse themselves and begin a new life of penance and reparation[34]

As the church in France got back onto its feet after the Revolution, the problem of the quality of the clergy lessened, and Eugène de Mazenod and the Oblates were able to follow the example of the Sulpicians by focusing on seminary formation so as to ensure that there would be priests who were worthy stewards of the mysteries of the Savior.

Trained to Minister in Parish Missions

Eugène de Mazenod's missionaries came together primarily to evangelize the abandoned people in the poor villages of Provence. They did this by preaching prolonged parish missions of some four to six weeks in each village (and longer if the town was larger). It was a method of evangelization that had existed in Europe for many centuries, but it was

---

[32] 1818, *Part One, Chapter One, §3 Article 1.*
[33] Ibid., Article 2.
[34] Ibid., Article 3.

Bérulle and his followers in France who gave it a particular imprint. Vincent de Paul, Jean Eudes, and the Sulpicians each brought their own characteristics to the method.[35]

Eugène de Mazenod imbibed all this and adopted these methods for the Oblate missions. Oblates were to imitate the twofold mission of Jesus Christ: to be bearers of salvation and to evangelize the poor. With the pastoral "heart" of the French School, the missionaries aimed to be close to the people by visiting them in their homes, being available for direct encounters, especially in the confessional, and adapting their language and ceremonies to the understanding and culture of the villagers. The Oblates instructed people, who had been untouched by the church as a result of the Revolution, with sound catechetical knowledge and then accompanied them as they entered into a deeper and more committed relationship with God. The success of the missions was gauged by the numbers of people who came to confession and received communion.

It was at St. Sulpice that Eugène de Mazenod learned this methodology that was used by a succession of Oblates throughout the world for many decades.

Reaching Out Through Works of Charity

The French School of spirituality was known not only for its theological reflection, but was marked by its outreach to the poor and needy. Vincent de Paul stands out as one of its outstanding examples. He was one of the formators of Jean-Jacques Olier, thus ensuring that his concern for the poor continued in the seminary as part of the training of future priests. Olier himself had adopted the principle: "Let us remember that Our Lord chose the poor to serve as a witness to the divinity of his mission, and to draw from it the unmistakable character of the truth of his doctrine; the members who most suffer of its members more particularly than the others they have a right of preference to our tenderness and our affection."[36]

Eugène de Mazenod had learned his lesson well, and echoed Olier's words in the first documented sermon that we have after his priestly ordination in 1813:

---

[35] Cf. Yves Krumenacker, "The French School of Spirituality," 339ff.
[36] Ibid., 318.

The poor, a precious portion of the Christian family, cannot be abandoned to their ignorance. Our divine Savior attached such importance to this that he took on himself the responsibility of instructing them and he cited as proof of the divinity of his mission the fact that the poor were being evangelized, *pauperes evangelizantur* [37]

As a seminarian, he had been formed to look out for the poor and the most abandoned in any situation. He taught catechism classes to a group of boys whom he described as "the poorest in the parish, children of tavern keepers, in a word, a vermin-ridden lot." [38]

The very groups that Vincent de Paul had concentrated on helping and evangelizing were the ones Eugène de Mazenod chose to work with after his return to Aix as a young priest: the prisoners, domestic servants, and the youth who were directionless because of lack of catechesis. [39] Later the Oblates were to join him and continue this ministry.

In 1837 Eugène de Mazenod became Bishop of Marseilles, and his well-trained heart and eyes were constantly on the lookout for the most abandoned in the diocese. A harbor city, it was the second-largest city of France and doubled in population during his episcopacy. The majority of those coming into the city were poor and needy. The bishop's imagination knew no limits and the list of groups he assisted was impressive, as was the number of people drawn into different works to minister to the needy.

Ten years after taking over the diocese Eugène de Mazenod exulted, in a pastoral letter, as he surveyed the works of charity undertaken in a decade:

> Admire how these works multiply. How many new institutions have a purpose formerly unknown! Childhood, old age, the sick, the poor, the workman bent from morning to night under the weight of the day and of the heat, innocence in peril, the vice that is disgusting and filled with remorse, the young prisoner already initiated into the habits which make convicts, the big criminals, the rich on their deathbed who are often so needy before God: charity embraces

---

[37] Homily instructions in Provencal, given at the church of the Magdalene in 1813, *Oblate Writings* I, 15, n. 114, 35.

[38] Letter to his mother, 1 February 1809, *Oblate Writings* I, 14, n. 44, 96.

[39] Yves Krumenacker, "The French School of Spirituality," 318.

everything. And for new needs, it invents new means, spiritual relief, corporal works, nourishing of the soul, sustaining of the body. . . . All kinds of good works are multiplied in the name of Jesus Christ.[40]

Conclusion

Today, two hundred years after the foundation of the Missionary Oblates of Mary Immaculate, it is a privilege to be able to recall with gratitude the role of the Sulpicians in their foundation and development. Fr. Emery and his community gave the young Eugène de Mazenod a solid foundation and education in his vocation. We could say that they gave him a "compass" and taught him how to use it so that he, in turn, would share this compass with his Oblate Family. The spirit of that compass continues to guide the Oblates today as they continue to preach the Good News of the Savior to the ends of the world.

[40] *Mandement de Monseigneur l'Evêque de Marseille, pour le carême de 1847* (Marseille: Marius Olive, 1847), 8–9.

CHAPTER THREE

A Distant Mirror:
Is the French School of Spirituality Still Relevant?

Ronald D. Witherup, PSS

Introduction

This chapter addresses the question of the ongoing relevancy of the "French school of spirituality."[1] The title poses a question. The reader can probably guess that the answer will be in the affirmative, but it might not be clear how or why. I am not the first to raise the issue of the relevance of the so-called "French school of spirituality." More than thirty years ago, one of my predecessors as superior general of the Sulpicians, Raymond Deville, PSS, who wrote extensively on the French school, authored a short article entitled "Actualité de l'école française?" in which he tried to address this relevance.[2] It appeared around the time the Sulpicians had begun to "return to the sources," as Vatican Council II (1962–65) had recommended to religious orders. His article was based upon the impetus that his predecessor as superior general, Constant Bouchaud, PSS, had given the Society to do more research on Sulpician founder Fr. Jean-Jacques Olier and the French school. This push from the Society's

---

[1] The author expresses his sincere gratitude to Fr. Ronald Rolheiser, OMI, president of the Oblate School of Theology, and to the organizers and moderator of the colloquium, for the kind invitation to participate in celebrating the bicentennial of the founding of the Oblates of Mary Immaculate.

[2] *Bulletin de Saint-Sulpice* 8 (1982): 42–54. Hereafter, *BSS* refers to this journal, which was published as an annual from 1975 to 2016 but now continues as an occasional publication of the Society of the Priests of St. Sulpice.

leadership led to an increasing interest in the history and spirituality of the seventeenth century, an interest which continues today. For the four hundredth anniversary of the birth of Olier (2008), the Society sponsored an academic colloquium in Paris at the Institut Catholique and eventually published two major works, which also attempt to address the issue of relevance, albeit in a manner different from my own proposal here.[3] The reason this task is still worthwhile is the availability of new materials in recent years, especially critical editions of the writings of Sulpician founder Fr. Olier, whose works will be the main source throughout this article.[4]

Before proceeding, we need briefly to clarify two aspects of this study: the French school itself and the meaning of relevance.

In contrast to other well-known "spiritualities" in Church history— Benedictine, Franciscan, Dominican, Carmelite, Cistercian, Jesuit (Ignatian), etc.—the French school is far less known. A recent example of how regularly the French school is overlooked can be seen in a new book billed as a "comprehensive" overview of the Catholic tradition of prayer.[5] There are chapters on Franciscan, Carmelite, Dominican, Benedictine, Salesian, Augustinian, Jesuit (Ignatian) traditions of prayer, and even that of the Sisters of Mercy, but there is no chapter on the French school!

Even more serious is the fact that some scholars question the designation "French school" for this seventeenth-century phenomenon.[6] They believe it misleads one to conceive that there was an organized, formal school of thought. Was there really a "French school of spirituality"? Its

---

[3] See the *BSS* 34 (2008), "Jean-Jacques Olier (1608–2008). Hier et aujourd'hui," 411; and Maurice Vidal, ed., *Jean-Jacques Olier: Homme de talent, serviteur de l'Évangile (1608–1657)* (Paris: Desclée de Brouwer, 2009).

[4] See *Jean-Jacques Olier, Correspondance: Nouvelle édition des lettres suivies de textes spirituels donnés comme lettres dans les éditions antérieures*, ed. Gilles Chaillot, Irénée Noye, and Bernard Pitaud, Mystica 3 (Paris: Honoré Champion, 2014); Jean-Jacques Olier, *Introduction à la vie et aux vertus chrétiennes, avec une seconde partie inédite, de la conformité à l'extérieur des mystères*, critical edition in accord with the manuscripts, ed. Mariel Mazzocco, Mystica 6 (Paris: Honoré Champion, 2016); and the first critical biography of Fr. Olier, Bernard Pitaud, *Jean-Jacques Olier (1608–1657)* (Namur: Lessius, 2017). Unfortunately, few resources are available in English.

[5] Robert J. Wicks, ed., *Prayer in the Catholic Tradition: A Handbook of Practical Approaches* (Cincinnati: Franciscan Media, 2016).

[6] The major resource for the French school is Yves Krumenacker, *L'école française de spiritualité: Des mystiques, des fondateurs, des courants, et leurs interprètes* (Paris: Cerf, 1998).

founder and seminal thinker was Cardinal Pierre de Bérulle, founder of the French Oratory, who quickly gathered a group of disciples around him who were fascinated by his deep spiritual insights. If, however, by "school" is meant an organized, well-identified spiritual movement within the Church, purposefully founded on precise principles with easily recognized "markers" for its spiritual thought, then the term "school" is likely an over-statement. The phenomenon the term describes was rather an amorphous spiritual and mystical movement in the Church in seventeenth-century France that describes a forceful and intentional attempt to reform the Church from within. Its influence would mark succeeding generations of Catholics into the eighteenth and nineteenth centuries, especially the founders of numerous religious orders of men and women, including St. Eugène de Mazenod, founder of the Oblates.

Regarding the meaning of "relevance," my approach is simple. What interests me is what is useful or practical. So studying aspects of the French school is not merely looking for traces of theology or thematic interests but practices, teachings, or ideas that might actually apply to our modern, twenty-first century context. As I read through some of the many publications of members of the French school, especially Fr. Olier, founder of the Sulpicians, I believe there is relevant material that can be attractive today. In this chapter we will examine five touchstones from the French school that seem particularly relevant: context, pastoral orientation, baptism and a relationship with Jesus Christ, Word and sacrament, and a feminine dimension.

Context

We begin with the context in which the French school was born, an element that might easily be glossed over as irrelevant, given the exigencies of periods of history. I remember being taught by one of my professors during doctoral studies that a text without a context is a pretext! The same can be said with movements in history. The French school of spirituality came into being in a particular context that should be recalled and that is pertinent to the question of relevance to our own time. The French school, as mentioned above, was really a loose movement of religious leaders in the seventeenth century who were interested in and concerned about the reform of the Church. In fact, one cannot understand the French school without seeing it as part of a larger movement in the

Church after the Council of Trent (1545–63) which was concerned about the reform of the Church. In light of the 500th anniversary (2017) of the beginning of the Protestant Reformation (October 31, 1517), we should remember that, despite its excesses and sad legacy of division in the church, Martin Luther's main point was not entirely false. The condition of the church in the sixteenth and seventeenth centuries was embarrassing. It was largely in disarray, had lost sight of many key aspects of the gospel message, and was seen as corrupt. The state of the clergy was also abysmal, with a serious lack of education and formation, scandalous moral behavior, and ignorance of Scripture. The church ultimately, if grudgingly, acknowledged that the church by the sixteenth century had become bloated with accretions and was sorely in need of reform. Thus, the main purpose of the Council of Trent was to address long-needed reforms within the church, ideally in a way that would not jeopardize its unity.[7] It was a reform council. If previously Trent and its aftermath led to the vocabulary of the Counter-Reformation, today it has become more current to speak of "Reformations" (in the plural), because the reform-minded developments after 1517 were much more complex than previously recognized.[8]

Fr. Olier and other members of the French school understood their task as nothing less than reforming the Church. But Olier thought that the key to this reform lay in reforming the clergy. If one could reform the priests themselves, then the flock would follow. Three brief citations illustrate this goal. Olier writes:

> God wishes me to renew his Church by instructing many priests in the ecclesiastical spirit so they will then go forth to serve God where He is pleased to call them.[9]

---

[7] The best current, accessible study of the Council of Trent is John W. O'Malley, *Trent: What Happened at the Council* (Cambridge, MA: Belknap, 2013), which is largely based on the magisterial study of Hubert Jedin, *A History of the Council of Trent*, trans. Ernest Graf, 2 vols. (London: Thomas Nelson, 1957–61).

[8] See, for example, Christopher M. Bellitto, *The Reformations* (Rockville, MD: Now You Know Media, 2012), 12 lectures on audio CD or video DVD; Christopher M. Bellitto, *Renewing Christianity: A History of Church Reform from Day One to Vatican II* (New York/Mahwah: Paulist, 2001); and Carlos M. N. Eire, *Reformations: The Early Modern World, 1450–1650* (New Haven/London: Yale University Press, 2016).

[9] *Mémoires* 3, 83. Fr. Olier's unpublished *Mémoires* in both autograph and typed format are privately kept in the Sulpician Archives in Paris and are only available to qualified researchers.

Elsewhere he writes:

> I see now that there has to be a large number of pastors throughout
> the Church who will seek reform. . . . That is the Order of Jesus
> Christ, the first Pastor of souls, which must now reform itself to
> bring about the reform of the universal Church.[10]

Olier, following the example and encouragement of his friend Vincent
de Paul, with whom he had been ordained and who became for a time
his spiritual director, decided that the means for such reform lay in the
founding of seminaries, which the Council of Trent had envisioned. (Keep
in mind that one of Luther's main complaints was the lack of education
of the clergy, as well as proper formation in spirituality and morality.)
Olier regularly speaks of the need for an "apostolic spirit" (*esprit apos-
tolique*) needed among the clergy to succeed in this reform. He writes:

> If there were three apostolic men in a seminary filled with humility,
> kindness, patience, zeal, charity, and poverty, with the knowledge
> and wisdom needed for this heavenly work, they would be able to
> sanctify a whole diocese. . . . They would sanctify many people and
> would be able to affect not only the seminary of a diocese, but a whole
> kingdom. Such is the power of the apostolic and selfless spirit.

In essence, Olier's vision is about putting into practice the call of the
Council of Trent for reform of the Church by reformation of the clergy.[11]

Now consider our own context. Like the members of the French school,
we are living in a period within five decades of the end of a major ecumenical council that, in the estimation of some, turned the world upside
down. Although clearly many of the historical and cultural circumstances
are different, nevertheless, it is fair to say we live in a time when church
reform is also a preoccupation. Such a postconciliar time causes considerable tension and movement back and forth like a pendulum. Thus,

---

[10] *Mémoires* 3, 332–33.

[11] One should note, however, that the Catholic Church did not use the words "reform"
or "reformation" in official documents until Vatican Council II. The 1964 Decree on
Ecumenism (*Unitatis Redintegratio*), while avoiding the expression *Ecclesia semper reformanda est* characteristic of Protestant formulations in the twentieth century, speaks of
the need for "continual reform" in the Church: "Christ summons the church, as she goes
her pilgrim way, to that continual reformation [*perennem reformationem*] of which she
always has need, as she is a human institution here on earth" (6).

Pope Francis—who sees himself as elected Supreme Pontiff to oversee the reform of the church in our day—has consistently evoked the need for the church to become less administrative, less triumphant, humbler, more welcoming, while other forces are calling for a so-called "reform of the reform" and seeking a smaller, holier, more purified church. In his December 2016 address to the Curia, the pope specifically addressed the question of the need for ongoing reform and tied it closely to the notion of conversion. He said explicitly, "reform is first and foremost a sign of life, of a Church that advances on her pilgrim way, of a Church that is living and for this reason *semper reformanda*, in need of reform because she is alive."[12] This and earlier addresses of the pope clearly indicate his vision for the necessary reform of the church in our time.

Those who know their history understand well that it often takes the church a century or so after a major ecumenical council to find her "sea legs," if you will, or solid footing. Our own context may have its unique aspects, such as the effect of social media, the extremely rapid rate of scientific inventions, and the evolving means of communication, but in many ways we share some of the uncertainties of the seventeenth century that led it to be a wellspring for spiritual transformation in the church through the members of the French school.

Pastoral Orientation

A second, related theme from the French school that I find pertinent today concerns its pastoral orientation. The word "pastoral," unfortunately, can be misleading. Some think immediately of something that is soft, easy, undisciplined, or without solid doctrinal foundation. In seminary curricula, one finds an attitude at times that pastoral placements and pastoral courses are second-class dimensions of priestly formation. This is not what I mean by "pastoral," nor is it what the French school would reflect. Rather, pastoral evokes its original sense: all that pertains to being a good shepherd, one who properly cares for those entrusted to his or her care.

The members of the French school were anything but soft on doctrine. The writings of the French school are filled with deep, profound reflections on the basic truths of Christianity and the Catholic faith, especially

---

[12] Pope Francis, Address to the Roman Curia, December 22, 2016.

the incarnation. They read the Scriptures, the church fathers, and medieval theologians with insight. They also wrestled to explain elements of the faith in a controversial context, as cited above, in the wake of the Protestant Reformation. One can thus find elements of apologetics in some of their writings. But what most strikes me is the profoundly pastoral orientation of many members of the French school. They really wanted the faith to be understood by the faithful, and thus they wanted priests to be properly trained so that they could impart the faith authentically and explain it in understandable terms. Let us turn once more to Olier for illustration.

Olier's very orientation must be seen as pastoral. When during a retreat in December 1641 he had his vision to found a seminary and to form a community of diocesan priests to train diocesan priests, he quickly oriented his vision toward the parish that he would direct as pastor between 1642 and 1652. This was St. Sulpice, then on the outskirts of Paris and under the jurisdiction of the Abbey of Saint-Germain-des-Prés and not far from the little village of Vaugirard where Olier founded his first seminary. He wanted the seminarians to participate in parish life and so learn step-by-step good pastoral practice. In addition, as a means of helping to educate his parishioners as well as his charges in seminary formation, he would eventually write a catechism in simple question-and-answer format (novel at that time) to explain basic elements of the faith.

To give an example of Fr. Olier's pastoral sensitivity, I quote a letter he wrote to a woman who was clearly anxious about many circumstances in her life and whose dejection apparently had become overwhelming.

> You must have confidence in the goodness of God. Everything he has done for your salvation is an indication that he loves you, and his merciful acts are much greater for you than you can ever conceive. . . . I advise you often to have before you his infinite mercy, which absorbs every sin like a burning furnace consumes in an instant a piece of straw, or like the vast ocean absorbs into its depths a grain of sand thrown into it. The mercy of God has no limits; it is immense, and standing before it our sins are nothing but a tiny particle. Its great glory is to gobble up the most serious of crimes. The more it absorbs them, the more dazzling it appears. It makes its power known in the face of our numerous sins and our enormous miseries, and it exalts in the infinite grandeur of its goodness. This is the great basis for Christian confidence, of which you should often

avail yourself to overcome your dejection and to fortify yourself against your fears.

These are the words of a highly sensitive pastor, one who was seeking to comfort and strengthen someone who was experiencing great personal difficulty in her life.

Olier's approach to the mercy of God, at least to my ears, cannot help but reflect the message of Pope Francis, who has repeatedly called for a pastoral orientation in the Church. He has eschewed the approach of some bishops and priests as "princes" and has instead called for true pastors. In his emphasis on mercy, even in the face of difficult doctrinal issues like marriage and divorce, he has called for a pastoral approach, one that attempts to meet people where they are suffering and offer them hope.[13] Indeed, I suggest that Pope Francis's approach is very much in the spirit of Vatican Council II as conceived by St. Pope John XXIII as a "pastoral" council. It was never intended to proclaim new dogmas but was instead to help express the faith in ways that would make it more comprehensible to the modern world. This was not a "soft" approach to doctrine, but a pastoral one. Doctrine and pastoral practice are not polar opposites; rather they are complementary ways of trying to make church teaching more accessible and more easily understood. So, by its pastoral orientation, the French school offers us another insight into applying religious beliefs in our day.

Baptism and the Relationship with Jesus Christ

If a certain amount of shared similar context and pastoral orientation is insufficient to uphold the relevancy of the French school today, certain key themes help us move in this same direction. My third point, then, focuses on the importance of baptismal identity and the personal relationship with Jesus Christ that accompanies it.

To set the stage, we should recall that the French school is often perceived as having promoted clericalism. While it is true that Fr. Olier and all the members of the French school possessed an enormous respect for and love of the priesthood, and thereby largely focused their efforts on

---

[13] See Pope Francis's Bull of Indiction, *Misericordiae Vultus* (2015), which announced the Year of Mercy (2015–16).

the reform of the clergy, what is forgotten is that they also held in equally high esteem the baptismal identity of each Christian. By virtue of baptism, every Christian becomes a part of the royal, priestly people affirmed in the Scriptures. I cite Olier again:

> The Christian is made in himself, which is the summit of every dignity. . . . The Christian possesses the Spirit of Jesus. Now whoever is a priest cannot be stripped of this dignity: "You are a priest forever (Heb 5:6 and Ps 109:4)." He also carried this dignity in himself wherever he lives. That is why each faithful person in Jesus Christ is a priest: "You are the royal order of priests, the holy nation, the people God has chosen (1 Pet 2:9)." Faithful ones in Jesus Christ, you are kings and priests, [and] your priesthood will be eternal like that of Jesus Christ.[14]

Even more surprising, perhaps, is the use of a certain vocabulary that we normally identify with the priestly charism conferred by holy orders. For Olier, baptism first makes of each and every Christian an *alter Christus* (another Christ). This transformation begins by baptism and is at the basis of Christian identity. Being an *alter Christus* is not reserved for the ordained. Every Christian is called to this dignity, although our later theological understanding of priesthood draws attention to this title in a special way for those who participate in holy orders.

Once this special grace of transformation has begun in baptism, it continues in the growth of the relationship with Jesus Christ to which we are called. Olier was insistent on the importance of developing this relationship with the Lord. One of the most striking passages in Olier uses two Pauline citations to underscore the dramatic and transformative nature of this baptismal identity. For Sulpicians, this passage is particularly important, because it constitutes the first article of Olier's seminary project that he envisioned. He writes the following in his little tract (written in Latin) called *Pietas Seminarii Sancti Sulpitii*:

> The first and final goal of this Institute (i.e., the Sulpicians) will be to live supremely for God in Christ Jesus, Our Lord, in such a way that the interiority of his Son will penetrate our heart intimately and each one will be permitted to say, along with Saint Paul, "It is no

---

[14] *Mémoires* 11, 55–65.

longer I who live but Christ who lives in me." This will be the one ambition, the one thought, the one action of all: to live the life of Christ inwardly and to show it outwardly in our mortal body.[15]

While it is true that this passage is written in the context of Olier's vision of founding his community of priests for the purpose of initial and ongoing formation of priests, it is also clear that the spirituality it expresses impregnates his overall thought. The famous passage from Galatians that he cites—"It is no longer I who live but Christ who lives in me"—constitutes almost a refrain in Olier's writings but also in those of other members of the French school. They are fascinated by St. Paul's concept of the total transformation of the Christian that begins at baptism. We no longer live ourselves, but Christ lives in us! Moreover, the insistence on the uniformity between interior attitudes and exterior actions is noteworthy. We might say it is a very Pauline idea: Become what you are! Let the world see Christ in action by what we say and do.

This intensely Pauline spirituality, or what might properly be called "mysticism," is characteristic of Olier's approach to the Christian life and to the life of priests. Similar language appears in some of his letters to his multiple correspondents, many of whom were laity and religious. In one letter he sends this advice:

> We must become a living being for God in Jesus Christ. We should be filled with Jesus; our work, says Saint Paul, is that Jesus Christ be everything in everyone (cf. Col 3:9-11). We have to work carefully at this, my dear Mother, and between you and me, to tell the truth, that is how we must begin, knowing how to establish Jesus in us, who banishes the "Adam" within us. May his humility chase away our superiority, his love [become] pure love; his Spirit take the place of our own. In short, may the new man [human being] banish the old. We have to love and adore Jesus greatly to hold on to him in ourselves. . . . My Mother, understand well when I speak to you of being filled up with Jesus that you be filled with his dispositions,

---

[15] *Pietas Seminarii Sancti Sulpitii*, art. 1. The text contains references to the following Pauline passages: Rom 6:11; Gal 2:20; and 2 Cor 4:10-11. One cannot exaggerate the importance Fr. Olier gave to the letters of Paul. He quotes from them assiduously, and much of his spirituality is based upon Pauline conceptions. See Gérard Gaudrault, "L'influence de la pensée de Saint-Jean et Saint-Paul sur la pensée de M. Olier," *BSS* 34 (2008): 117–57.

enter into his same sentiments, even into his interior life to become
a participant there, adoring him and continually giving yourself
to him.[16]

In this passage, as in others, we see Olier's profound appreciation for
certain aspects of Pauline theology that served as a basis for his ecclesio-
logical understanding.

In what way might these ideas resonate today? To me, the answer is
again rather evident. One of the great outcomes of Vatican II was a re-
discovery of the universal call to holiness and the shared baptismal identity of each Christian who is called to become like Christ in all that we
think, say, and do. *Lumen Gentium*, the Dogmatic Constitution on the
Church (1964), affirms the universal call to holiness:

> All Christians in whatever state or walk in life are called to the full-
> ness of christian life and to the perfection of charity, . . . following
> in his footsteps and conformed to his image, doing the will of God
> in everything, they may wholeheartedly devote themselves to the
> glory of God and to the service of their neighbor. (LG 40)

Only after the Constitution outlines this universal call in the following
words, does it address the various distinctions within the church like the
hierarchy:

> The forms and tasks of life are many but there is one holiness, which
> is cultivated by all who are led by God's Spirit and, obeying the
> Father's voice and adoring God the Father in spirit and in truth,
> follow Christ, poor and humble in carrying his cross, that they may
> deserve to be sharers in his glory. All, however, according to their
> own gifts and duties must steadfastly advance along the way of a
> living faith, which arouses hope and works through love. (LG 41)

---

[16] J.-J. Olier, Letter 84, to Mère de Bressand, in G. Chaillot et al., *Jean-Jacques Olier, Correspondance*, 188–89. The reference to "Adam" is an obvious allusion to Paul's creative christological teaching that Jesus is the "last Adam" who replaces the first Adam and has all the capabilities to obey God's will that the first Adam did not have (see Rom 5:12-14; 1 Cor 15:22, 45-49; and perhaps Phil 2:6-11). Olier sees remnants of the first Adam in each human being that must be banished by Christ, the new Adam, who comes to dwell in us.

It is also interesting to see that the very same passage from Galatians that Olier uses over and over again to reinforce this baptismal identity and call is cited in *Lumen Gentium* in a similar context: becoming more and more Christlike is the call of every Christian. Pope Benedict XVI, too, citing *Lumen Gentium*, reinforced this point in a General Audience (April 13, 2011): "The saints expressed in various ways the powerful and transforming presence of the Risen One. They let Jesus so totally overwhelm their life that they could say with St Paul 'it is no longer I who live, but Christ who lives in me' (Gal 2:20). Following their example, seeking their intercession, entering into communion with them, 'brings us closer to Christ, so our companionship with the saints joins us to Christ, from whom as from their fountain and head issue every grace and the life of the People of God itself.'"[17]

Word and Sacrament

A fourth element in my proposal concerns the careful balance of Word and sacrament that I believe is evident in the French school of spirituality. While it is true that all the members of the French school had a deep love for the sacraments, especially the Eucharist, it is also true—and a neglected point—that most members of the French school had a strong devotion to the Bible, the Word of God. What is all the more remarkable about this observation is that these were Catholics living in the wake of the Protestant Reformation and subject to the tendency in Catholicism at the time to define itself over and against the Reformers by emphasizing the sacramental life of the Catholic faith. Where Luther and other Protestants clearly emphasized the importance of Sacred Scripture and downplayed (or reduced in number) the sacraments, Catholics tended to do the reverse. But what do we find in Fr. Olier?

Reflecting on many diverse elements of Holy Orders, Olier writes the following:

> God has two treasures for which he made the Church a depository: the first is his body and precious blood; the second is the Word or His Scripture, His divine testament, which is the deposit of His se-

---

[17] *Lumen Gentium* 5. Note the use of the passage from Galatians so evident in the writings of Fr. Olier.

crets and divine wishes. . . . Because this sacred treasure of Scripture has been given with confidence into the hands of the Church, which has then confided it to the priest so that it may be heard by and explained to the people, . . . it should be accorded the greatest respect and reverence it merits, as Saint Augustine remarks when he says that he wants us to give the same respect to the least syllables of Scripture that we give to the particles of the Blessed Sacrament, because they are like envelopes, curtains and sacraments which contain the Holy Spirit, being the ordinary instrument through which He acts in the Church.[18]

In this citation, we notice the balance between Word and sacrament which is conveyed not only by the mention of the two as special ministries of the priesthood but also by the fact that both demand the same proper respect. Why? Using an allusion to a passage from St. Augustine, Olier speaks of each syllable of Scripture as comparable to each particle of the consecrated host at Eucharist. Both communicate the divine "real presence." Pope Benedict XVI, in his postsynodal apostolic exhortation on the Word of God, *Verbum Domini*, actually makes a similar point, speaking about the same way the Scripture and the Eucharist should be approached. He quotes a contemporary of St. Augustine, the curmudgeon St. Jerome.

Saint Jerome speaks of the way we ought to approach both the Eucharist and the word of God: "We are reading the sacred Scriptures. For me, the Gospel is the Body of Christ; for me, the holy Scriptures are his teaching. And when he says: whoever does not eat my flesh and drink my blood (Jn 6:53), even though these words can also be understood of the [eucharistic] Mystery, Christ's body and blood are really the word of Scripture, God's teaching. When we approach the [eucharistic] Mystery, if a crumb falls to the ground we are troubled. Yet when we are listening to the word of God, and God's

---

[18] Jean-Jacques Olier, *Traité des Saints Ordres (1676) comparé aux écrits authentiques de Jean-Jacques Olier (†1657)*, ed. Gilles Chaillot, Paul Cochois, and Irénée Noye (Paris: Compagnie des Prêtres de Saint-Sulpice, 1984), 125–26. This text is the critical edition from diverse writings of Olier assembled by Louis Tronson, PSS, third superior general of the Sulpicians. While the form of the text cannot be considered definitive, it is a reasonable reconstruction. The allusion to Augustine is Sermo CCC, Migne, *Patrologie Latine* 39, 2319.

Word and Christ's flesh and blood are being poured into our ears
yet we pay no heed, what great peril should we not feel?"[19]

My point is to assert that the sentiment from Olier is not that far from
modern Catholic thought and especially Vatican II which, in *Dei Verbum*,
the Dogmatic Constitution on Divine Revelation, affirms:

> The church has always venerated the divine scriptures as it has
> venerated the Body of the Lord, in that it never ceases, above all in
> the sacred liturgy, to partake of the bread of life and to offer it to the
> faithful from the one table of the word of God and the Body of
> Christ. (DV 21)

The Constitution on the Sacred Liturgy makes a related point by emphasizing the multiple types of real presence of the risen Lord during the
liturgy, one of which is during the proclamation of the Scriptures. The
Constitution affirms:

> Christ is always present in his church, especially in liturgical cele-
> brations. He is present in the sacrifice of the Mass both in the person
> of his minister, "the same now offering, through the ministry of
> priests, who formerly offered himself on the cross," and most of all
> in the eucharistic species. By his power he is present in the sacra-
> ments, so that when anybody baptizes it is really Christ himself who
> baptizes. He is present in his word since it is he himself who speaks
> when the holy scriptures are read in church. Lastly, he is present
> when the church prays and sings, for he has promised "where two
> or three are gathered together in my name there am I in the midst
> of them" (Mt 18:20).[20]

This incredibly rich notion of the equality between Word and sacrament
was characteristic of Olier's thought, all the more remarkable when, as
mentioned above, one remembers the context of the Protestant Reformation and post-Tridentine reforms.[21]

---

[19] *Verbum Domini* 56; quoting Jerome, *In Psalmen* 147: CCL 78, 337–38.

[20] *Sacrosanctum Concilium* 7.

[21] See Pierre Bougie, "Table des Écritures et Table eucharistique chez le fondateur du
Séminaire de Saint-Sulpice," *BSS* 34 (2008): 268–89.

The Feminine Dimension

My final point touches on a most delicate question, the role of women.[22] Despite the highly sensitive nature of the topic today, when the question of women's role in the church is often tied to the issue of ordination, it may come as a surprise that members of the French school of spirituality worked closely in ministry with women, and some women were extremely influential in guiding the mission of congregations they founded or co-founded. Think of Vincent de Paul and Louise de Marillac (1591–1660) and the founding of the Daughters of Charity, or Jean Eudes and Marguerite de Saint-Sacrement. Or a precursor of the French school and a person who greatly influenced Fr. Olier by his preaching, François de Sales and his work with Jeanne de Chantal. Fr. Olier himself was greatly influenced by several women who proved important to sustaining him and his vision of reform for the Church: Marie Rousseau, who helped him get through his personal struggles; Blessed Agnès de Langeac, prioress of the cloistered Dominicans in Langeac in the Auvergne region of France who helped Olier from a distance sustain his commitment to the priesthood; and others such as the Mère de Bressand. Of course, one should also remember that such cooperation between women and men in ministry is found earlier than the French school. One thinks of siblings like Benedict and Scholastica, or Francis of Assisi and Clare, or even the like-minded spirituality of John of the Cross and Teresa of Avila. The fact is that the French school exhibits a remarkable openness to the thought of women, especially those who were perceived as possessing incredible wisdom and a deep sense of mysticism, which marks much of the thought of the French school.

Most important of these feminine dimensions, albeit of a different character, is the well-developed devotion to the Blessed Virgin Mary. This is a characteristic of the French school that several members, beginning with Cardinal de Bérulle, deepened in their reflections and writings. This path would expand in the spiritual thought of Louis-Marie Grignon de Monfort whose Marian devotion would find broad success in popular devotions, as well as in Eugène de Mazenod's teachings for the Oblates

---

[22] For a brief overview, see Agnes Cunningham, "The Role of Women in the French School," in *The French School of Spirituality: An Introduction and Reader*, ed. Raymond Deville, trans. Agnes Cunningham (Pittsburgh: Duquesne University Press, 1994), 214–35.

of Mary Immaculate. Olier is no exception in this development and indeed made his own distinctive contribution. In particular, Olier emphasizes the importance of Mary as a model for priests! In fact, he sees in
her the perfection of priestly commitment. Her *"fiat voluntas tua"* is
nothing less than the absolute acceptance of the will of God that a priest
must make at his ordination. Note well that Olier and his contemporaries
would never have thought to connect this Mariology with the question
of the ordination of women, which may be a lightning rod in our own
time but was far from their minds in the seventeenth century. What is
important is to see that, both in their spirituality and in their pastoral
practice, there was a feminine dimension that served the mission of evangelization well.

This connection to Mary as Mother of Priests, Queen of the Clergy,
has resounded in our own day in teachings from every modern pope,
from Paul VI to Francis. John Paul II, in fact, called the famous Prayer
of Fr. Olier—actually, an adaptation of the prayer formulated by his
spiritual director, Charles de Condren, and one recited regularly by
Sulpicians—a perfect summation of Mariology.[23] The prayer reads:

> O Jesus, living in Mary,
> Come and live in your servants,
> In the spirit of your holiness,
> In the fullness of your power,
> In the perfection of your ways,
> In the truth of your virtues,
> In the communion of your mysteries:
> Overcome every oppressing force
> In your Spirit,
> For the glory of the Father. Amen.

What is striking about the prayer is the opening line, which evokes both
a Mariology and a Christology at the same time. Olier's Christocentric
thought is ever present in his reflections on the role of the Jesus' Mother.
"Jesus, living in Mary . . ." evokes both the conception of Jesus Incarnate
in the womb of his mother and his ongoing action in the world as risen

---

[23] Comments made after a Lenten retreat preached by Cardinal James A. Hickey in
February 1988. See James A. Hickey, *Mary at the Foot of the Cross* (San Francisco: Ignatius
Press, 1988).

Lord. In one passage Olier also alludes to a certain eucharistic imagery in which a connection is made between Mary as the receptacle of Jesus and the tabernacle where Jesus still dwells to be adored.

> Jesus Christ in Mary is in a tabernacle where he wants to be adored;
> Jesus Christ in Mary is on a throne where he wants to be honored;
> Jesus Christ in Mary is an oracle where he wants to be heard; . . .
> Jesus Christ in Mary is in his bed of justice where he wants to forgive;
> Jesus Christ in Mary is in his place of repose where he wants to be congratulated. . . . O, who can understand what is Mary to Jesus Christ and what is Jesus in Mary![24]

Olier obviously reflected deeply on the mystery of Mary's role in the history of salvation, beginning with her immaculate conception, which was not yet a dogma of the faith in the seventeenth century but certainly in active discussion, through her role in the incarnation, and even to her presence at the foot of the cross with the disciple whom Jesus loved (John 19:25-27). This was an image for Olier of the birth of the new community of faith, the church. Olier's devotion to Mary also explains his choice of November 21, the feast of the Presentation of Mary in the Temple, as the patronal feast of the Sulpicians, which is celebrated to this day. As Mary was given in service to God in the Temple, so Olier envisioned his followers and the seminarians they formed as equally called to surrender themselves totally to the service of God and God's holy people.

The use of Mary as a model for priests has continued strongly in various modern teachings, such as John Paul II's postsynodal apostolic exhortation *Pastores Dabo Vobis* (1992).[25] But we should also emphasize that the French school was careful generally to avoid exaggerated forms of Mariology that the church would find unacceptable.[26] Their approach was simultaneously theological and affective. Their image of Mary is never wholly disconnected from Christology or even Trinitarian theology. Mary

---

[24] *Mémoires* 9, 250–51.

[25] *PDV* 82.

[26] Unfortunately, editions of a book falsely attributed to Fr. Olier continue to appear under his name and promote the kind of exaggerated Mariology the Church finds suspect. I refer to *Vie intérieure de la Très Sainte Vierge Marie* (Paris: Poussielgue Frères, 1866), which was actually a work of Sulpician Fr. Etienne-Michel Faillon (1800–1870), loosely based upon fragments of a manuscript of Olier's.

is perceived as a vehicle through which God reached out to offer salvation to the world through the gift of his own Son, the incarnate Word-made-flesh. Mary's role was critical in this divine economy of salvation, but it also has appropriate limits.

The feminine dimension I outline here is but a mere sketch of what could be said. The essential point is that this dimension resonates well with the later Mariology of the church as it developed in history and also can inform our contemporary devotion to Mary from a theological and spiritual perspective. Moreover, although one awaits further concrete steps by Pope Francis to ensure a greater role for women in Church governance, he has spoken numerous times about the need to respect the unique role of women in the Church.

Conclusion

With these five touchstones, I have suggested the French school indeed remains relevant today. Yet we must not minimize the challenge one confronts in reading the writings of the French school. One must be attentive to a distinctive vocabulary, as well as to the unique historical and cultural context of the seventeenth century. Understanding some passages from Bérulle or Olier is not easy. At times the images are jarring and even incomprehensible. But then we must remember we are often dealing with men and women of a distant era who were essentially mystics and who therefore sometimes touched the deepest mysteries of faith in ways hard to describe.

Yet I believe my main point is valid. In proposing these five topics I have tried to address the task assigned to me, to speak about the French school whose tradition also lives on in the Oblates of Mary Immaculate on the occasion of their bicentennial. I have asserted that the French school, despite its relative obscurity in Roman Catholic circles today, remains profoundly relevant. I have only chosen five evident themes—context, the pastoral orientation, the role of baptismal identity and life in Christ, the balance of Word and sacrament, and a feminine dimension. Other themes strike me as equally relevant, such as evangelization and the need to foster the Church's mission of outreach, incarnation and its importance for understanding how God reaches out to humanity in friendship, or the nature and power of prayer. All of these have potential for enhancing our appreciation of the French school's teachings and their applicability today.

What I have attempted to show is, to borrow a phrase from Barbara Tuchman's masterful treatment of the fourteenth century, that looking closely at the seventeenth-century French school of spirituality is like peering into a "distant mirror" in which we find ourselves more clearly reflected than we ever could have imagined.[27] If the times have changed significantly, we find ourselves nevertheless confronting some of the same challenges faced by the members of the French school. We are still struggling to implement the vision of a major ecumenical council. We still have the arduous task of trying to restore the unity of a church sadly injured by sharp divisions and ongoing theological and practical differences. We still work at overcoming the serious scandals of clergy, especially seen in the scourge of sexual abuse of minors, cover-ups, and misuse of finances. We still seek to affirm each individual's baptismal identity, their call to personal relationship with Christ, and the recognition of their human dignity. We still work to bring Word and sacrament together in a way that uniformly nourishes the church's life and promotes true unity. We still desire to be eminently pastoral in our approach to people while not compromising on essentials of the faith. And we obviously wrestle with the question of how to promote the full participation of the feminine dimension in the Church in a way that respects the dignity of women but also respects the authentic living tradition of the Church.

In multiple ways, this distant mirror challenges us to learn from the history and theology of our ancestors in faith in the French school. What can we learn from them and their experience? How can we better respond to the call to follow Christ in our own day?

To conclude, I recall here the closeness of Eugène de Mazenod with Jacques-André Emery, the Sulpician superior general at the time of the French Revolution and its aftermath. Fr. Emery, whom Sulpicians consider a second founder because he saved the Society during the difficult period of the Revolution and the Terror, recognized in young de Mazenod a devout and dedicated seminarian whose potential was evident. So, when de Mazenod was ordained, he was immediately invited to join the Sulpician seminary faculty at a time when Napoleon had suppressed the Society of St. Sulpice and the Sulpicians were dispersed. What is clear from this and subsequent history is that de Mazenod was imbued with the same zeal found in the major figures of the French school. The same

---

[27] See Barbara Tuchman, *A Distant Mirror: The Calamitous 14th Century* (New York: Ballantine, 1978).

apostolic Spirit evident in Sulpician history from the time of Olier finds a home in the ongoing vision of de Mazenod and his successors in Oblate ministry all over the world. We might say that de Mazenod peered into the mirror and perceived exactly that call, that identity that would direct his energetic missionary efforts that continue today. This is the great grace one can find by examining the living tradition of the French school.

Further Reading

Deville, Raymond. *The French School of Spirituality: An Introduction and Reader*. Translated by Agnes Cunningham. Pittsburgh: Duquesne University Press, 1994. See also the new, expanded French edition: *L'École française de spiritualité, édition revue et augmentée*. Paris: Desclée de Brouwer, 2008.

Thompson, William M., ed., *Bérulle and the French School of Spirituality. Selected Writings*. Classics of Western Spirituality. New York/Mahwah: Paulist, 1989.

PART TWO

CHAPTER FOUR

Captured Yet Free:
The Rich Symbolism of the Heart
in French Spirituality

Wendy M. Wright

It was an era of the heart. Not simply in the sense of an emerging focus on human emotion or affections. Rather, the period in Western Europe spanning the early to late modern periods was an era in which the heart as symbol and as sign was utilized in myriad ways. Casting a wide gaze upon the denominationally diverse early modern European world, the predominance of the heart image is captured in the phrase "the religion of the heart" coined by historian Ted A. Campbell to describe those approaches to the Christian life, including Pietism, Methodism, Jansenism as well as the Moravian and Hasidic movements that shared a concern with experience as a source of knowledge and emphasized an affective relationship with God.[1] This certainly was also true of Roman Catholic spiritual currents of the same era—the Ignatian and Salesian specifically—that took a decidedly humanist stance when considering the relationship between human and divine and the extent to which human beings were intrinsically oriented toward God through a reciprocal bond of love. All these spiritual schools, movements, or denominations made liberal use of both the language and the visual image of the heart: a heart strangely warmed, a converted heart, the knowledge of the heart, the discernment of the direction of desires of the heart, the exchange of

---

[1] Ted A. Campbell, *The Religion of the Heart: A Study of European Religious Life in the Seventeenth and Eighteenth Centuries* (University of South Carolina, 1991).

hearts, the wounds of the heart, a universe of conjoined hearts, the Sacred Heart, the Immaculate Heart. These and many other visual and verbal images of the heart proliferated in Christian discourse and appeared in material devotional artifacts of the period.

Moreover, during this era the physical heart itself was revered as the distilled essence of a person: among relics of venerated Catholic deceased, the heart was most treasured. This had long been true for European royalty: Richard the Lionheart of England (d.1199), for example, had instructions that upon his death his heart be separately embalmed and entombed in Rouen, and Robert the Bruce of Scotland (d.1329) requested that his disembodied heart be taken on a tour of the Holy Land before being returned to his natal land. The tradition continued, especially in Catholic countries, into the seventeenth and eighteenth centuries: James II of England/James VII of Scotland (1633–1701), a convert to the Roman church and promoter of religious liberty in his Protestant realm, fled to the continent after being overthrown by his successors. Upon his death James's heart was placed in a silver-gilt locket and enshrined in a reliquary in the Visitation of Holy Mary Monastery in Chaillot, France. The heart of his widowed queen, Maria di Modena (1633–1701), was also enshrined there as was the heart of Henrietta-Marie of France (1609–1669), the convent foundress, daughter of French monarch Henri IV (1553–1610), and wife of England's Charles I (1600–1649), who sought refuge within the monastic walls after the execution of her husband during the English Civil Wars.

Promoters of the Catholic cause throughout the centuries of our concern gloried in the practice of venerating the physical heart of saintly figures. During the Catholic reformation those deemed saints were promoted as witnesses to the prestige and spiritual vitality of the Church of Rome. Defenders of the Catholic faith and the *ancien régime* during the turmoil of the French Revolution also clung to the practice of venerating the relics of revered figures. Savoyard bishop François de Sales's (1567–1622) heart, which along with other body parts had at his death been fought over by devotees, had been enshrined in the monastery of the Visitation in Lyons when, threatened with extinction during the Reign of Terror (1793–74), the monastic community fled and embarked on a perilous journey across the Alps to Mantua in Italy. They carried with them their founder's heart, stripped of its valuable golden reliquary that had been seized by the functionaries of the revolutionary forces. The lengths to which the possession-less community went to abscond with and secrete away their "treasure of inestimable value" is worthy of a detective thriller.[2] A less dramatic but not less venerated story concerns the adulation of the revered Vincent de Paul's (1581–1660) incorrupt heart that was, as custom dictated, separated from the remainder of his body. It resides to this day housed in a much-visited reliquary in the historic motherhouse of the Daughters of Charity at Rue de Bac in Paris.

France

Narrowing focus to French spirituality of the seventeenth to the long nineteenth centuries reveals a rich profusion of heart symbolism in the main Roman Catholic spiritual currents. Special devotional attention was paid to the hearts of the seminal figures of the faith: Jesus Christ and his mother Mary. But there was also focal attention paid to the human heart in the spiritual literature and practice of the time, the heart being seen as central in the drama of spiritual transformation and maturation. For the most part, the term "heart," when used at this time in reference to the human heart, was firmly rooted in its biblical meaning and connoted the whole person where the intellect, memory, and their attendant capacities including the affections or desires converged. It did not merely refer to the human affections or emotions or passions.

Scriptural images of the human heart and of allusions to the hearts of Jesus and of Mary and of the divine heart had, of course, long been part and parcel of the language of Christianity. One thinks, for example, of late traditional meditations on Mary's "pondering" or "keeping" things in her heart" (Luke 1:29, 2:19, 2:51) or the Lukan prophecy (2:35) voiced by Simeon that the mother's heart would be pierced as a sign of the shared destiny in which Mother and son participated. These were part of the "Joyful Mysteries" prayed as part of the Rosary. But something new was emerging in early modern Catholic spirituality that would give nuance and depth to the symbol of the heart. Historian Donna Spivey Ellington has described the significant cultural transition from an oral to a literate

---

[2] *I Leave You my Heart: A Visitandine Chronicle of the French Revolution: Mère Marie-Jéronyme Verot's Letter of 15 May 1794*, ed. and trans. Péronne-Marie Thibert, VHM (Philadelphia: Saint Joseph's University Press, 2000).

society that was taking place in the early modern world.[3] This, she claims, gave rise to a new type of spirituality. In oral culture, knowledge derives from the concrete, and religious expression tends to the bodily and externalized, while literacy in contrast fosters a mindset that favors inner awareness and individualism. Spivey Ellington chronicles the gradual replacement of a medieval, exteriorized, concrete piety with a more "spiritualized," inward faith that accorded with the more privatized and individual piety that is bred in a literate culture. She links this to the early modern era's increased ecclesial attention to private sacramental confession, privatized devotion, the popularity of spiritual direction, as well as the acquisition of virtue as being hallmarks of an increasingly literate society. A parallel idea is advanced by historian Mosche Sluhovsky who holds up the era's popular practice of "general confession," an introspective recounting of one's entire life dispositions for the purpose of spiritual renewal and regeneration, as evidence of the emergence of modern notions of the self. [4]

This inward turn was of great interest to all the reformers of the late sixteenth and seventeenth centuries, Catholic and non-Catholic alike. The capacity for self-reflection, for interiority, was key to their understanding of the reformed and well-lived Christian life. The new inward, reflective, and thus the idealized human person is glimpsed, in Spivey Ellington's narrative, through images of the Virgin Mary. If in the medieval (oral) culture, she argues, Mary was honored for her bodily contribution, her motherhood, and for her objective role in the history of salvation, in the early modern period the Virgin became first and foremost the self-controlled, silent contemplative whose humility and obedience were her virtuous crown. Her inner life, the qualities of her heart, now commanded attention.

Newly stressed was Mary as role model, someone whose piety and receptivity to God's word could be imitated by all Christians. Certainly, for monastics in the medieval era the Virgin had functioned as a model of contemplative receptivity but what was new in the early modern world

---

[3] Donna Spivey Ellington, *From Sacred Body to Angelic Soul: Understanding Mary in Late Medieval and Early Modern Europe* (Washington DC: Catholic University of America Press, 2001).

[4] Mosche Sluhovsky, "General Confession and Self-Knowledge in Early Modern Catholicism," in *Knowledge and Religion in Early Modern Europe: Studies in Honor of Michael Heyd*, ed. Tamar Herzig, Michael Heyd, Asaph Ben-Tov, and Yaacov Deutsch, 25–46 (Brill, 2013).

was the emphasis on her as an imitable model of the virtues for everyone including the laity. Especially important were the virtues of humility and obedience that were virtues the Church urgently wanted to cultivate in the Catholic people of Europe in the sixteenth and seventeenth centuries. These were traditional virtues associated with the contemplative life as well as virtues or qualities of heart that would well serve a reforming ecclesial community bent on uniformity of practice and belief.

In the same vein, it is interesting to note that devotion to the Immaculate Heart of Mary would flower as the seventeenth century unfolded and captured the collective Catholic imagination. This newly expanded devotion focused on Mary's interior virtues, on the *quality* of her heart. In the early and medieval church it had been primarily Mary as God-bearer (*Theotokos*), the cosmic Throne of Wisdom, the intercessory Queen of Heaven and Queen of saints that captured the loyalty of the faithful. While devotion to Mary's heart was not utterly new in the early modern era— Anselm of Canterbury and Bernard of Clairvaux are credited with prayers to her as the human contemplative ideal who disposed self to become Mother of God, and Bernardine of Siena preached rapturously of the fiery heart of the Virgin—it was not until the late seventeenth century that a formal devotion to the Heart of Mary gained momentum and took on a distinctively early modern cast. The devotion is one that clearly owes its existence to the era's shift toward interiorized piety. The same could be said of devotion to the Sacred Heart of Jesus and spiritual reflection on the interior life lived in *imitatio Christi*. The new reflexive piety led to new conceptualizations of the nature of divine love revealed through the crucified heart of Christ, a devotional focus on the qualities or virtues of the Savior's heart, and new understandings of the process of incorporation into the life of the grace.

A World of Hearts

Of the Catholic spiritual reformers from the early modern "century of saints," Savoyard François de Sales's spiritual vision is most steeped in the imagery and language of the heart. As a young man de Sales was trained in the Christian humanist curriculum taught by the Jesuits at their Parisian college of Clermont. Thus he was conversant with literature, rhetoric, and the sciences as well as with the depth of scriptural, patristic, and medieval theological and spiritual reflection and devotional practice.

The Jesuits had already inherited the ancient popular devotion to the heart of Christ that had taken visual, poetic, and prayerful forms in the medieval European Christian world and they passed this on to their students. From patristic times the Savior's pierced heart (John 19:34) had been allegorized as the salvific fountain from which flowed the sacramental streams of baptism and Eucharist. The medieval monastic world had explored the Savior's heart as the source of divine wisdom that a contemplative disciple might lean upon in intimate union (John 13:23). Devotional poetry rhapsodically celebrated the side of the Savior as the bridge to heaven bowered with herbs and fragrant flowers. Visionaries such as Gertrude the Great (1256–1302) reported vivid encounters with Jesus displaying his immeasurable love for his people as he opened his breast to reveal the eucharistic heart. Folk images portrayed the wounded heart flanked by the nail-studded feet and hands pinned upon the cross. All this was part of the patrimony to which François de Sales was heir.

Trained by his Jesuit mentors to be attentive to the interior movements of desire—consolation and desolation—and to be an exegete open to the mystical reading of the Scriptures, the young François de Sales was captivated when he encountered the *Canticle of Canticles*, opened to him in a class taught by Benedictine Scripture scholar Gilbert Génébrard. He thus came to conceive of the drama of human life as a compelling love story, an astonishing story of a world of intertwined human and divine hearts bridged by the crucified heart of Christ.

The devout Christian life was best conceived, the Savoyard came to believe, as an "exchange of hearts": the gentle, humble crucified heart of Christ (revealed in Matthew 11:29-30) gradually exchanged for the human heart through prayer and the practice of the "little virtues," those ordinary relational habituated practices such as gentleness, humility, simplicity, cordiality, and patience. The mystical trope of the exchange of hearts familiar in the era through the stories of mystics such as Catherine of Siena was, in a sense, laicized and domesticated by François who taught that all devout persons in all walks and circumstances of life were called to this heart-transformation. He saw the realization of a God-directed transformed world especially in the cultivation of loving relationships, being with one another heart to heart.

Chief among these heart-centered relationships was spiritual friendship, a unique form of equal and reciprocal love he referred to as the "bond of perfection." Taking his cue from the Gospel of John in which Jesus calls his disciples to the love of friendship with himself and each other and demonstrates the length and breadth of divine love by laying down his life for his friends (John 15: 13-15), de Sales put the heart at the center of the mystery of salvation. Just as the Son from the beginning was in the heart of the Father, knowing the secrets of the divine heart, so the beloved disciple leaned on the breast of the Son to share the secrets of that heart, thus all disciples are called from servitude to friendship, to love one another, to love as they have been loved, to communicate with God and with each other heart to heart, because friends, unlike servants, are privy to the secrets of the master's heart.

For the Savoyard bishop, as for his contemporaries, the Virgin Mary was both the focus of veneration and the model of the human person fully realized and showing forth the graces of redemption. She, who was closest to her son, the Savior, carried the Redeemer beneath her heart, was most intimate with him in reciprocal love and obedience, and shared his sufferings, her own heart being pierced by his sorrow. It was Mary who modeled the exchange of hearts to which humankind was destined. De Sales expounded on Mary's visit to her cousin Elizabeth narrated in the Gospel of Luke:

> Charity and humility] it was these two virtues which motivated her and made her leave her little Nazareth, for charity is never idle; it burns in the hearts where it dwells and reigns, and the most Blessed Virgin was full of it, because she bore Love Itself in her womb. . . . She also loved her neighbor in a most perfect degree. . . . She not only possessed charity, but had received it in such plentitude that she was charity itself. She had conceived Him who, being all love, had transformed *her* into love itself. [5]

The women's religious congregation that he founded in 1610 with widowed Frenchwoman Jeanne de Chantal (1572–1641), the Visitation of Holy Mary, was to model this Marian way of being in community to the conflicted world of the times through the practice of the little virtues of gentleness, humility, and mutual cordiality. In one of her letters to the burgeoning Visitation monastic order, Mother Superior Jeanne de Chantal encouraged her sisters in religion to embody this vision of a world of conjoined hearts.

---

[5] *The Sermons of Francis de Sales on Our Lady*, ed. Lewis Fiorelli, trans. Nuns of the Visitation (Rockford, IL: Tan Books, 1985), 50–52.

Ah, my dear sisters, our beloved Visitation is a tiny kingdom of
charity. If union and holy cherishing do not reign, it will soon be
divided and consequently, laid waste, losing the luster which all the
ingenuity of human effort could never regain. . . . Let us therefore
all pray that the Spirit of Love, uniter of hearts, grant us this close
and living union with God by the total dependence of our will to
His and between us by a perfect cherishing and reciprocal union of
heart and spirits and in our little Institute by a mutual and exact
conformity of life and affection without talk of "yours" and "mine"
ever occurring among us, and with our amiably serving each other
to the greater Glory of God.[6]

The Visitation spread rapidly in France. By the time of Jeanne de
Chantal's death in 1641 there were eighty-six foundations. The sisters
carried with them the hidden practice of the exchange of hearts. Alongside this, François de Sales's best-selling writings, *Introduction to the
Devout Life* and *Treatise on the Love of God* (the former written for lay
persons embarking on the spiritual journey, the latter for those more
advanced in devotion) spread the interiorized Salesian vision of a world
of intertwined hearts across the Catholic spiritual landscape. To
"Philothea" his imagined female lay reader and in his characteristic
rhetorically rich manner, de Sales wrote of the heart transformed by
devotion and the exercise of virtues.

Amid the difficulties that you experience in the exercise of devotion
remember our Lord's words: "A woman in labor is sorrowful because
her time has come, but once her child is born, she no longer remembers her anguish for the joy of having brought someone into the
world." You have conceived the world's noblest child, Jesus Christ,
in your soul. Until he is completely born you cannot help but suffer.
But have courage. When these sorrows pass, eternal joy will remain
for having given such a one to the world. You shall have brought
Him forth fully when you have completely formed him in your heart
and in your words by imitating his life.[7]

---

[6] Sainte Jeanne-Françoise Frémyot de Chantal, *Sa Vie et ses oeuvres*, Tome III (Paris:
Plon, 1874), 341.

[7] *Oeuvres de Saint François de Sales*, Édition complète d'après les autographs et les
éditions originales, par les soins des Religieuses de la Visitation du première monastère
de la Visitation d'Annecy (Annecy: 1892–1932), III, *Introduction de la vie dévote*, 137.

Devotion to the Sacred Heart and the Immaculate Heart

A half century after de Sales's death a young member of the Visitation monastery at Paray-le-Monial, Marguerite-Marie Alacoque (1647–90), received a series of visions between 1673 and 1675 of Jesus revealing his heart and commissioning her to be the "Apostle of the Sacred Heart": visions during which she vividly experienced the searing exchange of her own heart for that of the Savior. The first of these visionary encounters took place while she was praying before the Eucharist on the December 27 feast of John the Evangelist, named by tradition as the "beloved disciple," who had leaned on the master's breast, becoming privy to the secrets of the divine heart.

> He said to me "My divine heart is so impassioned with love for humanity and for you especially. It cannot contain the flames of its burning charity inside. It must spread them through you and show itself to humanity so that they may be enriched by the previous treasures I share with you, treasures which have all the sanctifying and saving graces needed to draw them back from the abyss of destruction." . . . He asked for my heart. I begged him to take it and he did, placing it in his own adorable heart. He let me see it there like a little atom consumed in a burning furnace. Then he returned it to me and placed it where it had been saying. . . . "It will serve as your heart . . . and you will be given the joy of shedding your blood on the cross of humiliation.[8]

The instructions given to this new Visitandine apostle were to advocate for the institution of a series of devotional and liturgical practices to give honor to and make reparation for the perceived abuses directed toward the eucharistic heart of Christ. Marguerite-Marie experienced Jesus asking her to establish a feast of the Sacred Heart in the liturgical octave following the feast of Corpus Christi (the Body and Blood of Christ, a feast whose genesis had been in the revelations of a twelfth century visionary), as well as an hour of prostration between Thursday night and Friday in honor of Christ's agony in the garden, and the practice of observing the First Friday of each month to adore the eucharistic heart and

---

[8] *Vie et oeuvres de Sainte Marguerite-Marie*, presentation Professeur R. Darricau (Paris-Fribourg: Editions St. Paul, 1991), 1:82–84.

make reparation for what were perceived as the abuses heaped upon it: failure to participate in the Eucharist due either to a false notion of human unworthiness and divine judgment or simply laxity.

Marguerite-Marie's visions took devotion to the Sacred Heart in a new direction as it became tinged with the flavor of the Bérullian or French School of spirituality with its emphasis on adoration as the primal stance to be taken before the divine, as well as shaped by the current French political and cultural moment. Jansenism as a theological proposition had been officially condemned in 1642, yet a Jansenistic spirit still permeated much of French Catholic life: a vivid sense of human unworthiness prevailed and eucharistic reception was in decline. While she was a vowed religious of the order of the Visitation of Holy Mary and thus a daughter of François de Sales and his vision of a conjoined world of human and divine hearts, the context of Marguerite Marie's spiritual flowering was quite different from her Savoyard founder's.

Although it took decades (not until 1856) for the Catholic Church to officially establish the Feast of the Sacred Heart as obligatory for the entire church, the liturgical and devotional practices Marguerite-Marie envisioned in the seventeenth century were, after some hesitation, adopted by her own Visitation community, then quickly championed by a series of Jesuits. First her confessor at Paray-le-Monial, Claude de la Colombière (1641–82) who came to believe that her visions were authentic, then Fathers Jean Croiset (1656–1738) and Joseph de Gallifet (1663–1749) took up the effort to write her biography and vigorously promote the practices she had advocated. Within a half century French Catholicism had adopted the Sacred Heart as patron and protector, and cities were consecrated to the Heart of Jesus to avoid the plague and other natural disasters.

The French School and Devotion to the Hearts

A contemporary of Marguerite-Marie Alacoque, Jean Eudes (1601–80), priest-founder of the Congregation of Jesus and Mary and the Order of Our Lady of Charity, raised devotion to the Sacred Heart of Jesus and the Immaculate Heart of Mary to new theological and spiritual heights. Eudes's thinking was deeply shaped by the Bérullian or French school of spirituality but he also drew from the heart-centered vision of François de Sales. As did the Savoyard bishop, Eudes saw the heart of Christ as the "new heart" of the children of God. He expanded this notion to apply to the Church, those incorporated into the Mystical Body of Christ through the sacrament of baptism. Eudes saw the new heart as given so that humans might love God and neighbor just as Jesus did and honored the heart of Christ as the center of the universe, the point of connection between God and the created world.

The first liturgical offices for the celebration of the Sacred Heart of Jesus and the Immaculate Heart of Mary were composed by Eudes and he dedicated the seminary chapels of his priestly community, the Congregation of Jesus and Mary (the Eudists), to the twin hearts of the Son and his Mother. The feast of the Heart of Mary was celebrated publicly for the first time in 1648, and that of the Sacred Heart of Jesus in 1672.

In keeping with the era's emphasis on Mary as the human person most loved by God and most entirely swept up in the divine embrace, Jean Eudes focused on the innumerable qualities of the Virgin's heart that exemplified the apex of divine-human reciprocal love. In his rhapsodic *The Admirable Heart of Mary*, the native of Normandy presented the term "heart" as signifying both the material, corporeal heart of the Virgin—her memory, intellect and will, the highest point of her spirit which turns directly toward God—and the entirety of her interior life. The term as he used it also included the Holy Spirit Itself and the Son of God who is the "heart" of the Father. All these, he claimed, are present in the heart of the Virgin herself. The treatise explored in cascades of imagistic language the innumerable rich metaphors and exemplary qualities that Eudes asserted can be ascribed to Mary's heart: sun, center, fountain, sea, garden, burning bush, harp, throne, sanctity, power, truth, mercy, justice, zeal, peace, glory, patience, humility, and so forth. In chapter 5 he contemplated the image of the fountain, drawing prayerfully on Scripture and tradition to exclaim how the Virgin is admirable in all the perfections and virtues that issue from her incomparable heart.

> The fourth symbolic picture of Our Lady's most blessed heart is the wonderful fountain that God caused to spring from the ground at the beginning of the world, as described in the second chapter of Genesis. "A spring rose out of the earth, watering all the surface of the earth." Bonaventure tells us that this fountain was a figure of the Blessed Virgin Mary. . . . But we have equal reason to say that this represented her heart, which is truly a living fountain whose heavenly waters irrigate not only the whole earth but every created thing

in Heaven as well as on earth. . . . So holy and impenetrable is the heart of Mary that only God, Who enclosed within His treasures of grace and put His seal upon it, can know the quality, quantity and price of the graces hidden in this sealed fountain. All we can say is that Mary's Immaculate Heart is a fountain of living and life-giving water, a fountain of milk and honey, a fountain of wine. . . . Finally it is the source of an infinity of blessings and goodness.[9]

Eudes wrote as well and with equal fervor about the mystery of the Sacred Heart of Jesus.

Jesus' heart loves boundlessly. The uncreated, divine love which fills that heart is quite simply, God's own self. Because God is unlimited, God's love is also unlimited. Since God is everywhere, God's love is everywhere, in all places and things. The Sacred Heart loves us not only in heaven but on earth. In the sun, in the stars, in everything created. We are loved in all the hearts in heaven, we are loved in all the hearts of everyone on earth who has some care for us. All the love in heaven and on earth shares in the love of Jesus' Sacred Heart. Jesus even loves us in our enemies' hearts. I say boldly that we are loved even in hell, in the hearts of the damned and demons, in spite of their anger and hatred, because divine love is everywhere, filling heaven and earth like the presence of God.[10]

Later exponents of the French School continued and expanded on heart-centered devotion. In the writings of Louis de Montfort (1673–1716), Parisian priest and founder of the Company of Mary (the Montfort Fathers), the Virgin was extolled as Queen of Hearts. De Montfort was an ardent promoter of the Rosary and is considered one of the chief architects of modern Marian devotion, placing her at the center of the plan of God and at the core of the spiritual practices that he promoted in order to transform human hearts.

Mary has received from God a great dominion over the souls of the elect; for she cannot make her residence in them as God the Father

---

[9] St. John Eudes, *The Admirable Heart of Mary*, trans. Charles di Targiani and Ruth Hauser (Buffalo: Immaculate Heart Publications, 1947), 46–47.

[10] Adapted from "Other Meditations on the Sacred Heart," in *The Sacred Heart of Jesus by John Eudes*, trans. Dom. Richard Flower (New York: Kenedy and Sons, 1946), 121–22.

ordered her to do, and as their mother, form, nourish and bring them forth to eternal life, and have them as her inheritance and portion, and form them in Jesus Christ and Jesus Christ in them, and strike the roots of her virtues in their hearts and be the inseparable companion of the Holy Ghost in all his works of grace—she cannot, I say, do all these things unless she has a right and dominion over their souls by a singular grace of the most high. . . .

Mary is the Queen of Heaven and earth by grace, as Jesus is the King of them by nature and by conquest. Now as the kingdom of Christ consists principally in the heart or interior of humanity—according to his words, "The Kingdom of God is within you"—in like manner the kingdom of Our Blessed Lady is principally in the interior of a person; that is to say, the soul.[11]

De Montfort believed that since it was through the Virgin that the redemption of the world was begun, so through her it must be consummated. With a strong sense that he was living in consciousness of the last times when the second coming of Christ is imminent, de Montfort taught that

Being the sure means and the straight and immaculate way to go to Jesus Christ and to find him perfectly, it is by her that the souls that are to shine forth especially in sanctity have to find Our Lord. He who shall find Mary shall find life, that is, Jesus Christ, who is the Way, the Truth and the Life. But no one can find her who does not seek her; and no one can seek her who does not know her; for we cannot seek or desire an unknown object. It is necessary then, for the greater knowledge and glory of the Most Holy Trinity, that Mary should be more than ever known. [12]

At the core of Louis de Montfort's spiritual program was total consecration to Mary's heart. The devotee was to surrender him- or herself to the Virgin through a variety of interior exercises designed to regenerate the person from within: honor Mary as Mother of God, meditate on her virtues and grandeurs, make acts of praise and gratitude to her, unite with her, and begin, perform and end all actions with the view of pleasing her.

[11] Adapted from Louis de Montfort, *True Devotion to Mary*, trans. Frederick Faber (Rockford, IL: TAN Books, 1985), 22.
[12] Ibid., 29.

In addition there were exterior practices which included joining a Marian association or order, giving alms, wearing Marian scapulars or the Rosary, reciting the Rosary or Little Office or Psalter of Our Lady daily, adorning her altars, carrying her image, singing canticles in her honor, and most importantly, making a solemn consecration to her heart. The formula emphasized the continuity with and deepening of the baptismal life as well as the sense of human nothingness without God that is so central to the spirituality of the French School. This Marian-focused devotion was carried throughout the Catholic world by the Association of Mary Queen of Hearts, a lay confraternity under the sponsorship of the Company of Mary.

Expansion of the Devotion to the Hearts of Mary and Jesus

The profound disruption of French Catholic life and French religious communities during the Revolution and the subsequent social and political upheavals of the late eighteenth and into the long nineteenth centuries cannot be overestimated. Yet when faithful practitioners loyal to Roman Catholicism gradually emerged again and were able to haltingly establish presence and practice, the central symbols under which they most often aligned themselves were the Hearts of Mary and of Jesus. This was sometimes a controversial identification as the image of the Sacred Heart was intertwined with the ecclesial tensions of the day: the Sacred Heart was almost solely identified with the Bourbon monarchy and the triumph of Ultramontanist over the French church's Gallicanist factions.

By the eighteenth century the trajectory of devotion to the Sacred Heart in France would move well beyond the realm of pious exercise and become the major ecclesial symbol of resistance against the republican government to champion a Catholicism aligned against the modern world. In fact, at the time of the Revolution, the Sacred Heart became the most identifiable emblem of the Counterrevolution. The emergent republic was characterized in counterrevolutionary circles as a conspiracy against altar and throne and the Sacred Heart as France's salvation and shield. In 1875 construction of the Basilica of Sacré Coeur on Montmartre in the center of Paris began. Known as the Church of the National Vow, the church was to be a sign of reparation and repentance that atoned for the sins of spiritual infidelity that had caused the defeat of France at the hands of Germany in 1870.

Eventually the image of the Sacred Heart expanded beyond the borders of France and when in 1864 Pope Leo XIII consecrated the entire human race to the Sacred Heart, it became the defining symbol of Catholic identity, situating the church in opposition to the secularism, scientism, and rationalism of the modern world. Gradually the image would lose some of its anti-modernism association and by the mid-twentieth century would once again serve primarily as a devotional image communicating the generosity of divine love, albeit an image with strongly eucharistic overtones.

Yet in the early modern era the heart was not only a political image but also a consoling and attractive image, a visual symbol of the immeasurable love of God that was, the Church of Rome asserted, the font of salvation from which poured the sacraments of Eucharist and baptism. During this later period of our inquiry and running parallel to the monarchist-nationalist strain of Sacred Heart imagery, and the anti-modernist and antisecular tone of Marian veneration, the more specifically spiritual strain of devotion to and understanding of the heart continued to flourish. Just as the heart of Christ functioned both as a devotional image, a model of human spiritual maturity, and a standard for the Catholic cause, so Mary with her Immaculate Heart also served all these functions in late modern France.

By the nineteenth century Catholic spirituality was turning away from the rigorous and severe Jansenist tendencies that had predominated in the preceding century. In keeping with the Romantic movement sweeping the continent, French Catholic figures turned anew to the heart-centered teachings of François de Sales and to the works of Alphonsus Liguori (1697–1787), moral theologian and founder of the Redemptorist Order, who championed frequent communion, robust and affective devotional practice, and encouraged pastoral sensitivity that challenged the sterile rigorism and legalism that had crept into French clerical practice. At the center of Liguori's devotional vision was the love and mercy of God expressed in the Sacred Heart of Jesus.

As the nineteenth century approached and Catholic resurgence began in earnest, numerous congregations of women and men were founded in the religious vacuum left in the wake of the social and ecclesial disruptions. They drew upon the language and imagery of the heart for patronage and as spiritual inspiration. Most of these late modern foundations were of active orientation, allowed to form to fill the need for education, health care, and social services in a fragmented society. But catechesis and evangelization were also on the minds of the founders, most of whom decried the secularization of France and many of whom, during the official suppression and disbanding of religious communities, had remained loyal to the Church of Rome, even going underground or fleeing: only emerging when shifting civil governance allowed. Many of these institutes took as their patrons and spiritual orientation the Sacred Heart of Jesus, the Immaculate Heart of Mary, or the Two Hearts. Three examples will have to suffice.

Pierre Coudrin (1768–1837) was one of those late modern champions of the new Catholic religious institutes emerging in France. Pierre was in the process of training for the priesthood when his local seminary of Poitiers was closed. Making his way to Paris, he secretly took holy orders in the library of the Irish seminary since revolutionary forces occupied the seminary chapel. The young priest then went into hiding and for a number of years maintained an underground ministry in Poitiers and Tours. During this time he met Aymer de Chevalerie (1767–1834), a young aristocratic woman who with her mother has spent time in prison for harboring a Catholic priest. The two dreamed of establishing a group to promote devotion to the Two Hearts. Gathering a few companions, the pair made their respective vows in October and December of 1800 and devoted themselves to teaching and preaching the love of the Sacred Hearts. As the political climate changed, Pierre purchased buildings on Rue Picpus in Paris for the Congregation of the Sacred Hearts of Jesus and Mary with its men's and women's branches and established their headquarters. The spirituality that sustained them was cemented by consecration to the Sacred Hearts of Jesus and Mary. The members engaged in the contemplation of and announcement of God's love made flesh in Jesus and exemplified by Mary whose heart was joined with her son's and who thus was associated with his saving work in a singular way. The Congregation of the Hearts of Jesus and Mary received official papal recognition in 1817 and focused on founding schools for poor children and seminaries to train the priesthood of their institute and on giving parish missions throughout Europe.

A second example of the prevalence of the spirituality of the heart is discovered in Madeleine-Sophie Barat (1779–1865) foundress of the Society of the Sacred Heart (RSCJ). Early in her life she had imbibed the stern spirit of postrevolutionary Catholicism under the tutelage of her cleric brother. The two of them hailed from Joigny in Burgundy, a Catholic region famous for its decidedly Jansenistic leanings. Constantly wary of God's condemnation, convinced she was unworthy to partake in the Eucharist, abusive of her body through penance and overwork, Madeleine-Sophie found herself, nonetheless, chosen to lead a teaching congregation of women who would revive the faith and follow a modified Jesuit rule. During a brief 1821 visit she made to Chambery, she met Joseph-Marie Favre (1791–1838) who was preaching a mission to one of her fledgling communities in the region. Her life was forever changed. Favre was a noted spiritual director, an early adopter of Liguorian theology and a convinced disciple of François de Sales. When she encountered Favre with his fervent message of God's love expressed in the Sacred Heart, she was captured. For seventeen years until his death, Favre was her primary spiritual guide. Despite the fact that her congregation had previously been named for the Sacred Heart of Jesus, the inner meaning of that potent symbol had never unfolded in Madeleine-Sophie's own heart. It was Favre who began to chip away at the impregnable fortress of Madeleine-Sophie's fear-filled conscience. Her director's words began to take hold and transform the inner world of the foundress and she attained a measure of inner peace. Spiritual leadership of the Society became centered on the love of God revealed in the Heart of Christ. Barat was committed to a deep life of prayer and reflection and invited the members of the Society to see this as the basis for their inner lives and for whatever tasks they undertook. The motto of her educational mission became: One heart and one mind in the Heart of Jesus.

Not only were the newly emerging communities plumbing the depths of the heart image but older congregations were as well. In November of 1830 in the chapel of the Parisian Mother House of the Daughters of Charity on Rue de Bac, a young novice of that religious congregation founded by Vincent de Paul (1581–1660) and Louise de Marillac (1591–1660), was the recipient of a Marian apparition. This was the second appearance that novice Catherine de Labouré (1811–76) had witnessed and the girl reported to her confessor that in this one Mary showed herself as a light-filled presence standing on a globe of the world and offering another globe heavenward in her outstretched arms. This latter globe Catherine understood especially to represent embattled France. Around the Virgin an oval frame contained the words "O Mary, conceived without sin, pray for us who have recourse to Thee." Catherine was then commanded to have a medal of the image struck with the promise that wearing the medal and reciting the prayer would bestow divine grace. As she watched the oval frame rotate and the back of the medal was revealed, she saw the letter M surmounted by a cross and surrounded by twelve stars under which were the two hearts of Jesus and Mary, one surrounded by a crown of thorns and the other pierced by a sword. The "M" on the medal stood for Mary, and the interweaving of her initial and the cross visually communicated her singular connection with Jesus, her role as mother of the Church, and her part in human salvation. The two hearts— the Sacred Heart of Jesus and the Sorrowful Heart of Mary—represented the love of the Savior and his mother for humankind. The Miraculous Medal, as it came to be known, was struck with the permission of the Archbishop of Paris, gained immediate popularity, and spread across the globe.

The Rich Symbolism of the Heart

The spiritual and theological significance of the Heart of Jesus and the intimate connection between the hearts of the Mother and her son had long been a feature of Catholic reflection. In the seventeenth through the long nineteenth century, these two hearts became focal in both the spiritual and social-political identity of French Catholicism. Emerging from the bitter Wars of Religion and spanning the postrevolutionary French Catholic world, the two hearts of Jesus and Mary served as models of authentic discipleship and images of the transformed human heart. Through the symbol of the heart Catholic eucharistic and pastoral theology was communicated in visual form. The hearts of the son and Mother became the rhapsodic focus of liturgical and devotional veneration. The conjoined hearts were patrons of resurgent communities, miraculous talismans of protection, and animators of missionary evangelization on behalf of the Catholic cause. An incredibly rich intermingling of symbolic meanings and associations accrued to the symbol of the heart in early through late modern France. The symbol communicated the depths of human spiritual longing for union with the divine as well as the struggle to maintain and plant a faith in the face of opposition and challenge. For those who aligned themselves under the patronage and protection of the two hearts and for those who aspired to have their own heartbeats aligned with the sacred hearts of Jesus and Mary, the designation "captured but free" is fitting.

Selected Bibliography

Bérulle and the French School: Selected Writings. Edited by William M. Thompson. Translated by Lowell M. Glendon, SS. Mahwah, NJ: Paulist, 1989.

Croiset, Jean, SJ. *The Devotion to the Sacred Heart of Our Lord Jesus Christ*. Translated by Patrick O'Connell. Milwaukee, WI: International Institute of the Heart of Jesus, 1976.

De Montfort, Louis-Marie Grignon. *True Devotion to Mary*. Translated by Frederick William Faber. Rockford IL: TAN Books, 1941.

Deville, Raymond. *The French School of Spirituality: an Introduction and a Reader*. Translated by Agnes Cunningham, SSCM. Pittsburgh: Duquesne University Press, 1987.

Ellington, Donna Spivey. *From Sacred Body to Angelic Soul: Understanding Mary in Late Medieval and Early Modern Europe*. Washington DC: Catholic University of America Press, 2001.

Eudes, Jean. *The Admirable Heart of Mary*. Translated by Charles di Targiani and Ruth Hauser. Buffalo, NY: Immaculate Heart Publications, 1947.

Francis de Sales, Jane de Chantal: Letters of Spiritual Direction. Edited by Joseph F. Power, OFSF and Wendy M. Wright. Translated by Peronne Marie-Thibert, VHM. Mahwah, NJ: Paulist, 1988.

Guillon, Clement, CJM. *In All Things the Will of God: Saint John Eudes Through His Letters*. Translated by Louis Levesque, CJM. Buffalo, NY: St. John Eudes Center, 1994.

Jonas, Raymond. *France and the Cult of the Sacred Heart: an Epic Tale for Modern Times*. Berkeley: University of California Press, 2000.

Kilroy, Phil, RSCJ. *The Society of the Sacred Heart in Nineteenth Century France, 1800–1865*. Cork: Cork University Press, 2012.

Margaret Mary Alacoque. *The Letters of St. Margaret Mary Alacoque*. Translated by Clarence A. Herbst. Rockford, IL: TAN Books, 1954.

Wright, Wendy M. *Sacred Heart: Gateway to God*. Maryknoll NY: Orbis, 2002.

———. *Heart Speaks to Heart: the Salesian Tradition*. Maryknoll, NY: Orbis, 2004.

CHAPTER FIVE

Oasis of Gentleness in a Desert of Militancy: François de Sales's Contribution to French Catholicism

Thomas A. Donlan

According to the English historian Ralph Gibson, a remarkable theological and pastoral breakthrough occurred in nineteenth century French Catholicism in which Eugène de Mazenod and his Oblates of Mary Immaculate, among many others, were important actors. In his *A Social History of French Catholicism, 1789–1914*, Gibson states that across the eighteenth century a repressive rigorism, cultivated by Jansenists and non-Jansenists alike, had prevailed in the French Church.[1] A *pastorale de la peur* (or fear-based pastoral approach) through which the clergy strongly discouraged frequent communion and refused absolution to sinners in confession had become commonplace.[2] In this rigorist Catholicism, moreover, the faithful often imagined God as distant, angry, or disgusted by human impurity and sin. But during the early decades of the nineteenth century, Gibson maintains, France witnessed a "radical change" in Catholic attitudes and piety.[3] In seminaries, religious orders, and lay groups, Catholics began to emphasize God's mercy and the centrality of hope and love in their piety. Summarizing this change, which I will refer to as the "gentle turn" for reasons that will become obvious,

---

[1] Ralph Gibson, *A Social History of French Catholicism, 1789–1914* (London: Routledge, 1989), 260.

[2] Ibid., 261.

[3] Ibid., 260.

Gibson states that the French increasingly thought of and practiced their faith in terms of loving "reciprocity" or relationality with each other and with God.[4] This shift in mentality and practice is so striking to Gibson that he dubs it a "real Copernican revolution" in nineteenth century French Catholicism.[5]

Ralph Gibson's interpretation, supported by the work of other scholars, highlights Alphonse Liguori, the founder of the Redemptorists.[6] Although Liguori had died in 1787, his theology and pastoral methods grew in popularity in France, due, in part, to Eugène de Mazenod's Oblates of Mary Immaculate who favored Liguori's gentler, mercy-centered approach to human sin and imperfection. In this essay, I will widen the historical scope to explore an event preceding Alphonse Liguori which, I believe, is crucial for understanding the "Copernican revolution" in nineteenth century France. This event is François de Sales's reform of militant Catholicism during the French Wars of Religion (1562–1629).[7] Using the concept of *douceur* or gentleness, François de Sales fervently critiqued the aggressive, fearful piety prevalent among French Catholics in the sixteenth and seventeenth centuries, exhorting the faithful to a hopeful, merciful, and humble imitation of Christ. This essay will examine the Salesian reform of militant Catholicism, detailing how François embodied and promoted gentleness first in missionary work, second in the sacrament of penance and spiritual direction, and finally in his approach to asceticism. Following this examination, I will return to the "radical change" Gibson found in the 1800s and consider the place of François de Sales in it, examining in particular the influence of Salesian *douceur* on

---

[4] Ibid., 252.

[5] Ibid.

[6] Jean Delumeau, ed., *Alphonse de Liguori: Pasteur et docteur* (Paris: Beauchesne, 1987), 5; Gérard Cholvy, *La religion en France de la fin du XVIIIe à nos jours* (Paris: Hachette, 1991), 24–25; Jean Guerber, *Le ralliement du clergé francais à la morale liguorienne: L'abbé Gousset et ses précurseurs (1785–1832)* (Rome: Gregorian University, 1973), 2–4; Alfred Hubenig, *Living in the Spirit's Fire: Saint Eugène De Mazenod, Founder of the Missionary Oblates of Mary Immaculate* (Toronto: Novalis, 1995), 86.

[7] Traditional dates for the French Wars of Religion have been 1562 to 1598. Increasingly, however, historians are highlighting the enduring hostilities between Catholics and Protestants after the Edict of Nantes of 1598 and propose 1629, when Louis XIII's royal forces eliminated Huguenot's military strength, as the end date for the Wars of Religion. See Mack P. Holt, *The French Wars of Religion, 1562–1629*, 2nd ed. (Cambridge: Cambridge University Press, 2005), 1–6, for an excellent treatment of this topic.

Eugène de Mazenod. Here my goal will not be to challenge the role of Alphonse Liguori in the "gentle turn" of the nineteenth century but to locate it within a broader context of the Salesian reform, which I believe served as oasis of gentleness in French Catholicism in the 1800s much as it did in the 1600s.

Militant Catholicism in Early Modern France

It is only in recent decades that scholars of early modern France have begun to describe the militant religiosity prevalent among Catholics and Protestants in the sixteenth and seventeenth centuries and its role in the wars, persecution, and violence of the era. While historians had long used the phrase "French Wars of Religion" for the bloody Catholic-Protestant clashes erupting from the 1560s to the 1620s, they tended to reduce the conflict to class warfare, family feuds, and noble rivalries.[8] With the groundbreaking research of Natalie Zemon Davis and subsequent scholars in the 1980s and 1990s, however, we began to see how deeply fear and violence permeated Catholic and Huguenot pieties, fueling sectarian strife across the early modern period.[9]

The militancy of French Catholicism in the era is difficult to grasp without considering how tightly intertwined French national identity and Catholicism had become over the course of the medieval era. In the wake of the conversion of Clovis and the Franks in the early sixth century, the inhabitants of the French kingdom gradually came to view themselves as a uniquely holy, Catholic nation.[10] Medieval French political theory strengthened this self-perception by referring to France as the "eldest daughter of the Church" and proclaiming the kingdom to be the ultimate

---

[8] Mack Holt, "Putting Religion Back into the Wars of Religion," *French Historical Studies* 18, no. 2 (Autumn 1993): 524–51.

[9] Philip Benedict, *Rouen during the Wars of Religion* (New York: Cambridge University Press, 1981); Denis Crouzet, *Les guerriers de Dieu: La violence au temps des troubles de religion, vers 1525- vers 1610*, 2 vols. (Seyssel: Champ Vallon, 1990); Natalie Z. Davis, "The Rites of Violence," in *Society and Culture in Early Modern France* (Stanford: Stanford University Press, 1975); Barbara Diefendorf, *Beneath the Cross* (New York: Oxford University Press, 1991).

[10] Nancy Roelker, *One King, One Faith: The Parlement of Paris and the Religious Reformations of the Sixteenth Century* (Berkeley: University of California Press, 1996), 161.

protector of the papacy and Catholicism throughout Europe.[11] The prominence of the French in defining aspects of medieval Catholicism also
contributed to these lofty notions. French monks, for instance, founded
and propagated the Cluniac and Cistercian monastic movements, while
French knights often led crusading efforts in the Holy Land.[12] The Sorbonne theology faculty at the University of Paris, moreover, ranked
among the most prestigious institutions defending Catholic orthodoxy.
Given all of this, then, the French deemed themselves *un peuple saint* (a
holy people); indeed, some believed that they had inherited the "chosen"
status from the ancient Hebrews.[13]

When scores of French men and women began to turn to Protestantism in the 1530s and 1540s, therefore, many Catholics fell into shock and
sorrow. They had believed that, while Lutheranism might have taken hold
in German-speaking lands (starting in the 1520s), the "eldest daughter
of the Church" would never profane herself with heretical belief and
practice. Yet, at midcentury, several hundred Huguenot churches dotted
the French landscape, effectively extinguishing this Catholic optimism.
Deeming Protestantism a threat to tradition, national identity, as well as
salvation, French Catholics denounced Huguenots for rejecting the established "customs" enjoyed "since Clovis," and labelled Protestant piety
in France "execrable" and "pernicious to the honor of God."[14]

Before long, violent words led to violent deeds, giving rise to a Catholic
militancy affecting French history across the early modern era. In this
militant French Catholicism, there were two primary targets: heretics
and sin. Fearing (and hating) Protestants as a kind of heretical filth or
cancer within the body social, Catholics widely supported the killing,
injuring, or expelling of Huguenots as a necessary purification of society
willed by God.[15] This militant mentality contributed to brutal acts of
violence across many decades, including the execution of Protestants in
the *chambre ardente* in the 1530s and 1540s, the Vassy Massacre of 1562,

[11] Myriam Yardeni, *La conscience nationale en France pendant les guerres de religion: 1559–1598* (Paris: B. Nauwelaerts, 1971), 19.

[12] Marcus Graham Bull, *France in the Central Middle Ages, 900–1200* (Oxford: Oxford University Press, 2002), 36.

[13] Ibid., 17.

[14] David Potter, ed., *The French Wars of Religion: Selected Documents* (London: MacMillan, 1997), 44.

[15] Davis, "The Rites of Violence," 57–60; Diefendorf, *Beneath the Cross*, 152, 177.

the St. Bartholomew's Day Massacre of 1572, the assassinations of Henry III in 1589 and Henry IV in 1610, as well as the Revocation of the Edict of Nantes in 1685, which resulted in the forced conversion or exile of over 200,000 Huguenots.

As for the "war on sin" in the period, it is best understood in light of the belief that loose morals and lax piety among Catholics themselves gave rise to the Protestant heresy in the first place. If Catholics (lay and religious), had not indulged in pleasures of the flesh or neglected a rigorous observance of the faith, so the thinking went, then false religion would have never materialized in the kingdom.[16] Often accompanying this perception was the conviction that God's rising wrath over heretical belief and worship demanded urgent, painful satisfaction. Catholics, consequently, waged war on their bodies by means of extreme fasting and flagellation, sleep-deprivation, self-mutilation, and barefoot penitential processions.[17] In the words of Marie de Beauvilliers, abbess of a Montmartre convent, a zealous Catholic had to "practice hate" for "the body,"[18] through penances that caused "serious suffering."[19] This militant asceticism also assumed psychological and emotional forms consisting of constant self-denunciation and anxious self-doubt, as we shall see in a moment.

François de Sales and Militant Catholicism, 1578–1588

François de Sales's entire life unfolded during the French Wars of Religion (1562–1629) and evidence shows that in his youth he appropriated attitudes and behaviors of militant Catholicism. Residing, from the age of eleven to twenty-one, in the Latin Quarter in Paris, a hotbed of Catholic militancy, François rooted for the Holy League's war on Huguenots while also subjecting himself to severe mortifications including rigorous fasting, a hair shirt, and probably flagellation.[20] Additionally, François distanced

---

[16] Diefendorf, *Beneath the Cross*, 36–38.

[17] Ibid., 45–47, 53, 65, 161; David Nicholls, "The Theatre of Martyrdom in the French Reformation," *Past and Present* 121 (1988): 50.

[18] Marie de Beauvilliers, *Conferences Spirituelles d'une Superieure a ses Religieuses* (Paris: Toulouse, 1838), 9.

[19] Ibid., 32.

[20] André Ravier, *Francis de Sales: Sage and Saint* (San Francisco: Ignatius Press, 1988), 29–30; Roger Devos, ed., *Saint François de Sales par les Témoins de sa Vie* (Annecy: Gardet, 1967), 23.

himself from carnal temptation, avoiding games and festivals and, according to one biographer, spitting at a woman who expressed romantic interest in him.[21] François himself reveals the intensity of his penitential mindset. In personal notes from the 1580s, François states that if he fell short of his religious goals, he would impose "extraordinary" penances on himself. His mortification would be both "spiritual and bodily," characterized by "austerity, humility, and abjection." Through such asceticism, François explains, he would attain a piety that was "militant and triumphant."[22]

Fear of God and divine judgment also came to dominate François's devotion during his final years in Paris, touching off a painful spiritual crisis. Personal comments and prayers jotted down in 1586 and 1587 illustrate an anxious, troubled soul before an imposing, angry God. Among François's reflections are psalm-like laments, such as "Lord, have pity on me and heal my soul because I have sinned against you" and "Me, wretched, alas!"[23] François poses urgent, probing questions concerning his standing in God's eyes, among which are, "Will God forget to have pity? Or withdraw his mercy in anger?"[24] and "Will my soul not be given to God?"[25]

Eventually the fog of François's spiritual, emotional turmoil lifted as various people and places fostered his renewal. The camaraderie and fellowship among students and Jesuits at the Collège de Clermont likely played a role. François's love of the *Song of Songs* and his belief that the text revealed God's desire to be in tender, affectionate union with humanity seems to have strengthened him as well.[26] Healing also came in 1587 while praying in a Paris chapel before a statue of Our Lady of Deliverance, which depicts Mary holding the infant Jesus, gazing upon him with loving calm.[27] Through these experiences François's fear of divine punishment

---

[21] Ravier, *Francis de Sales*, 41.

[22] François de Sales, *Oeuvres de François de Sales, Evêque et Prince de Genève et Docteur de Eglise* (Annecy: J. Nierat, 1964), 22:11–12. These rules, written in the early- to mid-1580s, are found in the *Opuscules* (vols. 22–26) of the Annecy collection, consisting of miscellaneous prayers, musings, and notes from Francis's early life.

[23] Ibid., 17–18.

[24] Ibid., 23.

[25] Ibid., 17.

[26] Wendy M. Wright, *Heart Speaks to Heart: The Salesian Tradition* (Maryknoll, NY: Orbis, 2004), 24–25.

[27] Elisabeth Stopp, *A Man to Heal Differences: Essays and Talks on St. Francis De Sales* (Philadelphia: Saint Joseph's University Press, 1997), 42.

dissipated, as he gradually embraced the gentle Jesus revealed in the gospels as the true face of God. His attraction to militant-penitential piety also moved to the margins as he increasingly identified with a Catholicism of hope, compassion, and gentleness. Indicative of Francis's new life is his written comment that he would make it "to the mountain of Lord," whose name, after all, was not "damner" but "SAVIOR."[28]

"Douceur" in François de Sales's Missionary Work

In 1592 François was ordained a priest in his native Savoy, a duchy independent of the Kingdom of France, yet largely French in culture and language. François's work as a missionary from 1594 to 1598 in the Chablais, a predominately Huguenot region of northern Savoy, constitutes his initial reform of militant Catholicism. Prior to launching the mission in 1594, François had already committed himself to a Catholicism of *douceur*, preaching against the violence of the times. In a June 1593 sermon, for instance, François teaches that war is the product of sin and that to eradicate sin is to end war. If we "make peace with God," he told his listeners, "we will soon after have peace on earth."[29] François's critique of violence is strongly Christocentric, consistently presenting Jesus as the preeminent model to be imitated. On one occasion, he preaches that "gentle Jesus" bestows "peace to his people"[30] and in another sermon, he proclaims that Jesus is love itself and can therefore be "found only in places of concord."[31]

In the Chablais mission François labored tirelessly but nonviolently to share the Catholic faith with Huguenots. Initially, he relied on preaching, but this garnered only a handful of listeners. François then resorted to writing and disseminating catechetical pamphlets. In the latter stages of the mission, François made use of liturgical strategies, including the celebration of the Mass and Forty Hours celebrations.[32] The most striking and defining feature of François's approach in the mission, however, is

---

[28] François de Sales, *Oeuvres*, 22:66. The French text reads "mon nom qui n'est pas 'damnateur,' mais 'SAUVEUR.'"

[29] Ibid., 7:24.

[30] Ibid., 7:20.

[31] Ibid., 7:81.

[32] Jill Fehleison, "Appealing to the Senses: The Forty Hours Celebrations in the Duchy of Chablais, 1597–1598," *Sixteenth-Century Journal* 35 (2005): 375–96.

the centrality of what one might call "gentle relationality," that is, his reliance on compassionate interactions with Huguenots. Throughout his mission correspondence are references to respectful interactions and dialogue with Huguenots. In October 1594, for example, François discussed the Eucharist with a group of Protestants[33] and in early November of the same year he had several friendly exchanges with a certain Huguenot.[34] In 1595 François reports that he "never misses an opportunity to approach" town leaders to converse with them.[35] That François recognized the humanity and dignity of Huguenots is clear in mission documents where we find him referring to Huguenots as "learned,"[36] "erudite,"[37] and "gentlemen."[38] He appreciated a certain Huguenot by the name of Claude de Prez, in particular, because, as François writes on one occasion, "there is much virtue in him."[39]

Despite great risks, frustrating setbacks, and, at times, painfully slow progress in the Chablais, François refused to deviate from his gentle approach. In one instance, François, drawing on Psalm 20, states that he would continue to trust "in the name of the Lord" rather than in "chariots" and "horses." "May these words of David," he adds, "always be cited" in this era of "saber rattling."[40] When Catholics criticized François's irenicism he held his ground. His own father requested that he abandon the mission, asserting that only violence could persuade Protestants,[41] and a certain Capuchin friar encouraged François to use more "force" in the Chablais. To such suggestions, François replied that he did not care for coercion and intimidation. It is not with "force" that "I have entered the arena," he wrote, but "patience."[42]

---

[33] François de Sales, *Oeuvres*, 11:95.

[34] Ibid., 11:95–96.

[35] Ibid., 11:120.

[36] Ibid., 11:124.

[37] Ibid., 11:142.

[38] Ibid., 11:95 and 162.

[39] Ibid., 11:163.

[40] Ibid., 11:114.

[41] Charles-Auguste de Sales, *Histoire du Bienheureux François de Sales* (Lyon: La Bottière et Juillard, 1634), 94.

[42] François de Sales, *Oeuvres*, 11:115–16. It is important to note that at the close of the Chablais mission, Francis supported the decision of Charles-Emmanuel, Duke of Savoy, to forbid Protestantism in the Chablais. It is fair, at least from our vantage point today, to question whether Francis was as consistently and fully opposed to force in matters of religion as he believed he was.

In 1597 and 1598 the Chablais mission witnessed a remarkable shift, as thousands of Protestant men and women began to embrace the Catholic faith. While François did not bring about this dramatic development single-handedly (he was assisted by other clergymen and lay people), he was the head missionary and set the nonviolent tone of the mission. Although opposed to Protestantism, François viewed heresy as a pastoral issue to be addressed through preaching, education, and dialogue more than through force. Perhaps most crucial, François put gentle relationality at the heart of his missionary work, always conversing and interacting with Huguenots in a respectful, civil manner, affirming their human dignity. This humanization of Protestants called into question the militant Catholic narrative which insisted on the evil, threatening nature of Huguenots. And the success of the mission refuted the popular notion that violence was the proper and necessary response for negotiating the challenge of heresy.

"Douceur" in Confession and Spiritual Direction

In the years following the Chablais mission, François de Sales assumed the positions of provost, coadjutor bishop, and, then, in 1602, bishop, and, despite his countless administrative responsibilities, he devoted remarkable time and energy to providing pastoral care to the laity, including the sacrament of penance and spiritual direction. For certain priests during the French Wars of Religion, confession and pastoral care consisted of cultivating in the laity a hatred of sin, intolerance of imperfection, and fear of God's judgment. This could be an occasion of acute anxiety for some of the faithful as the purity and holiness of every Catholic were viewed as affecting the growth or regression of heresy, as well as the fate of the entire Catholic community before God.[43]

In the eyes of François de Sales, however, an effective pastor must develop a Christlike gentleness toward human weakness and sin, allowing a disposition of *douceur* to guide him as he shepherds sinners through self-examination, negotiating sin, and achieving spiritual growth. This is illustrated nowhere better than in his guidelines for confessors written in 1604.[44] In this document, François instructs priests that their primary

---

[43] Diefendorf, *Beneath the Cross*, 36–38.

[44] François de Sales, *Oeuvres*, 23:279–96. The guidelines are entitled "Avertissements aux Confesseurs."

charge in the sacrament of penance is to embody and communicate God's mercy. They have the responsibility, he explains, to be "the canals by which peace flows from heaven onto earth" and must therefore cultivate an attitude of openness and compassion prior to commencing the sacrament of penance.[45] Have a "paternal heart," François teaches and prepare to receive penitents with "extreme love."[46] Once confession has begun, the confessor must conduct himself "gently and amiably,"[47] remaining unfazed by the penitent's manner of speaking, lack of education, or depth of sinfulness.[48] A priest must avoid presenting himself, François explains, as some kind of "angel" that is shocked by impurity and imperfection;[49] instead, he must imitate the father from the prodigal son story who "hugs" and "kisses" his child despite his "nude, filthy, and smelly" condition.[50] In the case of profound shame and hesitation on the part of a penitent, François continues, the confessor must emphasize the depths of God's patience and desire to heal those who have committed serious sin. The greater "our misery" is, François insists, the more "God's mercy" is "glorified."[51] Even in the event of such heinous sins as "massacres" and "bestiality," the confessor and the penitent are to keep in mind that God's mercy is "infinitely stronger" than "all the sins of the world."[52]

In addition to these guidelines for the sacrament of penance, François provided his priests with a rubric for evaluating the spiritual growth of those in their care.[53] Here we find François urging the clergy to measure spiritual maturity in terms of *douceur*. A priest knows the faithful are moving in the right direction, François teaches, when they are "gentle and merciful to their neighbor."[54] This is especially important regarding how Catholics treat those who constantly fall into sin, due to moral "infirmity." A good pastor will encourage his flock to hesitate judging even these sinners and to incline, instead, toward "compassion."[55] François

---

[45] Ibid., 23:280.
[46] Ibid., 23:281.
[47] Ibid., 23:283.
[48] Ibid., 23:281.
[49] Ibid., 23:282.
[50] Ibid., 23:281.
[51] Ibid., 23:282.
[52] Ibid., 23:284.
[53] Ibid., 23:299–302. This document is entitled, *Avis aux Confesseurs et Directeurs Pour Discerner les Opérations de l'Esprit de Dieu et celles du Malin Esprit dans les Ames.*
[54] Ibid., 23:300.
[55] Ibid., 23:301.

maintains that human mercy should seek to emulate the mercy of God who "cannot hear the crying of the least of his creatures without offering aid" and avails himself "at the first tear flowing from a truly contrite heart."[56] François explains to his priests that Catholics who fail to see the gentleness of God and lack *douceur* in their relationships with others have probably fallen into a "false zeal," which prompts them to denounce others' sins with "horror and indignation," harping on their faults "without necessity" and "against charity." Such militancy, François provocatively asserts, may be influenced by the devil. This false zeal is also likely to mislead the faithful into imagining that God, full of "anger and extreme rigor," punishes the least faults with "dreadful vengeance." François exhorts his priests to discourage such a perception among the faithful, for God's mercy is revealed in "our Lord," Jesus, who comes to the faithful "gently."[57]

Years after writing these guidelines, François continued to counsel mercy and gentleness concerning human sin and imperfection, especially in the work of the clergy in confession and spiritual direction. Illustrating this is his *Treatise on the Love of God,* published in 1616, in which François once again critiques common blind spots in excessive religious zeal. In one discussion, François recounts the striking story of an early Christian monk, Demophilus, who engaged in both physical and spiritual violence."[58] In the account, two priests were standing near a church altar when a "notorious sinner" threw himself at the feet of a "good and worthy priest," desperate to confess his sins and yearning for "absolution" for his "faults." The good priest, François explains, "gently received this poor penitent" on the spot, for this was "his duty."[59] Outraged that this great sinner would dare to come "so close to the holy altar," however, Demophilus became violent, thrusting himself upon the sinner, kicking and punching him. After this, Demophilus denounced his fellow priest for welcoming the sinner and then, "running to the altar," removed all eucharistic vessels, fearing that the "sinner's presence" would "profane" them. Though perhaps the moral of the story was obvious, François nonetheless underscores its main point. The conduct of Demophilus was

---

[56] Ibid., 23:300.
[57] Ibid., 23:302.
[58] Ibid., 5:220.
[59] Ibid.

unacceptable for he allowed his zeal for holiness and purity to lead to violence, failing in his priestly obligation to "honor, love, and respect" the sinner.[60]

Salesian Reform of Militant Asceticism

Historians have, in recent decades, documented in great detail the militant nature of asceticism among the laity and religious in early modern French Catholicism. Barbara Diefendorf, for instance, has documented the punishing mortifications Catholics imposed upon their bodies in penitential processions, flagellating confraternities, and female religious communities.[61] The scholar Denis Crouzet, drawing on sermons, popular pamphlets, and learned treatises, has demonstrated the prevalence of religious anxiety, especially the fear of God and the end time, in French Catholic penitential practices.[62] In my own research, I have found the Acarie Circle and the Parisian *dévots*, more broadly, ranking among the most ardent and influential proponents of this militant asceticism, urging severe and constant self-punishment, both bodily and psychological. Take Pierre de Bérulle, for instance, who prescribes "continual combat" against oneself for, in his view, it is the ideal means by which the faithful are "purified" and "acceptable to God."[63] Or Benet of Canfield, who teaches that the "love of God" necessitates the "annihilation" of the self, an "annihilation" which is not "weak," but "forceful" and "violent."[64] And there is Barbe Acarie who prays for a "perfect abnegation" because she is entirely "wretched, execrable, detestable, and abominable."[65]

While François de Sales knew and respected Barbe Acarie and her fellow *dévots*, having met them in 1602, he eventually distanced himself

---

[60] Ibid.

[61] Diefendorf, *Beneath the Cross*, 38–44; Barbara Diefendorf, *From Penitence to Charity: Pious Women and the Catholic Reformation in Paris* (Oxford: Oxford University Press, 2004), 31–34.

[62] Crouzet, *Guerriers de Dieu*, vol. 1, 182–91.

[63] Pierre de Bérulle, Michel Dupuy, and Auguste Piédagnel, *Œuvres complètes*, vol. 3 (Paris: Oratoire de Jésus, 1995), 158 and 408.

[64] Benoît de Canfeld and Kent Emery, *Renaissance Dialectic and Renaissance Piety: Benet of Canfield's Rule of Perfection: A Translation and Study* (Binghamton, NY: Medieval & Renaissance Texts & Studies, 1987), 46 and 96.

[65] Bruno de Jésus-Marie, *La belle Acarie, Bienheureuse Marie de l'incarnation* (Paris: Desclée de Brouwer, 1942), 728 and 730.

from them and their piety. Indeed, François eventually developed the most effective and persistent critique of the militant asceticism they championed, a critique emerging out of his extensive pastoral experience. From roughly 1600 to 1610 (the same time frame in which he wrote his guidelines for his own priests), as François immersed himself in the pastoral care of the laity, he encountered many Catholics reeling from psychological stress and emotional upheaval. This is evident in his letters of spiritual direction and his *Introduction to the Devout Life*, where François laments the "affliction," "torment," "anxiety," and "fear" pervasive in Catholic piety.[66] Strikingly, François routinely describes his counselees as having a spiritual malady (*maladie spirituelle*), spiritual melancholy (*mélancolie spirituelle*), or malignity of spirit (*malignité d'esprit*).[67]

François responded to this militant, anxious asceticism by guiding Catholics from a notion of the faith as combat or confrontation to a practice of Catholicism rooted in gentle, affectionate relationality. Let us take François's counseling of Jeanne de Chantal as a case study. For years Jeanne subjected herself to punishing psychological and bodily penances, at one point knifing the name of Jesus into her chest.[68] Upon learning that Jeanne's spiritual director had encouraged this severe penitential piety, François accepted her as his counselee. In letters of spiritual direction, Francis calls on Jane to pursue her spiritual desires "gently" rather than "by force of arms."[69] He invites her to proceed with "gentleness" and "softness" rather than "force" and "violence."[70] In these efforts to persuade Jeanne to abandon aggressive asceticism, François cites the *douceur* of Jesus, urging her, for instance, to rest in the "gentle presence of Our Lord"[71] and to turn to the "gentle Jesus."[72]

---

[66] François de Sales, *Oeuvres de Francis de Sales, Evêque et Prince de Genève et Docteur de l'Eglise*, 26 vols. (Annecy: J. Nierat, 1892–1932), 12:85, 92, 94, 106, 135, 148, 170, 175, 197, 201; 13:29, 58, 68, 76, 79, 88, 95, 132, 157, 182, 187, 201; 14:21, 31, 80; François de Sales, "Introduction à la vie dévote," in *Oeuvres*, ed. André Ravier and Roger Devos (Paris: Editions Gallimard, 1969), 39, 130, 136, 137, 142, 172, 199, 210, 231, 269, 274, 276.

[67] François de Sales, Œuvres (Annecy), 3:34, 39, 210, 12:94, 177, 198, 13:46, 76, 14:38, 80.

[68] Stopp, *Madame de Chantal*, 82. Some accounts claim Jeanne had the name tattooed rather than carved. See R. Po-Chia Hsia, *The World of Catholic Renewal, 1540–1770* (Cambridge: Cambridge University Press, 2005), 150.

[69] François de Sales, *Oeuvres* (Annecy), 12:136

[70] Ibid., 12:148.

[71] Ibid., 12:186.

[72] Ibid., 13:56.

François de Sales taught these lessons to a wider audience in his *Introduction to the Devout Life* which became a best seller throughout Europe. In this work François exhorted Catholics to treat their bodies with gentleness, using the account of Balaam's donkey from the book of Numbers in the Hebrew Bible to make his case. In this story, Balaam's donkey refuses to move forward, sensing some kind of danger in its vicinity. Ignorant of the threat in their midst, Balaam beats his donkey mercilessly and ceases only after the donkey miraculously speaks, objecting to the violence of its master. François states that Catholics engage in the same brutality as Balaam with their unforgiving corporal mortifications. He invites the faithful to abstain from "excessive fasting, immoderate use of the discipline, and intolerable hair shirts," and to realize that their bodies need mercy like Balaam's donkey.[73]

François also taught ascetic gentleness on the psychological and emotional levels, especially with regard to negotiating one's own sins and faults. While militant Catholicism affirmed constant self-denunciation, François prescribed healthy doses of self-forgiveness. "Please," François entreats a counselee, "have patience with everyone, but primarily with yourself."[74] "Take a breath [and] breathe a little," he instructs another, for "if we must be patient with others, we must also be patient with ourselves."[75] In both his letters of pastoral direction and the *Introduction to the Devout Life* François de Sales called on Catholics to face up to personal sin honestly yet gently: "Regard your faults with compassion rather than indignation, with more humility than severity."[76] Sometimes François juxtaposed harsh, punitive self-correction with self-evaluations characterized by *douceur* to instruct the faithful. Upon realizing that we have succumbed yet again to the sin of vanity, for instance, we ought to avoid thinking in the following way:

> Aren't you wretched and abominable, you who have made so many resolutions and yet let yourself be carried away by vanity? You should die from shame. Never against lift up your eyes to heaven, blind insolent traitor that you are, a rebel against your God!

---

[73] François de Sales, *Oeuvres* (Paris), 199.
[74] François de Sales, *Oeuvres* (Annecy), 13:23.
[75] Ibid., 13:107.
[76] Ibid., 14:55.

Instead, one ought to try a gentler way of proceeding:

> Alas, my poor heart, here we are, fallen into the pit we were so firmly
> resolved to avoid! Well, we must get up again and leave it forever.
> We must call on God's mercy and hope that it will help us to be
> steadier in the days to come. Let us be of good heart. . . . God will
> help us; we will do better.[77]

Salesian "Douceur" and the Copernican Revolution

Let us now return to the nineteenth century and the "Copernican
Revolution" that Ralph Gibson finds occurring in French Catholicism in
this period. As stated earlier, Gibson views the dissemination of Liguorian
spirituality and pastoral methods as crucial factors in the shift toward
hope, mercy, and loving relationality in French Catholic piety. This as-
sessment, I believe, is quite accurate since, as much evidence shows, many
clergymen, including Eugène de Mazenod, his Oblates, as well as several
Jesuits were reading Liguori's works closely, administering confession
and other ministries in light of his teaching and example, as well as citing
him when critiquing Jansenist-rigorist approaches.[78]

I would like to propose, however, that Salesian *douceur* was more in-
strumental in the "gentle turn" of nineteenth-century French Catholicism
than has been appreciated, and that future research may even show the
influence of François de Sales surpassing that of Liguori. This possibility,
unaddressed in Gibson's analysis, is bolstered by several factors. First, we
must recall that Liguori deeply admired François de Sales, drawing on
him as he developed his own pastoral style and methods.[79] Indeed, Liguori
may rank among de Sales's strongest supporters in the eighteenth century.
Take Liguori's spiritual classic, *The Practice of the Love of Jesus Christ*,
published in 1768, for example. In this work, the founder of the Redemptorists invites Catholics to pursue a joyful, hopeful, and mercy-centered

---

[77] François de Sales, *Oeuvres* (Paris), 158.

[78] Guerber, *Le ralliement du clergé francais*, 358; Philippe Lécrivain, "Saint Alphonse:
Aux Risques du Rigorisme et du Liguorisme," in *Alphonse de Liguori: Pasteur et docteur*,
ed. Jean Delumeau, 250–54; Jean Leflon, *Eugene De Mazenod, Bishop of Marseilles, Founder
of the Oblates of Mary Immaculate, 1782–1861*, vol. 2 (New York: Fordham University
Press, 1961), 129–31.

[79] Wright, *Heart to Heart*, 112.

practice of the faith, citing François de Sales over fifty times, and praising him as "the master and model of holy meekness."[80] Well-versed in Salesian *douceur*, Liguori appeals to the authority of François de Sales as he exhorts Catholics to accept the gentleness of Jesus, to treat everyone (including enemies) with gentleness, to prefer gentleness over rigor in piety, and to receive communion frequently and joyfully.[81] It would seem, then, that when we witness a fondness for the generous, humane, and compassionate character of Liguori's theology and pastoral orientation in nineteenth-century France, we are also encountering, even if indirectly, an appreciation of Salesian gentleness.

Second, we must also keep in mind the scholarship on the "Salesian Pentecost" of the nineteenth century which has emerged since Gibson published his *Social History of French Catholicism* in 1989. The Salesian Pentecost refers to the remarkable proliferation of lay associations, devotional communities, and new religious orders founded in the name of François de Sales in the 1800s. Among these, as Wendy M. Wright beautifully describes in her *Heart to Heart: The Salesian Tradition*, are the Daughters of Francis de Sales, the Association of Francis de Sales, the Missionaries of Francis de Sales of Annecy, the Salesians of Don Bosco, as well as the Oblates and Oblate Sisters of St. Francis de Sales.[82] Many, but not all, of these new groups emerged in France, and it is likely that they contributed to the "gentle turn" of nineteenth-century French Catholicism.

Finally, an additional reason to anticipate a broader influence of Salesian *douceur* in the 1800s is the case of Eugène de Mazenod, himself, whose founding of the Oblates of Mary Immaculate 200 years ago we celebrated at the October 2016 conference. Indeed, it appears that before de Mazenod turned to Liguori as a mentor and guide, he had already developed a profound affection for François de Sales and his *Introduction to the Devout Life*. According to Jean Leflon, de Mazenod's appreciation of Liguori on a deep level likely occurred in the mid-1810s.[83] Yet, the eventual founder of the Oblates of Mary Immaculate had started reading

---

[80] Alphonse Liguori, "The Practice of the Love of Jesus Christ," in *The Ascetical Works of St. Alphonsus*, trans. Rev. Eugene Grimm (New York: R. Washbourne, M.H. Gill & Son, 1887), 316.

[81] Ibid., 318, 397, 319, and 284.

[82] Wright, *Heart Speaks to Heart*, 110–52.

[83] Leflon, *Eugene De Mazenod*, vol. 2, 129.

François de Sales at least as early as 1808, during the initial stages of his seminary training at Saint-Sulpice. This is revealed in an 1808 letter to his sister, Eugénie, in which he strongly recommends François de Sales's *Introduction to the Devout Life.*

> Read and do not stop reading St. Francis de Sales' "Introduction to the Devout Life"; you will find on this topic all you could desire, and further excellent guidelines for all the circumstances of your life. I have always found this book admirable but how much more excellent it appears since I have heard lectures on it in seminary and an explanation by one of our saintly Directors.[84]

De Mazenod's attachment to François de Sales is illustrated the following year when he prescribes the *Introduction to the Devout Life* to a loved one, yet again. In this 1809 letter, de Mazenod is even more laudatory, calling the *Introduction* "the most perfection Christian treatise after the Gospel":

> I will never cease to recommend that she read every day some chapter of the *Introduction to the Devout Life* by St. Francis de Sales [for] it is the best book she could read in her situation. . . . If only every sentence of that masterpiece of devotion were inscribed in indelible characters on her memory; it is, in the opinion of all the greatest masters of the spiritual life, the most perfect treatise on Christian perfection after the Gospel.[85]

It must also be noted that de Mazenod reveals an understanding of Salesian gentleness and the intention to practice it. This is evident in personal resolutions drawn up by de Mazenod on a retreat occurring at the start of his seminary training in October of 1808. Here de Mazenod makes peace with the decision to focus on an asceticism of the will rather than punishing mortifications on the body, citing François de Sales and the story of Balaam's donkey. "However light these penances are, I will content myself with them for the moment," de Mazenod writes, for "to follow the advice of St. Francis de Sales who says somewhere that one must not overemphasize the punishment of the body, a poor donkey who

---

[84] Eugène de Mazenod, *Écrits spirituels* (Rome: Postulation générale OMI, 1991), 56.
[85] Ibid., 74.

is not to bear all the blame . . . I will try above all to mortify my spirit."[86] These 1808 resolutions also show de Mazenod coming to trust in the mercy and gentleness of God, much as François de Sales had as he negotiated the spiritual crisis of his youth. In a moving passage, Eugène encourages himself to balance a fear of God with faith in divine mercy: "fear of the dreadful judgments of a just God must not so fill [my heart] that the trust I must have in his mercy cannot find entrance." And then, as if echoing the voice of François de Sales, de Mazenod affirms God's desire to hold, heal, and redeem the fallen: "This God of mercy came among us only to call sinners, it is to them he addresses his gentlest words, he runs after them, holds them to his heart, carries them on his shoulders."[87]

Other examples could be given illustrating the prominence of François de Sales and Salesian *douceur* in the religious imagination and personal piety of Eugène de Mazenod. Rather than pursuing any further evidence, however, I will close by suggesting that where de Mazenod and the Oblates of Mary Immaculate distinguished themselves from the Jansenists and quasi Jansenists of nineteenth-century French Catholicism, playing their part in the gentle turn of the period, they were standing on the shoulders not only of Alphonse Liguori but François de Sales as well.

Further Reading

Benedict, Philip. *Rouen during the Wars of Religion*. New York: Cambridge University Press, 1981.

Boenzi, Joseph. *Saint Francis de Sales, Life and Spirit*. Stella Niagara: DeSales Resource Center, 2013.

Bull, Marcus Graham. *France in the Central Middle Ages, 900-1200*. Oxford: Oxford University Press, 2002.

Cholvy, Gérard. *La religion en France de la fin du XVIIIe à nos jours*. Paris: Hachette, 1991.

Crouzet, Denis. *Les guerriers de Dieu: La violence au temps des troubles de religion, vers 1525-vers 1610*, 2 vols. Seyssel: Champ Vallon, 1990.

Davis, Natalie Z., "The Rites of Violence" in *Society and Culture in Early Modern France*. Stanford: Stanford University Press, 1975.

---

[86] Ibid., 43.
[87] Ibid., 40–41.

Diefendorf, Barbara. *Beneath the Cross*. New York: Oxford University Press, 1991.

Gibson, Ralph. *A Social History of French Catholicism, 1789-1914*. London: Routledge, 1989.

Holt, Mack P. *The French Wars of Religion, 1562-1629*, 2nd ed. Cambridge: Cambridge University Press, 2005.

Hubenig, Alfred. *Living in the Spirit's Fire: Saint Eugene De Mazenod, Founder of the Missionary Oblates of Mary Immaculate*. Toronto: Novalis, 1995.

Leflon, Jean. *Eugene De Mazenod, Bishop of Marseilles, Founder of the Oblates of Mary Immaculate, 1782-1861*. New York: Fordham University Press, 1961.

Potter, David. ed. *The French Wars of Religion: Selected Documents*. London: MacMillan, 1997.

Wright, Wendy M. *Heart Speaks to Heart: The Salesian Tradition*. Maryknoll, NY: Orbis, 2004.

CHAPTER SIX

Women and the French School of Spirituality

Mary Christine Morkovsky, CDP

Women certainly did influence and were influenced by the French School, and the influence continues to this day. The proliferation of congregations of women religious in France was unprecedented. They were suppressed in the following century during the French Revolution, but many reunited afterwards. The collaboration between St. Vincent de Paul and St. Louise de Marillac and between St. François de Sales and St. Jeanne de Chantal is well known. The rapid growth and influence of the Daughters of Charity and the Visitandines attest to the power of their cofoundresses. Instead of focusing on them, however, after a brief review of Bérulle's major insights, this paper concentrates on the women in the lives of Bérulle, Olier, Eudes, and de Montfort. All these men were founders who had influential women in their lives, and their influence continues today, even in this geographical area of San Antonio, Texas.

The theology of Cardinal Pierre de Bérulle (1575–1629) is abstract, and his spirituality is profound. His theology was influenced by neoplatonism and pseudo-Dionysius; they regarded God the Father's contemplation as emanating God the Son through whom all eventually returns to the One God in a series of *exitus-reditus*. But Bérulle rejected abstract mysticism. He insisted that each person appropriate interiorly the "states" of Jesus, which are the permanent qualities of the mysteries of Christ as lived in time. We adore today the God-Man who can enter souls as he entered the upper room when the doors were locked.[1] The mystic's contemplation is a sharing in Christ's exemplary adoration itself. Made one

---

[1] William M. Thompson, *Jesus, Lord and Savior* (New York: Paulist, 1988), 230.

with Christ through grace, we should dwell perpetually in Jesus as he dwells in the Father, freely giving ourselves to the God with whom we have fallen in love.[2] The human nature of Christ did not have its own subsistence but subsisted by the substance of the Word. In this "annihilation" of human personality, Bérulle saw an example of complete mortification, of total renouncing of all one has so as to be united with God.[3] Of the states and mysteries of Jesus, the incarnation and infancy are particularly meaningful for him. Meditating on them strengthens the conviction that self-gift or *anéantissement* is truly the ontological state of a creature, for we are nothing except what we have received from our divine Creator.

Bérulle's Mariology was an integral part of his spirituality. His original purpose in founding the Oratory was not to form clergy but to consecrate its members to the contemplation of the mysteries of Jesus and Mary, especially the incarnation.[4] His Mariology is not based on Marian apparitions or popular devotions but on theological insights. Since Jesus associated Mary in all his mysteries, one cannot appreciate the depth and grandeur of Jesus' self-gift or *kenosis* apart from her.[5] Bérulle advocated a vow of servitude to Jesus through Mary, whose own servitude gives her dominion over all the works of her son, not in a juridical sense but in a mystical and exemplary sense.[6]

Women Who Influenced Founders of the French School in the Seventeenth Century

Bérulle was a cousin of Madame Barbe Avrillot Acarie (1566–1618). Her house on the rue des Juifs in the Marais section on the Right Bank in Paris was the meeting place on Tuesdays for people most interested in the Counter-Reformation of the Church in France. The group had a total of about fifty four members and included Benet of Canfield, the English

---

[2] Anne M. Minton, "The Spirituality of Bérulle: A New Look," http://opcentral.org/resources/2015/01/12/anne-m-minton-The-spirituality-of-berulle-a-new-look/, accessed Aug. 1, 2016.

[3] Vincent R. Vassey, "Mary in the Doctrine of Bérulle on the Mysteries of Christ," *Marian Studies* 36, no. 2 (1985): 60–80, 72.

[4] Ibid., 60.

[5] William M. Thompson, *Christology and Spirituality* (New York: Crossroad, 1991), 57.

[6] Vasey, "Mary in the Doctrine of Bérulle," 66.

convert who became the Capuchin Benet de Canfield, François de Sales, Vincent de Paul, and the Sorbonne theologian André Duval as well as the wealthy and generous Marquise de Maignelay and Cardinal François de Sourdis.

The historian Henri Bremond considered Madame Acarie the most important religious figure between 1590 and 1620 because of her personal influence. She has been called "the conscience of France"[7] because she encouraged and directed almost all the important religious figures, both men and women, of her day. She exemplified the wealthy aristocratic woman of that time—articulate, self-confident with exquisite good manners and connections to influential people. These women did not have access to higher education, but they were well read and had the taste and leisure to take spiritual direction from priests and to advance in prayer. Many of them enjoyed mystical experiences. Many of them used their wealth to help the needy.

Barbe Jeanne Avrillot married Pierre Acarie at age sixteen and gave birth to six children. She became disabled as an adult after accidentally breaking a hip and a thigh. She began to have mystical experiences at age twenty four and received the stigmata a few years later. Not only did she help Bérulle found the Oratory, she also helped her cousin, Madame de Sainte-Beauve, establish the Ursulines in France to educate young girls. She supported the Benedictines and Sulpicians. St. Teresa of Avila told her in a vision to introduce the reformed Carmel in France, so she organized that project. The Carmelites of Spain refused to send sisters, so Madame Acarie sent Bérulle to Spain to negotiate. After overcoming numerous obstacles, the Carmelites, including two nuns formed by St. Teresa herself, arrived in Paris in 1604. Barbe herself had already formed their first French recruits in her home, calling the group the Congregation of St. Geneviève. Bérulle's mother entered the Carmel of the Incarnation in Paris in 1605.[8] All three of her own daughters later entered Carmel. By 1667, there were sixty three convents of reformed Carmelite nuns in France.

Barbe combined great charitable activities with deep contemplative prayer. She was humble, did not have a high opinion of herself, and rejected

---

[7] C. C. Martindale, SJ, *The Queen's Daughters: A Study of Women Saints* (New York: Sheed and Ward, 1951), 127.

[8] Raymond DeVille, *The French School of Spirituality*, trans. Agnes Cunningham (Pittsburgh: Duquesne University Press, 1994), 36.

insincerity. The key to her spirituality was faithfulness to the obligations of one's state in life. The incarnation was central for her, and she insisted "The Kingdom of God is within." She worked tirelessly for the reform of the Church, and the mighty consulted her. She broke off her association with Bérulle when he tried to make the French Carmelites take a fourth vow of servitude to Jesus and Mary, saying that was not part of their tradition.

After her husband's death in 1613, Barbe entered the Carmel in Amiens as a lay sister, Marie d'Incarnation. Although she was physically weak and ill, she continued to counsel people until she died in 1618. She was beatified by Pope Pius VI in 1791.[9]

Madeleine du Bois de Fontaines-Marans (1578–1637), another cousin of Madame Acarie and a close friend of Bérulle, entered the Carmel in Paris in 1604. She had been prepared by Barbe herself and became Mother Madeleine de St. Joseph, its first professed member, in 1604. She was elected prioress in 1608, 1611, and 1624 and served as mistress of novices for a time. Cardinal Richelieu asked for her advice. She encouraged the founding of the Oratory and advised her own father to enter it at the age of seventy four.[10] She influenced many important figures and trained many superiors and directors of novices.

The centerpiece of Mère Madeleine's spirituality was to desire only what God wants. Interior adherence of will to God is freedom of spirit. We should adore the unknown designs of God and leave the rest to God's mercy. Her ascetical writings and letters were theocentric. She promoted mystical Christocentrism, emphasizing interior adherence to the states and mysteries of Jesus, the incarnate Word. Contemplating Jesus' abasement and sufferings in his childhood leads to adoration and union with God. This preference no doubt influenced Bérulle's devotion to the infant Jesus, especially as promoted by the Carmel of Beaune. Mother Madeleine thought that adoration with love as its soul and life is preferable to thanksgiving because it is more extensive, less self-preoccupied and can moderate excessive sensitiveness.[11] Through adoration one enters into the holy person of Jesus Christ. But one cannot adore with Jesus Christ unless one is already living in Jesus Christ. She had a particular devotion to the

---

[9] See Robert P. Maloney, CM, "The Beautiful Acarie," *Vincentiana* 41, no. 3 (1997): article 7.

[10] Deville, *The French School*, 220.

[11] Ibid., 230.

Mother of God and taught her nuns that they were bound to love Christ and the holy humanity he took from Mary. As daughters of this Mother, they were continually to adhere to the states and mysteries of Christ and imitate the love and honor she gave her son. The Carmelite Order is especially favored by the Blessed Mother, but she claims it only to offer it to her son in a more worthy manner.[12] Mary shares with God the Father the right of property over the son, but this right is mystic and exemplary rather than juridical.[13]

Mother Madeleine's devotion to Mary led her to support devotion to the Eucharist, which contains all the mysteries and graces merited by Jesus. We cannot sacrifice ourselves to God physically, but in Holy Communion we offer Jesus and ourselves to God as a holy and acceptable sacrifice.[14] She received permission to have the Blessed Sacrament exposed every Thursday, day and night, and advised contemplating the divine presence rather than other realities of this mystery. She opposed quietism and false devotions. She shows the freedom of souls who are willing to let go of egocentric gratifications, greed, and grandiosity that separate us from God.

These women had effects in Bérulle's life. Other women were close to other representatives of the French School. Blessed Agnes Galand de Jesus Langeac, OP (1602–34), was a cloistered Dominican nun who began to receive mystical graces at the age of eight or nine. She did not know Jean-Jaques Olier (1608–57), who was to reform the huge parish of St. Sulpice in Paris and found the Sulpicians there in 1642. The Blessed Virgin Mary told her to pray for Olier's conversion. Indeed, the young man seemed to be headed toward a comfortable clerical life as a result of his natural intelligence and benefices such as the abbey of Pébrac which he received at the age of eighteen. Mother Agnes appeared to him twice in a vision in Paris, and he went to Auvergne for six months while she instructed him.[15] He was also challenged by Marie Rousseau, clairvoyant wife of a wine seller, who told him she had been praying for a long time for his conversion.[16] He was a friend of Jeanne Mance (1606–73), nurse and cofounder

[12] Ibid., 221.
[13] Vassey, "Mary in the Doctrine of Bérulle," 66.
[14] Deville, *The French School*, 231.
[15] http://nouvl.evangelisation.free.fr/ecole_francaise_t2_26.htm, accessed Sept. 7, 2016.
[16] http://www.sulpc.org/sulpc_fondateur.php, accessed Aug. 1, 2016.

of the city of Montréal.[17] Olier approved of Bérulle's insistence on abnegation and himself took the vow of servitude in 1643 and the vow of victim in 1645. He made an act of total submission to the Trinity through the Mother of God in 1651.[18]

St. Jean Eudes (1601–80), gifted orator and conductor of parish missions, left the Oratory in 1643 to initiate the Congregation of Jesus and Mary to conduct diocesan seminaries and do missionary work. He was told to examine the peasant Marie des Vallées (1590–1656) for possible demonic possession in 1641. She had begun to receive notable graces at a young age, but the rest of her life was not typical of the women mystics of that time. Between the ages of nineteen and twenty four she suffered abandonment like Jesus did on the cross as well as diabolical attacks along with great consolations. Eudes not only found no problems but witnessed one of her visions in 1649. He asked her to recommend to God his proposed Congregation of Our Lady of Charity of Refuge. (She not only did so but claimed the Blessed Virgin told her what habit the sisters should wear.)

Marie endured many exorcisms which apparently had little effect. At the age of twenty-five or twenty-six she renounced her own will and offered herself to God to atone for sins. In spite of wanting to, she could not receive Holy Communion for about thirty years. Jesus told her she had been given his passion instead of Holy Communion. All her torments were mental—anger, hunger, death, despair. Intermittently she suffered the pains of hell as well as abandonment like Jesus endured on the cross. She also received the stigmata, which were visible for more than nineteen years. Jesus told her that her sufferings made up for what was wanting in his passion, that he was suffering in her, and that her sufferings were redeeming souls. For seven years, she went through the "nights" of the spirit, senses, memory, understanding, and will as described by St. John of the Cross. The Virgin Mary guided her in all this, and the Sacred Heart revealed to her that the Heart of Jesus was one with the Heart of Mary.

---

[17] http://www.fondationlionelgroulx.org/Jeanne-Mance-et-les-pionnieres-de,595.html.

[18] Argiro Restrepo, PSS, "La Sagesse de la Croix dans l'Expérience Spirituelle de Jean-Jacques Olier," *Bulletin de Saint-Sulpice* 39 (2013–2014), 148. Olier is the author of the well-known prayer: "O Jesus, living in Mary, come and live in your servants, in the spirit of holiness, in the fullness of your power, in the perfection of your ways, in the truth of your virtues, in the communion of your mysteries. Rule over every adverse power, in your Spirit, for the glory of the Father. Amen."

In 1652, Jesus told her that her heart was united with Mary's and with his. (This was more than twenty years before the revelations to the Visitandine St. Margaret Mary Alacoque, which began in December, 1673.) Marie insisted that the shortest way to perfection was to give God one's life and receive divine life to the degree that one gave. When we are dead to self, she insisted, we can go to God and demand the salvation of our neighbor and of all that is necessary to obtain it.

Marie said many rosaries and made many pilgrimages. Jean Eudes claimed he received numerous special graces through her intercession and considered her a great saint. Cures and prophesies were attributed to her, but few understood her mission. Three bishops approved of her mystical experiences and said that she never lost her baptismal innocence. She was buried in the cathedral of Coutances. Eudes wrote a three-volume biography of her which was never published.[19]

Jean Eudes in 1641 also started the Congregation that came to be called the Good Shepherd Sisters (approved in 1666) for sisters to work with women of ill repute who were reformed and wished to do penance. Pope Leo XIII gave him the title, "Author of the Liturgical Worship of the Sacred Heart of Jesus and Holy Heart of Mary."

Some Women Influenced by the French School

Several prominent women who lived in the seventeenth century illustrate the great variety of ministries they started or supported. Jeanne Chézard de Matel (1596–1670), who was gifted with mystical graces from a very young age, felt she was called to found an order of women with the name of the Savior which would introduce God's "Son into the world so that he might be adored."[20] She was a friend of Jeanne de Chantal and knew Vincent de Paul and Jean-Jacques Olier. She helped Madame Marie Lumaque Pollalion (1599–1657) open a "House of Providence" for repentant women in difficulty. Thanks to the bishop of Lyon, Cardinal Alphonse de Richelieu (1625–53), who at first did not believe Jeanne and

---

[19] These details are given in http://www.touteslesprophetes.net/marie-des-vallees/, accessed Sept. 19, 2016. See Chas. Berthelot du Chesnay, "Marie des Vallées (1590–1656)," in *Encyclopaedia universalis* [en ligne], accessed Sept. 20, 2016.

[20] John M. Lozano, CMF, *Jeanne Chézard de Matel and Sisters of the Incarnate Word*, trans. Joseph Daries, CMF (Chicago: Claret Center for Resources in Spirituality, 1983), 19.

confiscated all her writings, her own accounts of her numerous visions and locutions have been preserved. By the age of twenty-four she was a daily communicant and enjoyed an awareness of the Blessed Trinity in her higher faculties, even during mundane tasks, which included begging alms for the poor. She liked solemn ceremonies and luxurious adornments.[21] Her accounts of her visions are very detailed, describing, for example, how she entered into the actual heart of Jesus or the womb of Mary. In 1625, she had a vision of the symbols which were to be on the habit of her order: a crown of thorns encircling the monogram IHS and containing a heart surmounted by three nails with the motto "*Amor meus.*" That year she and two companions moved into a house in Lyons formerly occupied by Ursulines. They followed the Rule of St. Augustine and added to the three traditional vows a vow of perpetual enclosure and a vow of fidelity to the mission of Christian education. She always insisted that her Order was both contemplative and apostolic; the sisters educated young girls inside their convents. Jeanne founded eight convents in her lifetime but did not make the traditional three religious vows until she was on her deathbed because, following the advice of priest-advisors, she needed to be free to travel and make important financial decisions.

The center of Jeanne's spirituality is the incarnation, not as such but as the person of the Word made flesh, uncreated and consubstantial with the Father and with us.[22] Her own spirituality unfolds as a spousal and maternal relationship with God the Son,[23] a grace she received from the Father. Typical of the seventeenth century, she did not see the Eucharist as a communal celebration but as a vertical relationship, an encounter with Christ, the exemplar of all being, even though she also discovered in the Eucharist the action of the Father and the Holy Spirit.[24] Adoration was to be a constant orientation, not restricted to prayer and to community life.[25]

Unlike Bérulle, however, Jeanne did not contemplate the incarnate Word to assimilate Christ's inner dispositions, humanity, and actions but rather to absorb and imitate the teachings of Jesus,[26] especially the Beatitudes, which were the nucleus of the rule of life of her order: to proclaim

---

[21] Ibid., 59.
[22] Ibid., 72.
[23] Ibid., 40.
[24] Ibid., 45.
[25] Ibid., 79.
[26] Ibid., 42.

the gospel of love and kindness.[27] She wrote two treatises on the Beatitudes and liked to imagine the soul as a circular temple with the Beatitudes as its outside pillars. Another preferred image was a crystal vase made of fragile glass and transparent in its simplicity. She sometimes imagined herself as a young eagle gazing fixedly at the divine Sun or as a dove, innocent and loving.

Jeanne devoted her life to establishing the religious order of the Incarnate Word, to which title the papal bull of approval added "and the Blessed Sacrament." Suppressed during the French Revolution, the Order revived around 1819 and, at the request of Bishop Jean-Marie Odin, CM, sent four sisters to Brownsville, Texas, in 1852. Then, in 1866, Bishop Claude-Marie Dubuis, CM, requested sisters for Victoria, Texas, and more foundations were made. Bishop Dubuis also obtained three sisters in Lyons in 1866, and they formed a "new branch" of sisters with simple vows dedicated to apostolic activity, the Sisters of Charity of the Incarnate Word (CCVI). There is a Houston and a San Antonio branch of CCVIs. In 1894 the IWBS Sisters started in Mexico, and by 1987 they had nine autonomous groups, five in Mexico and four in the U.S. Their most recent constitutions show they continue Jeanne's mission to extend the incarnation by contemplating, adoring, and imitating Jesus Christ, especially in his self-emptying.

Madame Marie Lumaque (or Lumague) Pollalion (1599–1657), a young widow, founded the House (or Seminary) of Providence in 1641 for young women in difficulty who had repented, and for converts. Becoming a third order Dominican and taking a vow of chastity on the advice of Vincent de Paul, Madame Pollalion and six other women formed the secular community of Christian Union, binding themselves by an act of association or *Regle d'Union* in 1647 to save souls and respond to all appeals from the Church. They tried to conform themselves to Jesus Christ and serve him in the person of the needy.

Anne de Croze and Renée Desbordes (1651–1707) were the first members of the Daughters of Christian Union which was initiated to convert heretics.[28] Theirs was a spirituality not of doctrine but of personal service. They also began to educate Catholic girls and offer retreats. Their purpose was to support Catholics, convert heretics, and baptize infidels. They

---

[27] Silvia Estela Mares, CVI, "Mother Jeanne Chézard de Matel," paper given at the CCVI Heritage Study Week, July 7–13, 1983, San Antonio, Texas, 3.

[28] *Heroines of Charity*, preface by Aubrey De Vere (New York: P.J. Kenedy, 1904), 115.

achieved this end by helping new converts to meet their material needs. At first they were supported by the Company of the Blessed Sacrament. From them later came houses of the Propagation of the Faith and of the *Nouvelles Catholiques* in Metz and Sédan, which were designed as asylums for converted Huguenot women.

Marie Madeleine Villeneuve de Vignerod du Pontcourlay (1604–1675), Duchess d'Aiguillon and a niece of Cardinal Richelieu, belonged to the Ladies of Charity of St. Vincent de Paul. She financed many projects, including some in Ireland and Africa, and helped establish the Daughters of the Cross in Paris after they had to leave Picardy in 1639. Their works were schools for the poor and retreats. She also financed in Canada the Hôtel Dieu and the Ursuline convent in Montréal as well as the Hôtel Dieu in Quebec.[29]

Catherine de Bar, Mère Mechtilde de Saint-Sacrement (1614–98) had Olier and Eudes as well as Vincent de Paul as advisors. She entered the Annonciades de Bruyères and was professed in 1634, but Swedish troops destroyed their convent in 1636. In 1637 she entered the Benedictines at Rambervillers. Four laywomen persuaded her to open a hospice in Paris, but Mother Mechtilde refused to be the superior. The women then funded in 1651 a monastery where in 1653 Mother Mechtilde started the Benedictines of Perpetual Adoration of the Most Holy Sacrament to make reparation for sacrileges. The nuns were cloistered the following year in the presence of Queen Anne of Austria and made the Blessed Virgin Mary their abbess. Their spirituality was to do the will of the Beloved and be faithful to observances out of love. They considered humiliations to be pledges of divine love. Their eucharistic piety consisted of total dedication to satisfy the justice of the Father. Forgetting self, they were given totally to the love of Jesus and the mercy of the Father. They were preoccupied with the glory of God and the salvation of souls. Mother Mechtilde founded seven or eight convents and wrote more than ten thousand letters.[30]

Marguerite Bourgeoys (1620–1700) joined a teaching Congregation in France, but left them to move to Canada, where she founded the Congregation of Notre Dame of Montréal in 1689. The members practiced a

---

[29] See https://richelieu-eminencerouge.blogspot.com/2007/09/duchesse-daiguillon .html, accessed June 27, 2016.

[30] http://voiemystique.free.fr/ecole_francaise_t2_347.htm, accessed Aug. 31, 2016. See also http://vultuschristi.org/index.php/2011/06/sayings-of-mectilde-de-bar/.

new form of consecrated life: secular, noncloistered wayfarers imitating the Virgin of the Visitation. Her sisters educated native peoples and orphan girls sent from France to start families in the New World. She opened the first public school and the first domestic training school in Canada. Evidence of the French School of Spirituality can be seen in her sense of the mystical, orientation toward an education focused on the meaning of life and growth in faith, and a spirit of hospitality and love as manifested in the first Christians. Her charism was compassion and solidarity with the poor, excluded, and oppressed. Her followers serve by letting people reveal their giftedness as well as their need and by inviting people to praise God.[31]

Another founder who shows the influence of Bérulle in his life and writings is Bishop Pierre Lambert de la Motte (1624–79). Helped by his wealthy relative, Madame Marie Bonneau de Rubelles Miramion (1629–96) and by the Duchess D'Aiguillon, he initiated what was to become the *Missions Etrangères* (Foreign Mission Society) in Paris in 1658. Named a Vicar Apostolic of Vietnam, he founded a congregation of women religious named Lovers of the Holy Cross in North Vietnam in 1670. The spirituality of the Lovers of the Cross is Christocentric; its members center their eyes and hearts on Christ crucified and on the mystery of the cross. Their charism is love of Christ crucified, whose salvific mission they continue through their prayer and service.

In 1649 Madame Miramion (1629–95) entered the Ladies of Charity which had been founded by Vincent de Paul in 1634 and made a vow of chastity. Among other projects, she built the large house of St. Pelagius, a refuge for rehabilitated prostitutes, with funds given by three pious women. She supported the Daughters of St. Geneviève, founded in 1636. The archbishop of Paris approved their statutes in 1658. She started the Daughters of the Holy Family in 1662 to teach girls, train teachers for country schools, and help the poor. The Daughters made no vows but were dedicated to good works. In 1665 they united with the community of St. Geneviève. Several other communities joined them, and they were called *Miraminnes*. Madame Miramion herself wanted to become a cloistered Carmelite, but never achieved that goal. During her lifetime, she started more than a hundred schools and more than two hundred missions.[32]

---

[31] See http://cnd-m.org/en/spirituality/charism.php, accessed Aug. 31, 2016.
[32] http://lefoudeproust.fr/2014/04/fiche-les-miramiones/, accessed Aug. 15, 2016.

Eighteenth Century

St. Louis-Marie Grignion de Montfort (1673–1716) is well known for promoting consecration to Mary as a means to arrive at union with the eternal and incarnate Wisdom. He and Sr. Marie-Louise of Jesus Trichet (1684–1759) founded the Daughters of Wisdom in 1703. He was the chaplain of the General Hospital in Poitiers at the time, and she became an inmate in order to help the sick. The first members of the Daughters were poor, sickly, crippled and blind women. He wrote their Rule as well as *The Love of Eternal Wisdom or the Secret of Mary*, stating that wisdom expresses love alone by giving self and losing self. The sisters aimed to acquire heavenly wisdom by imitating Jesus Christ, Wisdom incarnate. The means to imitate the incarnate Wisdom was special devotion to Mary. The Daughters describe themselves as called in community to seek and to contemplate Divine Wisdom, present in a world that hungers for meaning, justice, and compassion. They aim to bring the message of Jesus, incarnate Wisdom, to people experiencing injustice, violence, poverty and oppression, especially women and children.[33]

The Congregation of Divine Providence was founded in 1762 in France by a diocesan priest, Jean Martin Moye (1739–93), who manifests the vibrancy of the French School in the eighteenth century. In 1762–64 he published a brochure with comments on Bérulle's acts of offering one's self to Jesus incarnate and Mary. He also simplified and explained some prayers of Bérulle in 1766 so more people would be encouraged to use them. He did not use Bérulle's special vocabulary nor intersperse ejaculations such as "O divine gaze!" in his expositions, but he did sometimes use Bérulle's style of paradox such as a man God/God man, a virgin Mother/Mother of God, a God poor, suffering/and glorious at the same time, a Creator/ obedient to a creature, a judge of the universe/himself judged and condemned by his subjects.

Moye joined the Foreign Missionary Society in Paris and evangelized in China for ten years. There he published in Chinese *33 Reflections* that show Berullian influence. When he returned to France, he republished Bérulle's *Elévations* in 1786 because he found Bérulle's formulas to be solid, upright, and pure.[34] Moye often regards God as the ineffable and

---

[33] See http://www.montfort.org.uk/Life_MLT.php, accessed Oct. 3, 2016.

[34] Jean Guennou, *The Blessed John Martin Moye, 1730–1793, A Missionary Spirituality*, trans. Generosa Calahan, CDP (n.p., n.d.), 60–63.

absolute Other. Like Bérulle, he stresses abandonment as conformity to God in thought and action; detachment is its negative aspect. He is constantly aware of both the grandeur and the tenderness of God.

Moye accepts Bérulle's insight that the supreme reality on earth is the image of the Trinity and emphasizes our participation in this mystery *by grace*. One should always pray as a member of the Mystical Body. For Moye, this meant constantly offering the merits of Jesus and the saints rather than focusing on one's own needs and feelings.

Aided by two women in particular, Marie Morel and a Miss Fresné, Moye prepared young women to go, often alone, to live and teach children in poor rural hamlets in France as well as in China. Cognizant that most people of his time were ignorant of the mysteries that are the basis and foundation of faith, Moye gave unusually detailed instructions on how the sisters were to explain the mysteries of the Trinity, incarnation, and redemption to children. He even lists numerous sample questions that teachers can ask about these three profound mysteries.

His Christocentric spirituality consists in knowing, participating in (by grace), and adoring the mysteries of Christ's life, especially by entering into the secret sufferings of Jesus to obtain graces for the unknown needs of unknown souls.[35] He prefers to contemplate and imitate the *acts* of the Savior rather than his states or conditions. The young women he sent to remote hamlets to instruct children were to make their decisions and strengthen their motivation by imitating the Lord's actions.[36]

Bérulle's influence can be seen in Moye's recommendation of devotion to the Holy Child and recitation of Bérulle's "Litany of the Child Jesus." He told the sisters to honor *all* innocent children and ask for their protection. He also endorsed devotion to the Sacred Hearts of Jesus and Mary.

Nineteenth Century

Another congregation of women religious that claims to be influenced by the French School, especially the Eudists, is the congregation of the

---

[35] George Tavard, *Lorsque Dieu fait tout—la doctrine spirituelle du bienheureux Jean-Martin Moye* (Paris: Cerf, 1984), 86.

[36] Marguerite Kernel, SP, *De l'Insécurité selon J. M. Moyë* (Paris: Editions Franciscaines, 1976), 116, 128, 155; and Marguerite Kernel, SP, *Un Projet de Vie selon la Providence*, doctoral thesis, Université de Sciences Humaines, Faculté de Théologie Catholique (Strasbourg, France, 1974), 170–71, 177–89.

Sisters of the Sacred Heart of Jesus, originally known as the Sisters of St. Jacut. They were founded in Brittany by Angélique LeSourd (1767–1835) and her three companions in 1816. By 1854 they were approved by both the church and the French government. These sisters arrived in San Antonio in 1903 to work with the Missionary Oblates of Mary Immaculate.

The spirituality of the Sisters of the Sacred Heart is rooted in union with the heart of Christ, expressed in a charism of tenderness and mercy. Their vocation invites them to the unceasing contemplation of Christ in his filial and fraternal love. They try to manifest to all, especially the poor, the tenderness and merciful love of the Father revealed in Jesus. Humility, simplicity, and availability are their outstanding characteristics.[37]

Mary Elizabeth Lange (ca.1794–1882) was born in an ethnically French and Francophone community in Santiago de Cuba and stated that she was "French to her soul." She was educated in Cuba before she emigrated to Baltimore. She and a companion began to teach Black children in their home, for there were no schools for them. Early in 1828 Fr. James Nicholas Joubert, SSS, encouraged by Archbishop James Whitfield, asked her and Marie Balas to start a school for girls of color. He also asked them if they would consider starting a women's religious order. Fr. Joubert provided direction, solicited financial assistance, and encouraged other "women of color" to become members of this, the first religious congregation of women of African heritage. On July 2, 1829, Elizabeth and three companions pronounced promises of poverty, chastity, and obedience to Archbishop Whitfield and the chosen superior. They received papal recognition in 1832. The Sulpicians were replaced as their directors by Redemptorists in 1847, Jesuits in 1860, and Josephites in 1877.

Fr. Joubert wrote the first rule of the Oblate Sisters of Providence and incorporated the Sulpician ideal of following the rule and giving good example. Inner discipline rather than physical mortification was encouraged. The Congregation was bicultural, exhibiting classical French asceticism in an American mode. The sisters also adopted the "Holy Slavery of the Mother of God" promoted by Louis de Montfort. This may seem strange for a Congregation some of whose members were former slaves. However, for these women, devotion to the Mother of God was the most

---

[37] See http://www.soeursdusacrecoeurdejesus.com/Spirituality.html, accessed Nov. 6, 2016.

perfect means of being constantly united to Christ. They took the model of racism and made it a model of service and example of grace.

The sisters believe the suffering intrinsic to their Congregation from its beginning enables them to reach out to others with tenderness and compassion. They consider themselves called to bring joy, healing, and the liberating, redemptive love of the suffering Jesus to victims of poverty, racism, and injustice. Their prophetic role is to expose and overcome every form of racism which continues to divide society and the church and injure families.[38]

Fr. William Joseph Chaminade (1761–1850), represents the nineteenth century revival of Berullianism.[39] The spirituality of this founder of the Society of Mary is theocentric, promoting pure regard for God, adoration, and sacrifice. One must shed self-seeking and focus on God's majesty, infinity, and perfections. It is also Christocentric, incarnational, and Marian. Only through the incarnation is the Trinity revealed, and we are sanctified outside ourselves in Jesus Christ. Mary is "a pure capacity for Jesus." She enters into the power of giving her son to the world forever. Influenced by Olier, Chaminade stresses Sonship rather than servitude and regards Marian theology both as a generating principle and a means toward perfection.[40]

Adelaide Marie de Batz de Trenquelléon (1789–1828) and her companions helped Chaminade with his Sodality of the Immaculate Conception, and he helped her start the Institute of the Daughters of Mary Immaculate (FMI). Adèle and Jeanne Diché had founded an Association for mutual encouragement and spiritual support in 1804. Gradually they were accepted as a subgroup of Chaminade's Sodality of the Immaculate Conception. They became a religious order in Agen, France, in 1816. The sisters were to cultivate the spirit of faith or of mental prayer and remain hidden in the life of God. At first they were cloistered and took a fifth

---

[38] See http://www.oblatesisters.com/History.html, accessed Nov. 4, 2016; and Judith Weisenfeld and Richard Newman, eds., *This Far by Faith: African-American Women's Religious Biographies* (New York: Routledge, 1996), esp. Thaddeus J. Posey, OFMCap, "Praying in the Shadows."

[39] John A. Melloh, SM, "The Notion of Priesthood in the French School," in *Two Studies on the French School and Father Chaminade*, Marianist Resources Commission, Monograph Series, Doc. No. 18, Feb. 1975, esp. 26.

[40] Melloh, "An Overview of the Major Influences of the French School of Spiritual Doctrine of Fr. Chaminade," in *Two Studies*, 43–57, 75.

vow to teach the Catholic faith and Christian morals, but they were also to be missionaries with a unique "conquering zeal." By the time they arrived in San Antonio in 1949, they had shortened and simplified their Constitutions. After the Second Vatican Council, they were even more involved in local faith communities, women's concerns, and alleviating economic poverty.[41]

Jeanne Jugan (1792–1879), later Sr. Mary of the Cross, LSP, a shepherdess and maidservant, at age twenty five became an associate of the Congregation of Jesus and Mary founded by Eudes. She taught catechism and cared for the poor and other unfortunates. Joined by Françoise Aubert (aged seventy-two) and Virginie Trédaniels (aged seventeen), an orphan, they formed a small community in 1837. In 1839 they started taking elderly sick women into their home. From assisting such elderly abandoned women arose the Little Sisters of the Poor who to this day subsist by begging. Their spirituality is Christ-centered and Marian. She said "We must be so many other Christs on earth in order to continue here his life and work" and "to come to the heart of Mary is to come to Jesus." The Little Sisters of the Poor practice in particular simplicity and trust in Providence.[42]

Sr. Mary Euphrasia Pelletier (1796–1868) was a member of Eudes's Congregation of Our Lady of Charity of Refuge who started the Magdalenes, sisters who were consecrated to God for prayer and work. Today they are called Contemplative Sisters of the Good Shepherd. Seeing the need for a generalate instead of independent convents, in 1835 she founded the Congregation of Our Lady of Charity of the Good Shepherd.[43]

Amelie Fristel (1798–1866) entered Eudes's Third Order of the Sacred Heart in 1822. Its members did charitable works in parishes which included sponsoring a thrift shop and caring for the unemployed. In 1846 a benefactor gave her a large garden which she named Notre Dame de Chênes and used for the poor and elderly. The Bishop of Rennes would not let her form a religious congregation in 1849, but she did succeed

---

[41] See Joseph Stefanelli, SM, *Adèle, Aristocrat for the Poor* (Dayton, OH: North American Center for Marianist Studies, 1999).

[42] See http://littlesistersofthepoor.org/our-life/spirituality/, accessed Nov. 3, 2016.

[43] See https://viechretienne.catholique.org/saints/19131-sainte-marie-euphrasie-pelletier, accessed Oct. 28, 2016.

later and expanded its ministries in 1856. The spirituality of the Congregation of the Sacred Hearts of Jesus and Mary is to show compassion, mercy, and care of the poor—animated by deep faith in Providence.[44]

Twentieth Century

In 1943 a rather unusual congregation of women religious was founded in Canada by Rita Renaud (1918–2004) advised by Louis-Marie Parent, OMI (1910–2009). They are called *Adoratrices et Adorateurs Missionaires de la Famille Reclusienne,* Missionary Adorers of the Recluse Family (or hermits' family). Their model is Jeanne Le Ber (1662–1714) who lived most of her life as a recluse in Montreal. When its members were revising their Constitutions after the Second Vatican Council in the 1960s, they recognized their roots in the French School of Spirituality. They are aware of the importance and efficacy of *kenosis,* the self-emptying revealed in the Paschal Mystery. They try to enter into the feelings and attitudes of Jesus together with Mary his Mother, especially in the Annunciation, because the Word wishes to be born again in all hearts today. Eucharistic adoration is central in their life; they offer themselves as hosts with, in, and through Jesus, praying especially for priests and for all who further the Reign of God.[45]

This sampling of women connected to the French School for almost four centuries shows the important and continuing feminine influence. Do these women have anything in common? They identified the spiritual as well as material needs, many of which were new and unique to the people of their day. They met many of those needs with their own resources or found others who did so. They understood that one's total personal self-gift as well as close cooperation with others were necessary for the accomplishment of God's designs. We have reasons, especially in this geographic region, to be very grateful to God for their example and unselfish contribution to the life of the Church.

[44] See http://www.ssccjm.org/histoire/historique.html#, accessed Oct. 5, 2016.

[45] See http://reclusesmiss.org/wp/adoratrices-et-adorateurs-missionnaires/, accessed Nov. 2, 2016.

Bibliography of Further Reading

Deville, Raymond. *The French School of Spirituality*, Translated by Agnes Cunningham. Pittsburgh: Duquesne University Press, 1994.

Lozano, John M. ,CMF. *Jeanne Chézard de Matel and the Sisters of the Incarnate Word*, Translated by Joseph Daries, CMF. Chicago: Claret Center for Resources in Spirituality, 1983.

Melloh, John A., SM. *Two Studies on the French School and Father Chaminade*, n. p: Marianist Resources Commission Monograph Series, Doc. No. 18, Feb. 1975.

Posey, Thaddeus J., OFMCap. "Praying in the Shadows." in *This Far by Faith. African-American Women's Religious Biographies*, edited by Judith Weisenfeld and Richard Newman, 73–93. New York: Routledge, 1996.

Tavard, George. *Lorsque Dieu fait tout—la doctrine spirituelle du bienheureux Jean-Martin Moye*. Paris: Cerf, 1984.

Internet Resources

des Vallees. Marie. http://www.touteslesprophetes.net/marie-des-vallees/.

Minton, Anne M. "The Spirituality of Bérulle: A New Look," http://opcentral. org/resources/2015/01/12/anne-m-minton-The-spirituality-of-berulle-a-new-look/

Missionary Adorers of the Recluse Family. http://reclusesmiss.org/wp /adoratrices-et-adorateurs-missionnaires/

Sisters of the Sacred Heart of St. Jacut. http://www.soeursdusacrecoeurde jesus.com/Spirituality.html.

CHAPTER SEVEN

Saint Vincent de Paul: The Practical Mystic

Thomas F. McKenna, CM

"Mystical." The word conjures up a wide variety of experiences, all the way from ecstatic visions and out-of-the-body "elevations"(in Cardinal de Bérulle's expression) through a more widely diffused range of consoling, anchoring, and even emptying feelings, and finally to an overall intuition of divine presence spreading itself over all of life. Before locating Vincent de Paul along this spectrum, it is worthwhile to say something more general about the mystic life itself.

Mysticism is a subtype within the wider category of religious experience; that is, how it is that an encounter with the Holy Mystery registers in a person's awareness. Beginning in wonder at existence or at least some facet of it, the sensibility opens out onto a "religious" consciousness of a loving creator God who grounds reality, quickens it, and attracts it toward the future.

In this connection, the Bible speaks of "glory," as in what Moses experiences in the hollow of the rock as God's glory passes him by. In ordinary usage, the word connotes brilliance or radiance, but in the religious sense it takes on the additional meaning of weight or heaviness, the *Kabod Yahweh*. It is brightness with a profundity to it, carrying an importance that reaches down to the foundations. In Elizabeth Johnson's vivid description, this glory is "the weighty radiance of divine presence in the world, the heavy, plump, fat brightness of God's immanence close at hand to enlighten, warm and set things aright."[1] This brilliance radiates through

---

[1] Elizabeth Johnson, *Abounding in Kindness* (Maryknoll, NY: Orbis, 2015), 41.

all creation, permeating nature, persons, and the processes of human history.

The divine splendor shows itself in positive and negative emanations, on the one hand as God's grandeur ("shining like shook foil") in the beauty of creation and in the splendor of human freedom, and on the other as God's absence in the various depredations of the Holy in the destruction of nature and the desecrations of human dignity. This godly presence draws especially close to situations of tragedy, "bending over" suffering, injustice and death. Human response to all this is twofold: praise, adoration and thanks, together with efforts to cooperate with this holy closeness in deeds that bring God's compassion to earth.

Vincent de Paul's mysticism is not the visionary kind marked by rapturous encounters with the divine, but is of the more general type which for him happens mostly through interaction with other people (especially those in poverty), and involvement in the processes of history.

If there is a word that sets Vincent's mysticism off from much of the spirituality of his day, "practical" is that word. In reaction to the depredations and horrors of the Wars of Religion in the preceding era, the French Revival of the seventeenth century was marked by a strong penitential and ascetic tone with much emphasis on the interior life. While strong on interiority himself, Vincent paid at least equal attention to what was happening in the political and social events of the society around him. He was an early counterbalance to the otherworldly leanings that sometimes appeared in the adherents of this School.

The underlying theme of this book, *Surrender to Christ for Mission*, catches the longer term direction of the French Revival. The interplay of absorption in the enduring mysteries of Jesus' life and the taking up of his mission to the world led so many in subsequent centuries on the road to a signature blend of contemplation and gospel service. Vincent fits within its wider mainstream, but as will become evident he is nonetheless a distinctive voice within it.

Vincent and the French Revival

For sure Vincent swam in the currents of the era, both by his association with its main figures and just as much by the manner in which he took so many of its central tenets to himself.

a) As to *personalities*, he knew and associated with most all of the individuals in Henri Bremond's so called "French School." Arriving in Paris as a young cleric in search of an ecclesiastical career, Vincent put himself under the spiritual guidance of Pierre de Bérulle. Many of Bérulle's key themes and even characteristic words (e.g., adoration, subservience, kenosis, "honoring Christ's mysteries"; phrases such as "Ah", "Mon Dieu," "O Joy!") appear in Vincent's writings. But soon enough, for reasons having to do with his more pragmatic bent, he chose to move away from Berulle's circle and more out on his own. For a while, Vincent lived with Charles de Condren's Oratorians but decided not to join them, another instance of taking his own road. In the years to come, especially in the area of clergy and seminary transformation, he interacted with the reformers Jean-Jacques Olier and Jean Eudes, in addition to founding his own community (tellingly named the Congregation of the Mission).

In these years, Vincent had frequent face-to-face contacts with the renowned Bishop of Geneva, St. François de Sales, and greatly admired him. At de Sales's recommendation Vincent took on the role of spiritual mentor for St. Jeanne de Chantal and her Visitation nuns. André Duval, Madame Acarie, and the Abbé de Saint-Cyran of Jansenist fame are other celebrities of that fertile era whose paths he often crossed over his long (80 years) life. Vincent was "in the crowd" from almost beginning to end, but as we will see not entirely of it.

b) As to *themes*, the interweaving threads of "Surrender to Christ" and "Commitment to Mission" run all through Vincent's writings and activities. But again, they do so in a way that carries his unique stamp.

"Surrender to Christ"

The seventeenth-century French revival arose as a reaction to the abstract, overly propositional approach of the scholastics in the centuries before.[2] By contrast, it attempted to reground theology in lived faith and so focused on a fuller human experience, most centrally the experience of Jesus as he comes adoringly before his Father and totally empties himself before the Father's will as he moves through the events of his life, death and resurrection. The disciple is to participate in these eternally enduring mysteries by contemplatively entering into these "states" of Jesus' life ("honoring" them), and living them out effectively in the world. The tone was incarnational and Trinitarian through and through. Both

---

[2] William M. Thompson, *Christology and Spirituality* (New York: Crossroad, 1991), 65.

theology and spirituality arranged in this key are thoroughly meditative and contemplative.

Repeatedly we hear Vincent counseling his audiences to "honor" such and such a mystery of the Lord's life, that is, in prayer to put themselves on the inside of some incident or other of Jesus' journey to his Father. For instance, he advises the members of a prayer group for priests meeting at his headquarters in Paris to "honor the weariness of Jesus."

> In order to raise a soul to the highest perfection, God allows it to pass through dryness, brambles, and combats, causing it thereby to honor the times of weariness in the life of His Son, Our Lord, who suffered various kinds of anguish and abandonment.[3]

He is counseling them, both in their prayer time and in their daily ministry, to insert themselves into the dry and burdensome periods of Jesus life so as to let his endurance firm up theirs. The divine glory shines through each of the chapters of Jesus' life, and by honoring the different ones Vincent would open himself to that light.

Vincent consistently focuses on surrender to "The Lord Jesus." One of his most cited sentences comes in a letter written in 1635 to his close companion, Antoine Portail.

> Remember, Monsieur, we live in Jesus Christ through the death of Jesus Christ, and we must die in Jesus Christ through the life of Jesus Christ, and our life must be hidden in Jesus Christ and filled with Jesus Christ. And in order to die like Jesus Christ, we must live like Jesus Christ.[4]

---

[3] CCD:IV:37. CCD refers to the English translation of *Vincent de Paul: Correspondence, Conferences, Documents*, trans. Helen Marie Law, DC (vol. 1), Marie Poole, DC (vols. 1–14), James King, CM (vols. 1–2), Francis Germovnik, CM (vols. 1–8, 13a–13b [Latin]), Esther Cavanagh, DC (vol. 2), Ann Mary Dougherty, DC (vol. 12), Evelyne Franc, DC (vols. 13a–13b), Thomas Davitt, CM (vols. 13a–13b [Latin]), Glennon E. Figge, CM (vols. 13a–13b [Latin]), John G. Nugent, CM (vols. 13a–13b [Latin]), Andrew Spellman, CM (vols. 13a–13b [Latin]); ed. Jacqueline Kilar, DC (vols. 1–2), Marie Poole, DC (vols. 2–14), Julia Denton, DC [editor-in-chief] (vols. 3–10, 13a–13b), Paule Freeburg, DC (vol. 3), Mirian Hamway, DC (vol. 3), Elinor Hartman, DC (vols. 4–10, 13a–13b), Ellen Van Zandt, DC (vols. 9–13b), Ann Mary Dougherty (vols. 11, 12, and 14); annotated by John W. Carven, CM (vols. 1–14). Brooklyn and Hyde Park: New City Press, 1985–2014.
[4] CCD:I:276.

"For Mission"

It is for this second part of the formula, "Commitment to Mission," that Vincent is best known.

For one thing, his *apostolic output* was prodigious. The founder of two major religious societies and various lay confraternities ("The Charities") of both women and men, the organizer of thousands of parish missions in France and beyond, the creator of twenty new seminaries for diocesan priests throughout the realm, overseer of a home for the mentally disturbed, a force behind massive relief operations for the many war refugees streaming into Paris[5] and the tens of thousands of starving and destitute beyond, the cofounder with St. Louise de Marillac of numerous institutions for abandoned children, destitute elderly, single women and the sick poor, creator of programs for spiritual and pastoral renewal of the clergy (most notably his "Tuesday Conferences" held at his headquarters in Paris), initiator of foreign missions to Scotland, Poland, Ireland, and parts of Africa, advisor to the royal court on religious matters, fundraiser extraordinaire working with the rich and famous of the day, founder and Superior General of his own Congregation as well as of the Daughters of Charity (and in the process giving them a revolutionary juridical base that would make these apostolic societies such powerful pastoral agents for centuries to come), the list of his activities right up until the time of his death goes on and on. In the final year of his life, he expressed regret that he could not do more.

Vincent's correspondence was vast, directing such a far-flung and organizationally complicated array of enterprises. It is estimated that he wrote over thirty thousand letters just in the second half of his life. His correspondence and conferences today fill twelve volumes and this is only a fraction of his output. Many of his talks to his priests and brothers and to his own Daughters of Charity were never recorded, and this is not even to mention the hundreds of lost conferences he gave the Visitation Nuns and others over decades.[6]

---

[5] In 1652, he organized food collections in the city, gathering each week 5,000 pounds of meat, 3,000 eggs, and copious provisions of clothing and utensils. Robert Maloney, CM, *Go! On the Missionary Spirituality of St. Vincent de Paul* (Salamanca: Editorial Ceme, 2002), 162ff.

[6] Maloney, *Go!*, 165.

However, second was the *spiritual energy* fueling this activity that rose up from his intense and indeed signature encounter with the Holy. In large part, it was formed over a period of years during which he moved from what one commentator[7] has described as Vincent I, a bright ambitious cleric looking to work his way up the ecclesiastical ladder, to Vincent II, a disciple caught up in that "weighty" radiance of divine presence in the world, a man on fire with God's love in Jesus as he experienced it in both prayer and in people, especially the poor and the world in which they lived.

Soon after Vincent arrived in Paris as a young priest in search of a career, he was introduced to Pierre de Bérulle. Exposure to this director's meditative methods and Christocentric theology began to awaken in him an appreciation for the awesomeness and profundity of the Father's love, particularly in sending his Son. This led Vincent into a deeper contemplation of the mysteries of that Son's life in which he not only prayed about them but, as the terminology goes, came to "participate" in their enduring effectiveness (their glory). These Trinitarian and incarnational strands, so characteristic of the wider spiritual revival going on, suffused Vincent's spiritual and apostolic outlook ever after.

Most likely around the same time, almost it seems as something to do with his spare time, he started to visit a local city hospital given to the care of the many poverty-stricken of Paris. Before long, he began to notice a resonance between what was happening in his new prayer regimen and what he was sensing when meeting these sick poor. One experience seemed to open into the depths of the other, with the same "weighty radiance" revealing itself in both settings. This dawning awareness in these formative years was only a first glimpse for him of the link between God and God's poor ones. Vincent's encounter with a poverty-stricken man some years later in confession, an especially resonant homily he preached based on this encounter, and his organized response to the plight of a hungry family soon after were three particularly focusing events that solidified this earlier experience. In a phrase that has come to be associated with Vincent, he began to "see the face of Christ" both in prayer and in the eyes of these suffering poor. God's glory was passing by him in two intertwined ways.

---

[7] Hugh O'Donnell, "Vincent de Paul: His Life and Way," in *Vincent de Paul and Louise de Marillac*, Classics of Western Spirituality (Paulist: New York, 1995), 15ff.

One writer describes this as a "bi-spectacled" experience of the Holy; i.e., beholding God more or less simultaneously through the twin lenses of contemplation and service, each one affecting the other and bringing about a nondualistic vision of how God in Christ is at work in the world.[8]

This double-angled view, if we can so put it, gives Vincent special insight into that often elusive relationship between contemplation and action. For him the two are organically connected, coming together in a way in which they not only modify and enrich each other but act as mutual correctives. In him we see the interplay between "God's loving inflow"[9] and Vincent's attunement to that same love at work in the world. It is this contemplative base which rescues his astounding activity from activism, and conversely, it is his apostolic engagement which anchors his mystical experience in the things of this world. And so it is that Vincent's caring and contemplative presence to the poor becomes the locus of his encounter with his Lord. In his style of discipleship, doing and being lock hands.

There is a central text for Vincent which can serve as a special window onto his religious or mystical experience. It is the synagogue scene in Luke 4 where Jesus stands up to read a text from Isaiah which he then uses to announce his own Mission from his Father. In it Jesus testifies to both the source and the direction of his calling: "I have been sent (by God) to bring the Good News of his love to the poor." Meditatively entering this scene himself, Vincent catches sight of his own vocation and senses the shape of his own "being drawn" to the Father and doing the Father's will for the world. This is his version of his encounter with that "heavy, plump, fat brightness of God's immanence close at hand to enlighten, warm and set things aright!"[10]

Through this intermixture of his prayer and his action, Vincent "participates" in this opening event of Jesus' life, and like him goes forth to proclaim the Good News and release the captives. It is no surprise that, when choosing a motto for his own Congregation, these very words, "He has sent me to preach the Gospel to the poor" come to his mind.

---

[8] Thomas McKenna, CM, "Vincent de Paul: What Moved Him? And What Moved Him Toward Those Who Are Poor?," *Vincentian Heritage Journal* 32, no. 2 (2015).

[9] John of the Cross, *Selected Writings*, Classics of Western Spirituality series. New York: Paulist Press, 1987, 186.

[10] Johnson, *Abounding in* Kindness, 41.

This theme of adherence to Christ's mission surfaces in many other ways. Listen to Vincent as he lays out the core purpose of his own foundation of priests and brothers.

> May The Lord keep our lamps lit in His presence and our hearts always tending to His love and always devoted to clothing ourselves ever more with Jesus Christ. . . . Each individual then, has to strive to be conformed to Our Lord . . . to be bound in affection and practice to the examples of the Son of God, who became man like us in order that we might not only be saved, but, like Him, to be saviors. And this means cooperating with Him in the salvation of souls."[11]

Here again, Vincent is sharing in the incarnation, joining himself to the "states" of Jesus Christ as he, in servitude, carries on his Father's work in the here and the now.

Allied Themes

Although Vincent walks his own path, he nonetheless draws from core themes of the French Revival that show up elsewhere in this volume.

"Surrender of the Will"

Vincent constantly urged his missionaries and sisters to give themselves over to God's will. In a conference in the last year of his life, he prays:

> I always do God's Will. That's what His Son Our Lord, Wisdom itself, said and did. If it pleased His Divine Goodness to grant us the grace of doing always the Will of God . . . then we would be worthy of being in His school. But, my Lord, as long as we delight in our own will, we will be in no way prepared to follow You . . . nor have any part with You, as we will have if we truly renounce our own will for love of God.[12]

---

[11] CCD:XII:97. Letter on the Purpose of the Congregation of the Mission, 6 December 1658.
[12] CCD:XII:176. May 2, 1659, On Mortification.

Two weeks later he still more forcefully reiterates the point:

> Today I was reading the reflection of a saint, who says that openness
> to God's Will is the height of holiness, the sum of all virtues, and the
> destruction of vices. It's like fire, which not only aims at the core of
> love, but consumes everything that holds it back. . . . So my dear
> confreres, if openness to God's Will detaches our hearts from earth,
> they will be afire with the practice of the Will of God. When they
> stop loving others things, they will necessarily be filled with God's
> love.[13]

"Hiddenness"

The injunction to move out of the spotlight and be content with
anonymity is advice he gives repeatedly to his priests and sisters. To a
Daughter of Charity who is hurt because her service is not being noticed,
he advises, "Honor the hidden life Jesus lived in Nazareth." He means
that both in her contemplation and in the round of her daily actions, she
is to insert herself into this unobserved phase of Jesus' life and let his
unknown way of living through those years (especially his openness to
the will of his Father) suffuse hers.

In another place using one of his favorite analogies of gold in fire, he
praises both the unseen and the noticed moments in Gospel ministry.

> I thank God for having given the Company subjects who belong
> more to Him than to themselves, and who serve the neighbor at the
> risk of their lives! They are like unrefined gold, which becomes
> visible in fire and which would otherwise remain hidden under
> ordinary actions and sometimes under faults and failings.[14]

"Prominence of Women and Laity"

The collaboration of Vincent de Paul and Louise de Marillac is among
the best known instances of male-female "teaming up" in European
church history. The congregation they cofounded was revolutionary for
the time in moving religiously dedicated women outside the cloister as

---

[13] CDD:XII:188. May 15, 1659, On Indifference.
[14] CCD:IV:493. To Etienne Blatiron, Oct. 25, 1652.

well as opening up opportunities for many less educated rural girls to serve in ecclesial apostolates.

In his often quoted conference on "The End of the Congregation of the Mission," given on December 6, 1658, he asserts:

> Did the Lord not agree that women should enter his company? Yes. Did he not lead them to perfection and to the assistance of the poor? Yes. If, therefore, Our Lord did that, He who did everything for our instruction, should we not consider it right to do the same thing . . . so that God is served equally by both sexes?[15]

In his conferences to his Daughters of Charity he underlines the ideal of the mundane, unprotected, out-on-the-streets labor they were called to. His instruction to "poor country girls" (a term of endearment he and Louise de Marillac often used) is a classic in recasting the pastoral role women might take up in the Church.

> These women will have for a monastery the houses of the sick and the house where the superior lives. For a chapel, the parish church. For a cloister, the streets of the city. For an enclosure, obedience. For a grate, the fear of God. For a veil, holy modesty. For profession, continual confidence in Providence and the offering of all that they are.[16]

Vincent worked well with all classes of women. Particularly in his successful efforts as a fundraiser did he have extensive contact with the dames and ladies of the upper nobility, notably the Queen Regent and her Court.

Vincent's involvement with laity in ministry was far reaching. The associations he established in 1617, his Conferences of Charity, quickly spread through parishes in France and beyond. After his death they were a seedbed of inspiration for many organizations dedicated to the poor, most notably Frederic Ozanam's St. Vincent de Paul Society two hundred years later. Over the centuries, hundreds of lay-based groups have gathered around Vincent's spirituality, one that has proved itself especially adaptable to lay life.

---

[15] CCD:XII:77.
[16] CCD:X:530.

"The Heart, Focused on Mission"

Not only the Heart of Jesus but also the hearts of the people who collaborated with Vincent figure prominently in his preaching and exhortations.[17]

At a gathering of his Congregation of the Mission on 22 Aug, 1655, we hear him crying out, "Let us ask God to give this Company this spirit, this heart, this heart that causes us to go everywhere, this heart of the Son of God, the heart of Our Lord, the heart of Our Lord, the heart of Our Lord."

What God wants most, he continues, is the heart.

> God asks primarily for our heart—our heart—and that's what counts. How is it that a man who has no wealth will have greater merit than someone who has great possessions that he gives up? Because the one who has nothing does it with greater love; and that is what God wants especially.[18]

The Distinctive Tone Vincent Brings to the Movement

Though strongly influenced by these currents in seventeenth-century French spirituality, there are a number of areas in which his originality comes through. As mentioned earlier, while Vincent is *in* the movement, he is not entirely *of* it.

a) First is his *bent toward action*; that is to say, initiating deeds for sake of the Kingdom.

Though insistent on the indispensability of union with God in prayer, Vincent was at least equally resolute that the union be firmly grounded in time and space actions in this world. If prayer did not at some time spill over into purposeful and effective activity (especially on behalf of the needy sister and brother), he thought it suspect.

And so on the one hand we hear him exhorting his companions to pray.

> Let us give ourselves fully to the practice of prayer, since through it all good comes to us. If we persevere in our vocation, it is thanks to

---

[17] Cf. Robert Maloney, CM, "The Heart of Jesus in the Spirituality of Vincent de Paul and Louise de Marillac," *Vincentian Heritage Journal* 32, no. 2 (2015).

[18] CCD:XI:264.

prayer. If we succeed in our work, it is thanks to prayer. . . . If we remain in charity, if we are saved, all that is thanks to God and thanks to prayer.[19]

However, putting his foot just as firmly on the other pedal, he warns them:

And this is what we ought to be on the look-out for. There are many who, if they have a recollected exterior, and an interior filled with lofty feelings about God, rest there. But when it comes to deeds, and there is need for action, they stop short. They flatter themselves by the warmth of their imagination; they rest content with the sweet discourses they have with God in prayer; they even speak of Him like angels. But apart from this, should there be question of working for God, of suffering, of self-mortification, of instructing the poor, of going out to seek the lost sheep, of loving to be in want, of accepting illness or disgrace, alas! They are no longer to be found; their courage fails them.[20]

William Thompson comments on such "heaven directed," Quietist tendencies among some in the French School. He observes, "When adhering to the mysteries of Jesus there are moments of luminosity when The Transcendent exerts a profound 'pull' upon us. But for some worshippers, what begins as appropriate attraction can develop into an unbalanced absorption." Thompson cites Teresa of Avila's expression "boobishness" to describe this ersatz ecstasy.[21]

Vincent has a less technical, more down-home way of saying this, "Let us love God, my brothers. But let it be with the strength of our arms and the sweat of our brows."[22] And so it is not surprising, for instance, that Vincent distances himself from some of the more otherworldly teachings of Jean-Jacques Olier on the nature of contemplation.

b) A second and allied point is *the disclosive value he gives to events.* In a conference, he enjoins his coworkers to direct their attention to the here and now. "Let us do the good that presents itself"[23] he insists. Skeptical of overarching schemes and theories that flew above the concrete

---

[19] CCD:XI:361.
[20] CCD:XI:32–33.
[21] Thompson, *Christology and Spirituality*, 2.
[22] CCD:XI:32.
[23] CCD:XII:82.

happenings of the day, he looked to the unfolding historical process as an at least equally reliable medium through which God's direction would come.

Vincent's notion of Divine Providence follows from this. He images it as the leader in a race on whom all the runners back in the pack are to keep their eyes. "Do not run ahead of Providence," he repeatedly advises. "The works of God have their moment; his Providence brings them about at that time and neither sooner nor later. . . . Let us wait patiently . . . but let us act." [24] This combination of readiness to listen and willingness to follow through in deeds marked much of his life in the Spirit.

It was in the events of his time (wars, famine, the waves of beggars, refugees and abandoned children flooding into Paris, pastoral neglect of the rural areas, inadequate and even dangerous clergy training) that he heard the summons of Providence, a call he always joins to rigorous discernment.

"What must be done?" is a question some in our own time have singled out as Vincent's reflex response. To introduce his Rule for his priests and brothers, he cites the opening (and unambiguous) sentence of the Acts of the Apostles. "Our Lord Jesus Christ, sent on earth for the salvation of the human race, did not begin by teaching; he began by doing." [25] And bringing his practicality to the point, Vincent adds: "It is equally necessary to point out that Jesus is a model also for doing all things well, because whatever good we may do deserves blame rather than praise if it is not done well."

c) It goes without saying that for Vincent, the special ones to whom all this activity was to be directed were *people who were poor*. Attempting to encourage one of his priests at work in far off Algiers, he exclaims, "We cannot better assure our eternal happiness than by living and dying in the service of the poor, in the arms of Providence, and with genuine renouncement of ourselves in order to follow Jesus Christ." [26]

In that "Introduction" to his Rule just referred to, Vincent expands on that line of thinking. "My idea was that those who are called to continue Christ's mission, which is mainly preaching the Gospel to the poor, should see things from His point of view, and want what He wanted."

[24] CCD:V:400.
[25] *Common Rules*, chap. 1, 1.
[26] CCD:III:384.

These three leanings toward action, events, and the poor show up in a particularly stinging letter he sends to his priests.

> If there are any among us who think they are in the Congregation to preach the good news to the poor but not to comfort them, to supply their spiritual but not their temporal wants, I reply that we ought to assist them and have them assisted in every way, by ourselves and others. . . . To do this is to preach the gospel by word and work.[27]

d) Next to consider is what one might call his *virtue spirituality*, the vital place Vincent gives to the practice of certain New Testament traits and qualities. The ones he emphasized might be called the missionary virtues, the kind that enable and enhance missionary service especially to people who were poor. They were ideals, but even more so, behaviors and attitudes that required daily practice. The five he selects (humility, simplicity, mortification, zeal, and meekness) are singled out certainly because Jesus lived them, but also because they are especially needed by anyone who would minister to God's least ones. They empower a love that, in Vincent's phrase, is "not just affective, but effective."

And so, humility, the emptying of self so that God's presence could fill the heart of the missionary. Simplicity, that personal honesty and transparency without which the poor would not trust the evangelizer. Mortification, those many deaths-to-self required to keep the interest of the other in the forefront. Zeal, that inner fire driving the apostle out to the ends of the earth to preach the Good News. Meekness, a code word for the approachability needed by anyone who would convey an appealing and convincing word of God's caring love. Vincent uses David's "five smooth stones" as an image for this cluster, weapons to slay the opponents of Jesus' Way and Truth and Life.

As Vincent exhorts one of his own:

> Mon Dieu! Monsieur, how blessed are those who give themselves to God in this way to do what Jesus Christ did, and to practice, after His example, the virtues He practiced: poverty, obedience, humility, patience, zeal, and the other virtues! For in this way they are the true disciples of such a Master. They live solely of His Spirit and spread,

---

[27] CCD:XII:77.

together with the fragrance of His life, the merit of His actions, for the sanctification of souls for whom He died and rose.[28]

Again, the practical bent.

e) Vincent would be known today as an "*organization man,*" a person with the ability and talent to translate visions and ideas into institutional operation. The bulk of his correspondence is given over to the humdrum particulars of setting up and maintaining organizations. Here again, we see him bending much more toward concrete application than to theoretical underpinnings. Not bound to any particular system or ideology, he kept his eye rather on how things develop as they moved along and then adjusted to their changing circumstances.

f) Finally, there is Vincent's *language*. Compared to some of the other discourse of the day, Vincent's words were simple, unadorned, and to the point. Not only did he think this tamped down the preacher's temptation to show off, but it also had a sound more amenable to the ears of the poor. He promoted what he termed his "Little Method," a simple schema of nature, motives and means, by which the preacher could imitate the simple style of Jesus, the model evangelizer.

Conclusion

One of the most insightful of Vincent's modern commentators, André Dodin, suggests a helpful metaphor by which to draw together the parts of this sketch. [29] He contends that Vincent presents not so much a school or a theory as he does a "Way." It is while on The Way, in the very walking along the road of discipleship, in the present time following of the thinking and especially the doing of Jesus, that the person encounters that glory of God at work in the world. In the end, for Vincent it was through historical experience that God's "weighty radiance" showed itself. The divine drawing-near comes primarily through events and the people involved in them.

As Vincentian writer Hugh O'Donnell sums it up, "Vincent had been led beyond Berulle's elevations to the absolute conviction of God's presence in time and history. . . . This approach was radically incarnational,

---

[28] CCD:V:554.

[29] Andre Dodin, *Vincent de Paul and Charity: A Contemporary Portrait of His Life and Apostolic Spirit* (Brooklyn and Hyde Park: New City Press, 1993), 48–62.

historical, and existential."[30] For Vincent de Paul, God is here and now, to be discovered in a contemplation that is tightly mixed with the demands, tedium, and joys of everyday service, especially the service of those special ones who are God's poor.

---

[30] Hugh F. O'Donnell, "Vincent de Paul: His Life and Way," *Vincent de Paul and Louise de Marillac: Rules, Conferences and Writings*, Classics of Western Spirituality (New York: Paulist, 1995), 30.

CHAPTER EIGHT

Sanctification, Solidarity, and Service:
The Lay Spirituality of Antoine Frédéric Ozanam

Raymond L. Sickinger

Antoine Frédéric Ozanam is celebrated as the principal founder of the St. Vincent de Paul Society. The first conference of charity started in Paris by Ozanam and six other friends in April of 1833 was soon replicated elsewhere. As Ozanam saw the Society flourish throughout France and beyond, he became concerned about potential clerical challenges to this young lay Society. One such challenge occurred in Marseille during May of 1844 after a new conference was established there. According to André Dorval's account,

> a certain distrust began to be felt by the clergy. The pastors did not think it opportune to add another project to all those that already existed in this city. They feared the dispersal of energy and the exhausting effect on the generosity of the faithful. It was hard to understand that this association would be directed by a layman and that priests were not accepted as active members.

It was providential that Bishop Eugène de Mazenod intervened. He did not harbor the same reservations as his fellow clergy. He gave his blessing to the newly formed group of eight men, promising them his "help, assistance, and advice." Within a short time, the Oblates of Marseille allowed the members to conduct their weekly meetings in the crypt of their Calvary Mission. They eventually gave them access to their meeting hall because it was a larger and more comfortable gathering space. In December of 1844, Bishop de Mazenod praised the Society and recommended it to all of his clergy. His actions dispelled any further misgivings. Within two years the Society spread, expanding to over two hundred members and serving more than two hundred and eighty families.[1]

This incident not only highlights a significant connection between de Mazenod and the Society of St. Vincent de Paul, but also highlights the important issue of the role of the laity and lay spirituality. For Frédéric Ozanam the Society was to be run by laymen. The primary reason for its existence was to increase the holiness of its members by service to those in need and by building deep friendships. This triad of holiness, friendship, and service, or what I call sanctification, solidarity, and service, was an important contribution to nineteenth-century French lay spirituality.

The lay nature of the Society of St. Vincent de Paul was present from its inception. On Tuesday, 23 April 1833, at eight in the evening, a group of seven men met in the office of the newspaper, *Tribune catholique*, located at 18 rue du Petit Bourbon-Saint-Sulpice. The paper was run by Joseph Emmanuel Bailly.[2] Bailly not only welcomed the group to use the offices of his newspaper, but also joined them in this endeavor.[3]

Affectionately referred to by the young men as "le Père,"[4] Bailly was necessary to their success. He had experience to share. As a former member of the *Société des Bonne Études* (Society of Good Studies), he had "encountered students anxious to combine their academic efforts with religious formation." As a former member of the *Société des Bonnes Oeuvres* (Society of Good Works) he had visited the sick in hospitals. Both of these societies were part of the Congregation of the Blessed Virgin founded in 1801. After entering the Congregation's ranks in the spring of 1820, Bailly soon became one of its recognized leaders. The Society of Good Studies and the Society of Good Works eventually merged in 1828. Bailly managed them from a location he owned on *Place de l'Estrapade*.

---

[1] André Dorval, OMI, "Frédéric Ozanam and the Oblates of Mary Immaculate," *Oblate Communications* (August 10, 2012), http://omiworld.org/.

[2] Gérard Cholvy, *Frédéric Ozanam: Le christianisme a besoin de passeurs* (Perpignan: Éditions Artège, 2012), 62. The address is today 38 and is marked by a commemorative plaque on the side of the building.

[3] C.-A. Ozanam, *Vie de Frédéric Ozanam* (Paris: Librairie Poussielgue Frères, 1879), 187–89. See also Cholvy, *Ozanam: Le christianisme*, 59–60; and Kathleen O'Meara, *Frederic Ozanam, Professor at the Sorbonne: His Life and Works* (New York: Catholic Publication Society, 1891), 59–60.

[4] Charles L. Souvay, CM, "The Society of St. Vincent de Paul as an Agency of Reconstruction," *The Catholic Historical Review* 7, no. 4 (1922): 443.

But Paris at this time was politically unsettled. Groups like this were repressed after the fall of the restoration monarchy in 1830. The government feared that they could potentially become centers of political opposition.

In response to these closings, Bailly established the conference of history. It attracted talented students like Ozanam and his friends.[5] Unlike the earlier organizations that limited members to "a certain class of young Catholics of a particular shade of political thought," this new "Conference of History was open to every mind desirous of instruction, to every shade and difference of contemporary thought," all of which Frédéric Ozanam counted on winning over.[6] To support passionate students like Frédéric, Monsieur Bailly also opened his newspaper office as a gathering place; he even provided a wide selection of newspapers for them to read to keep up on current events. Lively discussion dominated his office; Bailly himself often joined in as an active and ardent participant.[7] He had much then to offer this budding group of young charity workers.

Although the first conference of charity formed in April of 1833 (it would become known as the Society of St. Vincent de Paul in 1835) was very similar to the *Société des Bonnes Oeuvres*,[8] there were important differences. The latter group had approved a regulation that "bound its members to aid one another in their worldly careers."[9] There was no such provision for the conference of charity or the Society of St. Vincent de Paul. There was more clerical influence in the *Société des Bonnes Oeuvres* because the Congregation of the Blessed Virgin required that the director

[5] Louise Sullivan, DC, *Sister Rosalie Rendu: A Daughter of Charity on Fire with Love for the Poor* (Chicago: Vincentian Studies Institute, 2006), 201–2. See also Ralph Middlecamp, "Lives of Distinction—Ozanam's Cofounders of the Society of St. Vincent de Paul," 3. Available at https://famvin.org/wiki/SVDP-Founders. Ralph Middlecamp, a member of the Society of St. Vincent de Paul for over thirty years, has spent many years researching the early days of the Society and has contributed to the Vincentian Encyclopedia on the Vincentian Family website (Famvin).

[6] Louis Baunard, *Ozanam in His Correspondence* (Dublin: Catholic Truth Society, 1925), 57.

[7] Sullivan, *Sister Rosalie*, 200–201. See also Cholvy, *Ozanam: Le christianisme*, 47; and Middlecamp, "Lives of Distinction," 3–5.

[8] One historian, Catherine Duprat, sees the Society of St. Vincent de Paul as an exact replica of the Society of Good Works at first. See Cholvy, *Ozanam: Le christianisme*, 60. See also Matthieu Brejon de Lavergnée, *Les Société de Saint-Vincent de-Paul au XIXᵉ siècle: Un fleuron du catholicisme social* (Paris: Les Éditions du Cerf, 2008), 118.

[9] Baunard, *Ozanam*, 71.

always be "a priest and authorized by ecclesiastical superiors."[10] As the historian Gérard Cholvy wrote: "The Society of Saint Vincent de Paul was founded by lay people, was run by them, and did not involve the Church."[11]

Ozanam may have already been familiar with the idea of visiting those living in poverty in their homes from a work entitled: *Le Visiteur du Pauvre* written in 1820 by the baron Joseph-Marie de Gérando, a Lyonnais. In this work, de Gérando sought to harmonize public beneficence and private charity. To achieve this end, he counseled that those in need must be befriended by speaking the same language as they do, building trust, and forming a deep friendship. This was very different from the more common practice of those in poverty visiting the homes of the wealthy on fixed days to receive some kind of assistance. The newly formed conference of charity discussed this approach and broached the idea with Bailly. He proved to be quite sympathetic. In fact, Bailly's wife had been visiting homes for the Daughters of Charity, but had confided in her husband that it was work better left to young men. Bailly took her recommendation to heart.[12]

On that night of 23 April, the group of seven discussed how they would conduct visits and how they would know who was in need. Jules Devaux was charged with obtaining a list of names from Sr. Rosalie Rendu, a Daughter of Charity in the Mouffetard District.[13] There is some evidence that Jules had already worked for Sr. Rosalie prior to this initial gathering.[14] It is no surprise that Bailly would have suggested Sr. Rosalie because his wife had been helping her and because his brother was a Lazarist priest.[15] Bailly's family also had a deep devotion to St. Vincent de Paul; he was well acquainted with the Vincentian family and its spirituality.[16]

---

[10] Marcel Vincent, *Ozanam: Une jeunesse romantique, 1813–1833* (Paris: Médiaspaul, 1994), 265.

[11] Gérard Cholvy, "Frédéric Ozanam and the Challenges of the Times," *Society of St. Vincent de Paul Bulletin of News* (13 February 2009): 2.

[12] Cholvy, *Ozanam: Le christianisme*, 61–62.

[13] Ibid., 62–63.

[14] Sullivan, *Sister Rosalie*, 206. See also Middlecamp, "Lives of Distinction," 12.

[15] Middlecamp, "Lives of Distinction," 6. See also Cholvy, *Ozanam: Le christianisme*, 63. Lazarist is the name given in France to the Congregation of the Mission priests who were founded by St. Vincent de Paul. In Paris they were at first located in the priory of St. Lazarus.

[16] Baunard, *Ozanam*, 67.

The small group was not disappointed. When approached by Jules Devaux, Sr. Rosalie warmly received him.

What Frédéric and his friends were undertaking as men was a remarkable innovation in the world of nineteenth-century charitable work. In particular, they offered an alternative to the model of men as one of honor, aggressiveness, and religious indifference prevalent in the nineteenth century. Instead, they offered a model based upon sensitivity and religious practice that was in large part countercultural.[17]

Once the early members chose the official name "Society of St. Vincent de Paul" in 1835, they prepared a Rule to guide their lay organization. The practices and procedures that had developed over the course of two years were now written down in the first Rule of the Society. The writing of the first Rule has generally been attributed to Emmanuel Bailly and François Lallier. There are some scholars, however, who strongly claim that Frédéric Ozanam helped to draft it and had an important influence on its content.[18] Given his close friendship with François Lallier, it is likely that he had significant input on the final draft. The Rule was not written immediately in 1833 because it was "necessary that it [the Society] should be well established—that it should know what Heaven required of it—that it should judge what it can do by what it already has done, before framing its rules and prescribing its duties."[19] This practice of embodying what was already proven to work is in the best tradition of St. Vincent de Paul and St. Louise de Marillac.[20]

---

[17] Brejon de Lavergnée, *Les Société de Saint-Vincent de-Paul*, 599–600.

[18] Sr. Louise Sullivan suggests that Bailly, Lallier, and Ozanam "were charged with the task." And she further emphasizes that as early as 1834 it was Ozanam who "had clearly seen the need for greater organization." See Sullivan, *Sister Rosalie*, 221. Fr. Edward O'Connor argues convincingly that, at the very least, the concluding portion of the Rule was composed by Ozanam. See Edward O'Connor, SJ, *The Secret of Frederick Ozanam: Founder of the Society of St. Vincent de Paul* (Dublin: M.H. Gill and Son, 1953), 56. According to Monsignor Baunard, Ozanam "was actively engaged in conjunction with Lallier, in the drawing-up of the Rule of the Society of St. Vincent de Paul." See Baunard, *Ozanam*, 106.

[19] *Rules of the Society of St. Vincent de Paul, and Indulgences*, Printed for the Council of New York (New York: D. & J. Sadlier, 1869), 9. This publication includes the original Rule of 1835 in translation, https://archive.org/details/RulesAndIndulgences. Quoted also in Sullivan, *Sister Rosalie*, 222. Original in *Règlement de la Société de Saint Vincent de Paul* (Paris: Imprimerie de E-J Bailly et Compagnie, 1835), 5–6.

[20] During the seventeenth century both Vincent de Paul and Louise de Marillac collaborated on various charitable works. It was their practice to see what worked first before forming any rules or guidelines in order to be certain of its efficacy and its divine approval.

The Rule set forth the Society's five purposes. Its primary purpose was "to sustain its members, by mutual example, in the practice of Christian life." Its secondary purpose was "to visit the poor at their dwellings, to carry them succor in kind, to afford them, also, religious consolations." "The elementary and Christian instruction of poor children, whether free or imprisoned," was the third. The fourth and fifth respectively were "to distribute moral and religious books . . . [and] to be willing to undertake any other sort of charitable work to which . . . resources may be adequate, and which will not oppose the chief end of the Society."

Growing in holiness, especially in service to those in poverty, was its ultimate and overarching goal.[21] Consequently, the Rule encouraged its lay members to be virtuous. In particular, it encouraged the practice of certain essential virtues. The first was *self-denial or self-sacrifice*:

> By *self-denial* we should understand the surrendering of our own opinion. . . . The man who is in love with his own ideas will disdain the opinion of others. . . . We should . . . willingly acquiesce in the judgment of others, and should not feel annoyed if our own propositions be not accepted. . . . Our mutual good-will should proceed from the heart. . . . We should . . . avoid all spirit of contention with the poor, and we must not consider ourselves offended if they should not yield implicitly to our advice; we must not attempt to make them receive it as from authority and by command.[22]

The second was *Christian prudence*:

> Among the poor, there are some who have the happiness to be good Christians; others are careless, and some, perhaps, impious. We ought not to repulse them, . . . remembering that Jesus Christ recommended His disciples to unite the wisdom of the serpent to the simplicity of the dove. Bounty opens the heart to confidence, and it is by charitable gifts that we prepare the way for spiritual benefits. St. Vincent de Paul often recommended not to try the latter until the former had been freely bestowed.[23]

---

[21] *Rules of the Society 1835*, 11–12. Quoted also in Sullivan, *Sister Rosalie*, 223. Original in *Règlement de la Société*, 8–9.

[22] *Rules of the Society 1835*, 13–14.

[23] Ibid., 14.

Christian prudence encouraged the members to be cautious when visiting those of the opposite sex:

> Now the poor are of either sex. As the *Society of Charity* is chiefly composed of young men, they should never forget that their mission is not to such of the other sex as are young, lest they should meet with their own destruction, whilst desiring to promote the salvation of others; moreover, it is necessary to shun even the appearance of evil, and all which might scandalize the weak.[24]

Christian prudence further required that politics be left at the door of the meeting room. Politics and political wrangling had no part in the structure of conference life:

> The spirit of charity, together with Christian prudence, will further induce us to banish political discussions forever from our meetings, as well general as ordinary. St. Vincent de Paul would not allow his ecclesiastics even to converse upon those differences which arm princes against each other, or upon the motives of rivalry which estrange nations. With more reason, those who wish to be of one mind, and to exercise a ministry of charity, should abstain from being inflamed by political leanings which array parties in opposition. . . . Our Society is all charity: politics is wholly foreign to it.[25]

The third virtue was *Love of our neighbor, and zeal for the salvation of souls*:

> This is the very essence of the *Conference of Charity.* He who is not animated by this twofold sentiment. . . . should not become a member. We must never murmur at the labors, the fatigues, nor even at the repulses to which the exercise of charity may subject us. We expose ourselves to all these things, in associating for the service of our neighbor. Neither should we regret the pecuniary sacrifices that we may make to our work, esteeming ourselves happy in offering

[24] Ibid. Discussion of this matter appears from time to time in the minutes of meetings. Carol E. Harrison is rather critical of the Society's concerns raised on this issue. See her *Romantic Catholics: France's Postrevolutionary Generation in Search of a Modern Faith* (Ithaca, NY, and London: Cornell University Press, 2014), 205–6.

[25] *Rules of the Society 1835*, 20–21.

something to Jesus Christ in the persons of the poor, and in being able to carry some relief to His suffering members.[26]

The fourth virtue was *meekness/humility*. Christ, the divine model, and St. Vincent de Paul, the patron, gave witness to the importance of being meek and humble:

> We should be kind and obliging to one another, and we should be equally so to the poor whom we visit. We can have no power over the mind, except through meekness. . . . The spirit of humility and meekness is more particularly necessary in giving advice, and in exhorting others to fly from evil and to practice [sic] virtue. Without gentleness, zeal for the salvation of souls is a ship without sails.[27]

The last in this list of virtues was the *spirit of brotherly love*:

> It is the *spirit of brotherly love* which will insure our *Society of Charity* becoming beneficial to its members and edifying to others. Faithful to the maxims of our divine Master and His beloved disciple, let us love one another. We should love one another now and ever, far and near, from one Conference to another, from town to town, from clime to clime.

All members were instructed as loving friends

> to bear with one another's failings. We shall never give credence to an evil report of a brother but with sorrow; and when we cannot reject the evidence of facts, even then, . . . in a spirit of charity, and with all the earnestness of sincere friendship, we will ourselves counsel our falling, or fallen brother, or cause advice to be conveyed to him; we will endeavor to strengthen him in virtue, or raise him from his fall.

Furthermore,

> If any member of the Conference should become ill, his brethren will visit him, will tend him, if it be necessary, will assuage the irksomeness of his convalescence; if his malady be dangerous, they should take the utmost care that he receive the Sacraments. In a

---

[26] Ibid., 14–15.
[27] Ibid., 15–16.

word, the troubles and the joys of each of us shall be shared by all, in accordance with the advice of the apostle, who tells us to weep with those who weep, and rejoice with those who rejoice.[28]

With the phrase "the troubles and the joys of each of us shall be shared by all," the Rule sought to establish a unity among members that would be a genuine "model of Christian friendship" and build authentic solidarity.

All five of these virtues reinforced not only the bonds of friendship, but also ensured that the dignity of each person—the person serving and the person served alike—was respected.[29] The Rule was clear:

> Our love of our neighbor, then, should be without respect of persons. The title of the poor to our commiseration is their poverty itself. We are not to inquire whether they belong to any party, or sect, in particular. Jesus Christ came to redeem and save all men, the Greeks as well as Jews, barbarians as well as Romans. We will not discriminate more than did He, between those whom suffering and misery have visited.[30]

Frédéric's wife, Amélie, provides an excellent example of how her husband took these virtues to heart:

> Frédéric loved the poor so much because in them he honored our Lord. This thought did not leave him and if charity was a great enjoyment for his heart, its goal has always been the propagation of the faith. The last winter that he spent in Paris, he was already very ill and my prayers could not prevent him from going weekly to . . . a lost and very ungodly old man. . . . Frédéric remained sometimes three quarters of an hour to one hour on his feet, exposed to all the winds, in the middle of the cries of market routes to educate, to persuade this man who was extremely bad. He was an old Septembrist jacobin, a terrorist who kept hating and blaspheming.[31]

---

[28] Ibid., 16–17. On these virtues see also Sullivan, *Sister Rosalie*, 222–24. See also *Règlement de la Société*, 7–10.

[29] *Rules of the Society 1835*, 17.

[30] Ibid., 20.

[31] For the source of the original French text see Amélie Ozanam-Soulacroix, *Notes biographique sur Frédéric Ozanam*, edition established by Raphaëlle Chevalier-Motariol, in Faculté de théologie Université catholique de Lyon, *Frédéric Ozanam: Actes du Colloque des 4 et 5 décembre 1998* (Paris: Bayard, 2001), 334. "Septembrist Jacobin": The

With great love, and patience, Frédéric persisted for two years. His efforts and prayers finally worked. The old man was persuaded "to forgive and to make his Easter communion which he did in very good feelings." When the old man died a bit later, "he died well."[32]

Frédéric Ozanam believed firmly in the "apostleship of the laity."[33] He fully understood, to borrow from Pope Paul VI's 1965 document on this concept, that the laity exercise

> their apostolate . . . when they work to evangelize people and make them holy; it is exercised, too, when they endeavor to have the Gospel spirit permeate and improve the temporal order, going about it in a way that bears clear witness to Christ and helps forward the salvation of humanity. The characteristic of the lay state being a life led in the midst of the world and of secular affairs, lay people are called by God to make of their apostolate, through the vigor of their Christian spirit, a leaven in the world. (*Apostolicam Actuositatem* 2).

In an 1835 letter to his friend Léonce Curnier, who was a member of the Society in Nîmes, Ozanam expresses in powerful and emotional language this very concept of the apostolate of the laity:

> Are we not, like the Christians of the first centuries, thrown into the midst of a corrupt civilization, of a collapsing society? Are we not as relegated to the catacombs in obscurity and beneath the contempt of those who consider themselves great and wise? Cast your eyes on the world around us. Are the rich and the favored much better than those who replied to St. Paul: "We will hear you another time?" And are the poor and the populace better instructed and are they better off than those to whom the apostles preached? The savants have compared the state of the slaves of antiquity with the condition of our workers and proletariat and have found these latter to have more to complain of, after eighteen centuries of Christianity. Then, for a like evil, a like remedy. The earth has grown cold. It is for us Catholics to revive the vital beat to restore it, it is for us to begin over again the great work of regeneration, if necessary to bring back the era of

---

Jacobins were a radical political group during the French Revolution. Septembrist refers to the September Massacres of 1792 during the French Revolution.

[32] Ibid.

[33] Didier Ozanam, "Frederic Ozanam," in Mary Ann Garvie Hess, trans., *Frédéric Ozanam*, special issue, *Cahiers Ozanam*, nos. 37/38/39, January–June (Paris: Society of St. Vincent de Paul, Council General, 1974), 11.

the martyrs. For to be a martyr is possible for every Christian, to be a martyr is to give his life for God and his brothers, to give his life in sacrifice, whether the sacrifice be consumed in an instant like a holocaust, or be accomplished slowly and smoke night and day like perfume on the altar. To be a martyr is to give back to heaven all that one has received: his money, his blood, his whole soul. This offering is in our hands; we can make this sacrifice. It is up to us to choose to which altar it pleases us to bring it, to what divinity we will consecrate our youth and the time following, in what temple we will assemble: at the foot of the idol of egoism, or in the sanctuary of God and humanity.[34]

Ozanam then used the story of the Good Samaritan to highlight for Curnier the necessary role a lay person could play in addressing both the physical and spiritual needs of those living in desperation:

Humanity of our days seems comparable to the traveler of whom the Gospel speaks: it also . . . has been attacked by the cutthroats and robbers of thought, by wicked men who have robbed it of what it possessed: the treasure of faith and love, and they have left it naked and wounded and lying by the side of the road. Priests and Levites have passed by, and this time, since they were true priests and Levites, they have approached suffering themselves and wished to heal it. But in its delirium, it did not recognize them and repulsed them.

He continued his narrative with insight into our own human frailty:

In our turn, weak Samaritans, worldly and people of little faith that we are, let us dare nonetheless to approach this great sick one. Perhaps it will not be frightened of us. Let us try to probe its wounds and pour in oil, soothing its ear with words of consolation and peace; then, when its eyes are opened, we will place it in the hands of those whom God has constituted as the guardians and doctors of souls, who are also, in a way, our innkeepers in our pilgrimage here below, so as to give our errant and famished spirits the holy word for nourishment and the hope of a better world for a shield."[35]

---

[34] "Letter to Léonce Curnier," 23 February 1835, in Joseph I. Dirvin, CM, trans. and ed., *Frederic Ozanam: A Life in Letters* (St. Louis: Society of St. Vincent de Paul, Council of the United States, 1986), 64. For the original French text see *Lettres de Frédéric Ozanam*, vol. 1, *Lettres de jeunesse (1819–1840)*, ed. Léonce Célier, Jean-Baptiste Duroselle, and Didier Ozanam (Paris: Bloud and Gay, 1960), n° 90, 166–67.

[35] Ibid., 64–65. For the original French text see ibid., 167.

Ozanam was convinced that he was called to this "sublime vocation God has given us."[36] This letter to Curnier remains one of the most eloquent expressions of the layperson's call to ministry in the world and dramatically reveals the depth of Ozanam's faith.

By the 1840s the Society of St. Vincent de Paul itself embraced this idea of an apostolate where "the laity participate in the priesthood of priests."[37] In fact, some of the members, including Ozanam, became actively involved with the work of the *Society for the Propagation of the Faith*. Started in Lyon by Pauline Jaricot in 1822, the *Society for the Propagation of the Faith* was intended to advance the faith through missionary activity. Ozanam actually edited its *Annals* or reports until 1848. Indeed, Ozanam referred to this work as "the peaceful crusade of the nineteenth century."[38]

Priests certainly had a role to play as spiritual advisors, but not as officers or active members, in the Society of St. Vincent de Paul . Although respectful of priests and all church authority, Frédéric was ever ready to defend the lay nature and leadership of the Society. It was in Lyon where he first encountered some significant challenges to the lay character of the Society. Ozanam wrote to François Lallier about his concerns:

> For some time we have been holding frequent meetings . . . to put an end to several serious discussions which have arisen on the part the clergy should play in our affairs. Some are already complaining of invaders, while others still accuse them of indifference and coldness. We have a right wing which would like to live in the shadow of the biretta, and a left wing which is still living according to the *Paroles d'un croyant*.[39] Outside both is your servant who, as you know, is rather centrist, finds himself greatly embarrassed, and calls on the help of your prayers.[40]

---

[36] Ibid., 65. For the original French text see ibid.

[37] Brejon de Lavergnée, *Les Société de Saint-Vincent de-Paul*, 172–73.

[38] Ibid., 172. For the phrase, see "Letter to Dominique Meynis," 25 August 1845, in *Lettres de Frédéric Ozanam*, vol. 3, *L'engagement (1845–1849)*, édition critique sous la direction de Didier Ozanam (Paris: Celse, 1978), n° 638, 122. For more information see Edward John Hickey, *The Society for the propagation of the faith; its foundation, organization, and success (1822–1922)* (Ulan Press, 2012).

[39] The biretta is the name given to a hat once regularly worn by priests. *Paroles d'un croyant* is the work written by Lamennais in 1834 that was condemned by the pope.

[40] "Letter to François Lallier," 1 August 1838, in Dirvin, *A Life in Letters*, 150–51. For the original French text see *Lettres*, v. 1, n° 181, 319–20.

Ten days later Frédéric again wrote to Lallier, who was secretary-general of the Society of St. Vincent de Paul, with a report and recommendations. As the president of the Society in Lyon, Frédéric informed the secretary-general of two concerns. The first was a laxity in observing religious celebrations. Some members wanted to "stimulate piety and the spirit of Christian brotherhood" in order to "preserve our conferences from degenerating to welfare bureaus."[41] The second was raised by other members who "were alarmed at certain acts of ecclesiastical protection, which seemed to them outside encroachments, and which could assimilate the Society into certain religious congregations, undoubtedly praiseworthy in themselves, but absolutely different in their end."[42]

Frédéric then offered a solution that would address both concerns by "drawing up unified measures capable of giving our work a character at once profoundly Christian and absolutely lay."[43] Five recommendations followed in his report.

The first was that

> from the time of the next general assembly, the active chairmanship of the meeting should be exercised not by the pastor of Saint-Pierre but by the president of the Society. . . . A place will be looked for within the two parishes of Saint-Pierre and Saint-Francois to avoid the inconvenience of meeting in a sacristy.

The second was that presidents of conferences would still have their proceedings approved by the clergy and would remind their members frequently

> that the end of the Society is especially to rekindle and refresh in the youth the spirit of Catholicism, that fidelity to meetings, and union of intention and prayer are indispensible [sic] to this end, and that visiting the poor should be the means and not the end of our association.

The third was that a request be made to extend to all the members of the Society the benefit of the indulgences from Rome now enjoyed only

---

[41] "Letter to François Lallier," 11 August 1838, in Dirvin, *A Life in Letters*, 151–52. For the original French text see *Lettres*, v. 1, n° 182, 320.

[42] Ibid., 152. For the original French text see ibid.

[43] Ibid., 152. For the original French text see ibid.

by the members in Paris. The fourth asked for a modification of the language of the Rule concerning "ecclesiastical superiors:"

> [T]he paragraph that deals with the deference owed ecclesiastical superiors, contains the following words: "They will accept with an *absolute docility the direction* that the superiors *will judge proper* to give them." Once we had received from the president general a clear interpretation, discussion was terminated on the sense which should be given it. But, since these words seem to *exaggerate* the thought they ought to present, the Council of Paris is asked to modify them in a next edition.

The fifth and final recommendation was that the

> "Council of Paris . . . meet more often and . . . enter into a more active correspondence with the provincial conferences, so as to prevent isolation and extreme individuality in some, and to rekindle languishing zeal in others." The recommendations ended with an acknowledgement that the conferences of Lyon understood "that their strength is in union and that the entire uniqueness of their work is precisely in its universality."[44]

Frédéric continued to foster both the spiritual life and lay character of the Society. One year later (1839), in correspondence asking Joseph Arthaud to be president of the conferences in Lyon, he insisted that the Society must "never wish to be either a grouping or a school or an association, unless it be profoundly Catholic without ceasing to be lay." He believed that Arthaud was the right person to insure the integrity of the Society in Lyon. He further shared with Arthaud his hopes that this lay apostolate could bring a true renewal:

> The work of St. Vincent de Paul is growing in importance without stop and . . . a magnificent mission has been given it, that it alone, by the multitude and status of its adherents, by its stable existence in so many diverse ways, and by its abnegation of all philosophical and political interest, can rally youth to the right paths, bring a new spirit little by little to the upper classes and the most influential ac-

---

[44] For these five recommendations see ibid., 152–53. For the original French text see ibid., 320–21.

tions, resist the secret associations which are menacing the civilization of our country, and perhaps in the end save France.[45]

It is also important to note that as a layman Frederic developed a deep spiritual life which embodied some of the essential features of seventeenth-century French spirituality. According to Raymond Deville, those in the French school of spirituality shared the following characteristics: "the history of their lives was the history of a spiritual and apostolic journey;" they had a strong relationship with Jesus and "the spirit of the risen Jesus" to which they abandoned themselves; they embraced a "mystical sense of the Church, the Body of Christ, the continuation and fulfillment of the life of Jesus;" they expressed a theologically sound, but "simple and pious, devotion to our Lady;" and they had a "vigorous, apostolic, missionary commitment aimed both inside and outside of France."[46] As evidenced throughout this study Ozanam participated in these characteristics. They were often his motivation as a Catholic layman.

In particular, his devotion to the Blessed Mother was pronounced. It was no surprise when Frédéric Ozanam proposed honoring the Blessed Virgin Mary as patroness of the Society of St. Vincent de Paul in February 1834. By that date he had already nurtured a strong devotion to the Blessed Mother. His friend Léonce Curnier recalled Ozanam's fervor:

> Notre Dame de Fourviere held for him a charm other than the splendid panorama which unfolded itself from the mountain. It was for him a place of prayer. He had a great devotion to the Mother of God, whose modest shrine bore on its walls many evidences of miracles obtained through her intercession. Ozanam, who knew the history of this holy place intimately, called up before my eyes the notable visitors of former times: Thomas à Becket, Innocent IV, Louis XI, Anne of Austria, Louis XIII, and, in our days, Pius VII, on his return from the coronation of Napoleon.[47]

---

[45] "Letter to Joseph Arthaud," 9 July 1839, in Dirvin, *A Life in Letters*, 163. For the original French text see *Lettres*, v. 1, n° 205, 353.

[46] Raymond Deville, SS, "The Seventeenth-Century School of French Spirituality," *Vincentian Heritage* 11, no. 1 (1990): 22–23.

[47] Quoted in Baunard, *Ozanam*, 15. For the original French text see Léonce Curnier, *La jeunesse de Frédéric Ozanam*, 4th ed. (Paris: A. Hennuyer, Imprimateur-Éditeur, 1890), 27–29.

Frédéric was only nineteen when in 1832 the first two thousand medals were struck according to the specifications of Catherine Labouré who had been visited by the Blessed Mother in 1830 and who had been charged by Mary to have a medal struck in her honor.[48] The year 1832 witnessed the terrible cholera epidemic in Paris. Although the medal was to be officially called "Medal of the Immaculate Conception," healing miracles were immediately attributed to it and the term "Miraculous Medal" soon became its most common reference.[49] There is a strong possibility that Frédéric wore one of the original two thousand medals when he and his friends met to form the first conference of charity in April 1833.[50] He certainly was fascinated by the story of the Jewish convert, Marie Alphonse Ratisbonne, who embraced the Catholic faith in 1842 supposedly because of the influence of the medal.[51] He actually helped to distribute accounts of that conversion.[52]

His devotion to the Blessed Mother was also revealed in the choice of his daughter's name, Marie. The Ozanams chose that name both to honor Frédéric's mother and to pay homage to the Blessed Mother, the "powerful patroness" who, in their opinion, was responsible for "this happy birth."[53] Unfortunately, when Marie was only eight years old, her loving father died. The day of his death was 8 September 1853, the Feast of the Nativity of the Blessed Virgin Mary. Given his lifelong devotion to Mary, it certainly seems fitting that he breathed his last on that Marian feast.

---

[48] Not far from the Chapel of St. Vincent de Paul is the motherhouse of the Daughters of Charity on the Rue du Bac. It was here that the Blessed Mother appeared to St. Catherine Labouré whose uncorrupted body still lies in state in the chapel of the Miraculous Medal at this location.

[49] Joseph I. Dirvin, CM, *Saint Catherine Labouré of the Miraculous Medal* (Rockford, IL: TAN, 1984), 116–17.

[50] "History of the Medal," *The Chapel Pamphlets* (July 2004), section 5, 2, http://www .chapellenotredamedelamedaillemiraculeuse.com/Carnets/carnetEN/HistoireMedaille -AN.pdf.

[51] "Letter to Dominique Meynis," 14 April 1842, in Dirvin, *A Life in Letters*, 289. For the original French text see *Lettres de Frédéric Ozanam*, vol. 2, *Premières années à la Sorbonne (1841–1844)*, edition critique de Jeanne Caron (Paris: Celse, 1978), n° 392, 280. The miraculous conversion of a French Jew who was an outspoken critic of the church is recounted in Dirvin, *Saint Catherine Labouré*, 166–71.

[52] "Letter to Dominique Meynis," 22 June 1842, in Dirvin, *A Life in Letters*, 301. For the original French text see *Lettres*, v. 2, n° 414, 310.

[53] "Letter to Théophile Foisset," 7 August 1845, in *Lettres*, v. 3, n° 636, 118.

As Ron Ramson notes, the spirituality of Frédéric Ozanam was "that of the person in the pew who burns with the desire to love God and neighbor and who, also, wants to put into practice that love." He was a man "of prayer and action, each supporting and fostering the other." The spirituality of Frédéric Ozanam was "the spirituality of humility, simplicity, mortification, meekness and zeal for souls." The spirituality of Frédéric Ozanam was "that of the Good Samaritan, the person who ardently practices the spiritual and corporal works of mercy." The spirituality of Frédéric Ozanam was "the spirituality of St. Vincent de Paul who believes and recognizes that it is truly Jesus in that person of the poor before him. For Frédéric, the poor person was the Risen Jesus; for Frederic, the poor person was the sacred image of the God whom he did not see." The spirituality of Frederic Ozanam was "the spirituality of compassion without judgement."[54]

The triad of sanctification (holiness), solidarity (friendship), and service was the fundamental foundation of Frédéric Ozanam's spirituality and the spirituality of the Society of St. Vincent de Paul established on his twentieth birthday in 1833. His was a lay spirituality that sought holiness by building solidarity and by seeking the face of Christ in those served. The Society embedded these principles in their Rule, making them a lasting legacy. Perhaps it would be fitting to leave the last word on spirituality to Frédéric:

> We are unprofitable servants, but we are servants, and wages are given according to the quality of work we are doing in the vineyard of the Lord in the portion assigned to us. Life is despicable if we consider it according to how we use it, but not if we . . . consider it as the most perfect work of the Creator, as the sacred vestments with which the Savior has willed to clothe himself: life then is worthy of reverence and love. . . . Let us go in simplicity where merciful Providence leads us, content to see the stone on which we should step without wanting to discover all at once and completely the windings of the road.[55]

---

[54] Ronald W. Ramson, CM, "Frédéric Ozanam: His Piety and Devotion," *Vincentiana* 41, no. 3 (May–June 1997): 159–60 (12). *Vincentiana* is online at http://cmglobal.org /vincentiana/. The online page numbers are given in parentheses.

[55] Letter to François Lallier," 5 November 1836, in Dirvin, *A Life in Letters*, 93. For the original French text see *Lettres*, v. 1, n° 136, 241.

Further Reading

Barbiche, Bernard & Christine Franconnet, eds. *Frédéric Ozanam 1813–1853: Un universitaire chrétien face à la modernité*. Paris: Les Éditions du Cerf; Bibliothèque Nationale de France, 2006.

Baunard, Louis. *Ozanam in His Correspondence*. Dublin: Catholic Truth Society, 1925.

Brejon de Lavergnée, Matthieu. *Les Société de Saint-Vincent de-Paul au XIXe siècle: Un fleuron du catholicisme social*. Paris: Les Éditions du Cerf, 2008.

Cholvy, Gérard. *Frédéric Ozanam: L'engagement d'un intellectual catholique au XIXe siècle*. Paris: Fayard, 2003.

Faculté de théologie Université catholique de Lyon. *Frédéric Ozanam: Actes du Colloque des 4 et 5 décembre 1998*. Paris: Bayard, 2001.

O'Meara, Kathleen. *Frederic Ozanam, Professor at the Sorbonne: His Life and Works*. New York: Catholic Publication Society, 1891.

Ozanam, Antoine Frédéric. *Oeuvres complètes*. 11 vols. Paris: Jacques Lecoffre et Cie, Libraires-Éditeurs, 1865.

Schimberg, Albert Paul. *The Great Friend: Frederick Ozanam*. Milwaukee: Bruce Publishing, 1946.

Sickinger, Raymond L. *Antoine Frédéric Ozanam*. Notre Dame, IN: University of Notre Dame Press, 2017.

———. "Faith, Charity, Justice, and Civic Learning: The Lessons and Legacy of Frédéric Ozanam." *Vincentian Heritage* 30, no. 1 (2010).

CHAPTER NINE

Abandonment and Apostolic Charity in Thérèse of Lisieux, Daughter of the "French School"

Mary Frohlich, RSCJ

Can the spiritual teaching of Thérèse of Lisieux be a resource for those who dedicate their lives to justice for the poor? Dorothy Day, who wrote a book on Thérèse,[1] certainly thought so. Several theologians have explored how Day found in Thérèse a colleague and patron for her development of the Catholic Worker ethos of mutuality and service among the poor.[2] In this essay my main focus is on a close examination of Thérèse's creative appropriation of the French School notion of "abandonment" and how it may pertain to this question of service among the poor. In my conclusion I will take another look at Day's claims in view of what I have discovered.

Thérèse and the French School

First, what exactly is Thérèse's relationship to the "French School"? Here I am following Krumenacher et al. in defining this rather contested

---

[1] Dorothy Day, *Thérèse* (Notre Dame, IN: Fides, 1960).

[2] James Allaire, "Dorothy Day and Thérèse of Lisieux," *Spiritual Life* 43 (1997): 195–200; Peter J. Casarella, "Sisters in Doing the Truth: Dorothy Day and St. Thérèse of Lisieux," *Communio* 24 (September 1997): 468–98; Frederick C. Bauerschmidt, "The Politics of the Little Way: Dorothy Day Reads Thérèse of Lisieux," in Sandra Yocum Mize and William L Portier, *American Catholic Traditions: Resources for Renewal*, 77–95 (Maryknoll, NY: Orbis, 1997); J. Leon Hooper, "Dorothy Day's Transposition of Thérèse's 'Little Way,'" *Theological Studies* 63, no. 1 (March 2002): 68–86.

term as primarily referring to the impact of the spiritual thought of Pierre de Bérulle (1575–1629). These scholars affirm that even by the eighteenth century, Bérulle's approach was no longer being transmitted integrally. Nonetheless, its derivatives continued to be taken up and transformed within hybrid movements that addressed new circumstances.[3] Thérèse's concept of "abandonment" is an example of an approach with deep roots in Bérulle, yet also showing signs of recontextualization and hybridism.

Bérullien language related to "abandonment" can sound rather alarming to twenty-first century ears. Words such as *abnégation* (abnegation, self-denial), *abandon* (abandonment, surrender), *dénûment* (deprivation, destitution), and *dépouillement* (austerity, stripping) are repeated like a sober drumbeat throughout Bérulle's writings. To set the scene, let us begin with a quotation from Bérulle that Thérèse may actually have read.

> To imitate [Christ's] destitution, you must be utterly stripped of your own being, so that you no longer do the actions or operations yourself, nor in yourself, but only in God. . . . My daughter, the first fundamental thought of abnegation is to have a low esteem for every created thing, for oneself more than any other thing, and a high esteem for God and his works, saying with the Apostle: I have regarded all things as mud, so that I may gain Jesus Christ.[4]

At first glance, Bérulle's extreme emphasis on divestment of one's self-esteem and, even more radically, stripping off one's very being appears to be the opposite of today's focus on developing spiritualities that enhance self-esteem and remove obstacles to self-fulfillment. Of even greater concern is the fact that spiritualities that counsel abandonment of self can easily be diverted into collusion with oppression or even abuse of those who are already poor or powerless.[5] Finally, the focus of this spirituality appears to be inward on "God and me" rather than on any concern

---

[3] Yves Krumenacker, *L'école Française de Spiritualité: Des Mystiques, Des Fondateurs, Des Courants et Leurs Interprètes* (Paris: Cerf, 1998), 11.

[4] My translation from Carmel of Tours, *Trésor Du Carmel, Ou, Souvenirs de L'ancien Carmel de France*, 2nd ed., vol. II (Tours: Paul Bouserez, 1879), 278, 281. Available for download at: https://books.google.com/books/about/Tr%C3%A9sor_du_Carmel_ou_souvenirs_de_l_anci.html?id=sRFapDpR64cC.

[5] See, for example, Lisa E. Dahill, "Reading from the Underside of Selfhood: Dietrich Bonhoeffer and Spiritual Formation," *Spiritus* 1, no. 2 (September 1, 2001): 186–203.

for justice for the poor through activism on behalf of social change. With awareness of these potential liabilities, let us explore how Thérèse retrieved and refreshed this spirituality of "abandonment" two and a half centuries after Bérulle.

Actually, from its very origins the spirituality of Carmel in France was hybridized with Bérullism. Bérulle was the primary force behind the persuasion of Teresa of Avila's sidekick Anne of Jesus to found Carmel in France. He and his close collaborators André Duval and Jaques Gallimard were then named its ecclesiastical superiors, thus remaining intimately involved in all facets of its development during its first decades.[6] Madeleine of Saint-Joseph, the first French prioress, was a devoted disciple and defender of Bérulle.[7] From the very beginning, the mentality, governance, language, customs, and practices of Carmel in France were deeply shaped by a unique hybrid of Carmelite and Bérullien influences. Thus it is fair to say that Thérèse's entire context was permeated with themes and practices rooted in what we today call the "French School."

In French Carmels, these traditions were passed down primarily by oral and interpersonal formation rather than textually. However, *Le Trésor du Carmel* was an anthology of quotations, rules, and exhortations—many of them from the founders Bérulle, Duval, Gallimard, Anne of Jesus, and Madeleine of St. Joseph—that was still revered in Thérèse's time. The above quotation from Bérulle is included in *Le Trésor*. Thérèse's superiors probably consulted this anthology when they prepared their instructions and exhortations for the community, and it is likely that some parts were read out loud to the nuns from time to time. Thérèse may even have had the opportunity to read parts of the text herself when she took on the charge of novice mistress or when she was preparing for her retreats. Even though there is little likelihood that Thérèse had much direct textual exposure to any other original sources of the Bérullien stream of French spirituality, the centrality of this anthology as a revered source for nineteenth-century French Carmelites confirms that the direct link to the French School remained very much alive in Thérèse's time.

---

[6] Stéphane-Marie Morgain, *Pierre de Bérulle et Les Carmelites de France: La Querelle Du Gouvernement 1583–1629* (Paris: Cerf, 1995).

[7] Stéphane-Marie Morgain, "Pierre de Bérulle et Madeleine de Saint-Joseph: Une Communion Au Service Du Carmel de France," *Teresianum* 40 (1989): 45–85.

Spiritual Childhood

Thérèse's focus on childlikeness and "the little way" is a key to her approach to "abandonment" as well as to her participation in the French School. Fernand Ouellette asks "whether the spirituality of Thérèse of Lisieux is not the logical culmination or accomplishment of the spirituality called 'French' in its most clear lines of force, of which the 'spirit of childhood,' so bérullien, is the summit?"[8] Bérulle is well known for his repeated meditations on the astonishing self-abasement of the Word who enfeebled himself by entering the womb of Mary as a helpless infant, then secretly lived there "a glorious and celestial life, a journeying life, a spiritual and interior life in the perfect use of his eminent grace."[9] For Bérulle, since Christ's mission involved abasing himself to childhood and dependency, our call to participation in his mission requires us to be united to him in doing likewise.

The affective mood of Thérèse's development of spiritual childlikeness, however, is generally much closer to that of François De Sales, who writes very movingly of the abandonment of the soul in the prayer of quiet as like a baby nursing contentedly at its mother's breast.[10] Salesian spirituality focuses on the tenderness, sweetness, and delight of the parent-child relationship, in contrast to the Bérullien emphasis on the infant's annihilating enfeeblement. De Sales was a contemporary and colleague of Bérulle, and their spiritualities share not only the milieu of origins but many similar themes and practices. While Krumenacher et al. do not regard de Sales as, strictly speaking, a member of the French School, the fact is that from early on in the Bérullien movement many of its most noted members included de Sales among their favored sources.[11]

In Thérèse's own life, the influence of Salesian spirituality was direct and pervasive.[12] Her mother's sister was a Visitation nun in Le Mans;

---

[8] My translation from Fernand Ouellette, *Autres Trajets Avec Thérèse de Lisieux* (Québec: Fides, 2001), 28.

[9] My translation from Roger Parisot, ed., *L'expérience de Dieu Avec Bérulle* (Fides, 1999), 102. The quotation is from *Oeuvres de piété*, 11.

[10] Francis de Sales, *The Love of God: A Treatise*, trans. Vincent Kerns (Westminster, MD: Newman, 1962), Book V, chap. 2; Book VI, chaps. 8–9.

[11] Krumenacker, *L'école Française de Spiritualité*, 302.

[12] Wendy M. Wright, "A Salesian Pentecost: Thérèse of Lisieux, Léonie Aviat, and Salesian Tradition," *Studies in Spirituality* 12 (2002): 156–77; Daniel J. Chowning, "The Spirituality of Francis de Sales and Thérèse of Lisieux," *Spiritual Life* 34 (1988): 91–108.

three of Thérèse's older sisters went to boarding school there; and her sister Léonie—the only one of the five Martin girls who did not become a Carmelite—entered another Visitation monastery. In fact, when the infant Thérèse had been on the verge of death, her aunt at the Visitation made a vow to François de Sales to save her life, and as a result Thérèse's baptismal name was Marie-Françoise.

Thérèse's mother Zélie read de Sales's *Introduction to the Devout Life* and a life of St. Jeanne de Chantal with great appreciation, writing to her daughter Pauline in 1875 (when Thérèse was two) that the biography was "all the more interesting to me because I love the Visitation Monastery very much, but now I love it more than ever."[13] Wendy Wright notes that the teaching given to little Thérèse by Pauline, who became her "second mother" after Zélie's death and then her prioress after both entered Carmel, carried "unmistakable echoes" of François de Sales's language and imagery.[14] Thérèse herself kept certain favorite quotations from de Sales in her cell throughout her life, and in an 1893 letter to her sister in the Visitation, Léonie, she commented that hearing the biography of de Chantal in the refectory was "a real consolation" because it "brings me even closer to the dear Visitation that I love so much, and then I see the intimate union that has always existed between it and Carmel."[15]

Thus we see that Thérèse's spiritual practices and reflections were strongly shaped by Bérullien and Salesian sources as well as by her Carmelite heritage.

Thérèse and Poverty

In order to reflect on the implications of Thérèse's practice of "abandonment" for service to the poor, we must first inquire as to what is meant by "the poor." Is poverty primarily economic destitution, or is it more fundamentally a spiritual condition (in which the economically destitute may or may not share)? Thérèse never lived outside of a sheltered and economically comfortable environment, yet it would be inaccurate to say

[13] Frances Renda, ed., *A Call to Deeper Love: The Family Correspondence of Saint Thérèse of the Child Jesus, 1863–1885: Blessed Zélie and Louis Martin*, trans. Ann Connors Hess (Staten Island, NY: St. Pauls, 2011), 206.

[14] Wright, "A Salesian Pentecost," 64.

[15] Thérèse de Lisieux, *Letters of Saint Thérèse of Lisieux, Volume 2, 1890–1897*, trans. John Clarke (Institute of Carmelite Studies, 1988), LT 154.

that she was oblivious to the difficulties faced by those lacking social and economic resources. Family biographer Stéphane-Joseph Piat notes that Louis Martin had at one point been a leader in the Catholic Worker Circles of Albert de Mun, who promoted a legitimist and counterrevolutionary version of social Catholicism.[16] Louis and Zélie took care to imbue their daughters with a variety of practices focused on charity for the economically poor. In *Story of a Soul* Thérèse recounted several examples of her family's care for the poor during her childhood, including providing a first communion feast, giving alms, and caring for the children of a sick woman.[17] Piat provides many other examples of the charitable acts of the parents, often involving considerable cost and personal inconvenience.[18] Dorothy Day pointed to Thérèse's zeal to pray for the depraved murderer Pranzini as early evidence of her consciousness of those who are most marginalized, both socially and spiritually.[19] Nonetheless, it is hard to argue from these few instances that Thérèse had a primary focus on the economically poor.

Thérèse's writings are, however, laced with the adjective *pauvre*. She loved to refer affectionately to herself and others as "poor" and "little." In most cases her intention seems to be to draw attention to the startling fact that the big, strong, and gifted are not the ones God preferentially seeks as coworkers; rather, God rushes to those who are poor and weak. To give just one of numerous possible examples, in August 1892 she wrote, "The Creator of the universe awaits the prayer of a poor little soul to save other souls."[20] The poverty that really fascinates and attracts Thérèse is the utter emptiness and impotence of the human person in contrast to God's infinite power. Rather than regarding this as depressing or disempowering, she grasps it as the ultimate empowerment. She rejoices because to be poor is, amazingly, to be God's preferred place of being manifested in the world.

---

[16] Stéphane-Joseph Piat, *Histoire D'une Famille: Une École de Sainteté, Le Foyer Où S'épanoit Sainte Thérèse de l'Enfant Jésus*, 4th ed. (Office Central de Lisieux, 1946), 135; Casarella, "Sisters in Doing the Truth," 478.

[17] Thérèse de Lisieux, *Story of a Soul: The Autobiography of Saint Thérèse of Lisieux*, trans. John Clarke, 3rd ed. (Washington, DC: ICS Publications, 1996), 21, 30, 38, 112.

[18] Piat, *Histoire D'une Famille*, 137–42.

[19] Day, *Therese*, 109–11; Hooper, "Dorothy Day's Transposition of Thérèse's 'Little Way,'" 82.

[20] Thérèse de Lisieux, *Letters 2*, LT 135.

For Thérèse, poverty in this sense is closely connected with abandonment. The realization that one is radically poor and powerless in relation to God confronts a person with a choice: to attempt to put up a front to mask one's poverty, or to surrender oneself with the trust of a little child. Drawing together both Bérullien awe at God's willingness to cross the infinite gap between divine majesty and human poverty, and Salesian delight in God's tender embrace of the childlike soul, Thérèse developed her personal perspective on abandonment.

Thérèse on "Abandonment"

In this section I will focus on tracing the trajectory of Thérèse's reflections on self-abandonment, placing them in the context of her life and writings.[21] Thérèse's first written use of the language of abandonment came in July of 1893 in three letters to Céline, who was the last sibling remaining at home to take care of their ill father. Céline was struggling mightily with feelings of sadness, regret, and spiritual aridity. Thérèse shares her own experience of feeling no consolation from Jesus and the way he learned simply to surrender to him. In the first of the three letters she writes: "He teaches me to do *all* through love, to refuse him nothing, to be content when He gives me a chance of proving to Him that I love Him. But this is done in peace, in *abandonment*, it is Jesus who is doing all in me, and I am doing nothing."[22] In the second letter she uses for the first time the image of abandoning herself into the arms of Jesus.[23] In the third letter she develops the image of a little child alone in a boat on a stormy sea, abandoning herself to the wind while learning to trust that although she sees no one, in reality Jesus is asleep in her boat and will bring it to shore.[24] In these letters we already see the essential concepts and images of childlikeness, trust, and self-surrender that Thérèse will develop with such power in her last years.

---

[21] For further discussion of Thérèse's language of "abandonment," see Conrad De Meester, *The Power of Confidence: Genesis and Structure of the Way of Spiritual Childhood of St. Thérèse of Lisieux*, trans. Susan Conroy (New York: Alba House, 1998), 305–7.

[22] Thérèse de Lisieux, *Letters 2*, LT 142, 796.

[23] Ibid., LT 143, 801. She had previously written of being "carried" in Jesus' arms; see, for example, LT 79 and LT 89.

[24] Ibid., LT 144, 803–4.

Before Thérèse entered Carmel, she and Céline had joined their father on a pilgrimage to Rome. There they visited the tomb of St. Cecilia, who, Thérèse later wrote, "became my saint of predilection, my intimate confidante."[25] Cecilia, the story goes, had vowed her virginity to God but was forced to marry. With complete confidence she went ahead with the wedding, and with God's miraculous aid was able to convince her husband to join her in consecrated virginity. Later the couple was heroically martyred. Thérèse saw Cecilia as the perfect model of abandonment and of "limitless confidence that made her capable of virginizing souls."[26] In April of 1894 Thérèse was deeply worried about Céline, who in addition to her interior struggles had indicated some potential interest in marriage. Thérèse wrote an elaborate poem on Cecilia's story and dedicated it to Céline as a gift for her twenty-fifth birthday.[27] In the letter that accompanied it, she wrote: "I would need a tongue other than that of this earth to express the beauty of a soul's abandonment into the hands of Jesus. . . . Céline, the story of Cecilia (the Saint of ABANDONMENT) is your story too!"[28]

At this point in Thérèse's life, it is clear that the language of abandoning oneself with total confidence in God has become a compelling ideal for her. In particular, it describes a way of actualizing faith in times when the expectation of God's care seems starkly contradicted by the reality of one's circumstances. She counsels both herself and her sister to be like Cecilia who walked confidently[29] into the darkness, trusting that God is present, faithful, and ready to act powerfully in the one who abandons herself to him. Yet the true radicality of her "little way" had not yet come to full formulation.

On September 14, 1894, after the death of their father, Céline finally entered Carmel. She took with her a notebook of quotations that included two Scripture texts that would become crucial catalysts for Thérèse's reflection on childlike abandonment. The texts were Proverbs 9:4, "Who-

---

[25] Thérèse de Lisieux, *Story of a Soul*, 131.

[26] Ibid.

[27] Thérèse de Lisieux, *The Poetry of Saint Thérèse of Lisieux*, trans. Donald Kinney (Washington, DC: Institute of Carmelite Studies, 1996), PN 3.

[28] Thérèse de Lisieux, *Letters 2*, LT 161, 850.

[29] A detail of the legend that impressed Thérèse as demonstrating total and joyful confidence was that "at the wedding festivities Cecilia went apart from the rest and sang in her heart the song of David." See Bertha E. Lovewell, *The Life of Saint Cecilia* (Boston: Lamson, Wolffe, 1898), 29.

ever is a LITTLE ONE, let him come to me," and Isaiah 66:13-12, "As one whom a mother caresses, so will I comfort you; you shall be carried at the breasts, and upon the knees they shall caress you." Conrad de Meester notes that in each of her five major letters written between February and November 1895, Thérèse identifies herself as "your very little sister" (or daughter). In his view, this is evidence that the seed of the "little way" has truly begun to sprout.[30]

Thérèse's "Act of Oblation to Merciful Love"

Meanwhile, in January 1895, Mother Agnes asked Thérèse to begin writing what scholars later termed Manuscript A, chapters one through eight of *Story of a Soul*. At the end of this autobiographical text, Thérèse wrote about making her *Act of Oblation to Merciful Love* on Trinity Sunday, June 9, 1895.[31] She concluded: "Oh! how sweet is the way of Love! How I want to apply myself to doing the will of God always with the greatest self-surrender (*abandon*)!"[32] The Oblation is essentially a testament of Thérèse's understanding of abandonment. It reaches its peak when she exclaims:

> In order to live in one single act of perfect Love, I OFFER MYSELF AS A VICTIM OF HOLOCAUST TO YOUR MERCIFUL LOVE, asking you to consume me incessantly, allowing the waves of *infinite tenderness* shut up within You to overflow into my soul, and that thus I may become a *martyr* of Your *Love*, O my God![33]

In nineteenth-century France, the devotional practice of offering oneself as a "victim of holocaust" was frequent among fervent women who apparently found the language of "victimhood" deeply compelling.[34] This spirituality has roots in Bérulle's controversial ideas about the "vows of

---

[30] De Meester, *The Power of Confidence*, 31–35.

[31] De Meester flags a section in chapter IV of *Story of a Soul* that closely parallels the *Oblation* and was probably written around the same time. Ibid., 178; Thérèse de Lisieux, *Story of a Soul*, 72.

[32] Thérèse de Lisieux, *Story of a Soul*, 181.

[33] Ibid., 277.

[34] Marcel Denis, *La Spiritualité Victimale En France* (Rome: Centre d'Études Génerale, 1981); Paula Kane, " 'She Offered Herself Up': The Victim Soul and Victim Spirituality in Catholicism," *Church History* 71 (2002): 80–119; Giuseppe Manzoni, "Victimale (Spiritualité)," in *Dictionnaire de Spiritualité Ascétique et Mystique, Doctrine et Histoire*, vol. 17 (Paris: G. Beauschesne, 1932), 531–45.

servitude." Stéphane Morgain says that for Bérulle, the purpose of the devotion of servitude was "to place oneself entirely in the hands of Jesus and his sacred humanity." It is a "disappropriation of self, a departure from self, an 'ecstasy' in order to subsist in the deified Humanity." One who makes the vow of servitude, then, no longer acts in one's own being but only under the immediate direction of the Spirit of Jesus.[35] Bérulle also frequently employed the language of "immolation" and "victimhood" to describe Jesus' self-giving in the Eucharist, saying, for example, that the eucharistic act "presents him to the eternal Father in the state of an immolated victim and gives him to human beings in the state of food, truly food and truly victim."[36] Similarly, the nineteenth-century vow of victimhood was an oblation modeled on the Eucharist. According to Manzoni, it implies "a community of life with Christ" manifested in "the *sanctification* (or separation) of the victim, its *oblation* (or offering), its *immolation,* its *transformation,* in order to enter into *communion* of love with God. . . . The veritable substance of the vow of victimhood is oblative love, in union with the reparative oblation of Christ to the Father for the salvation of the world."[37]

In her Oblation, Thérèse draws upon these traditions, yet stamps them with her own mark. Denis notes that she makes a fervent yet simple self-offering rather than going overboard with a full-fledged "vow" as was popular at the time.[38] While many understood the *victimale* devotion primarily in terms of the justice of God demanding victims who beg to endure extreme suffering with Christ in reparation for the sins of the world, Thérèse focused on the mercy of God completely permeating and immolating the victim as a willing participant in God's love pouring out into the world. Although she thanks God for "the grace of making me pass through the crucible of suffering,"[39] she does not ask for suffering but rather for enhanced capacity to hand herself over completely to participation in the action of divine love. This is her understanding of "abandonment."

In conversations recounted in her *Last Conversations* as well as in the beatification process, Thérèse is reported to have described an experience

---

[35] My translation from Morgain, *Pierre de Bérulle et Les Carmelites de France*, 263–64.

[36] Parisot, *L'expérience de Dieu Avec Bérulle*, 75. The quotation is from *Oeuvres de piété*, 280.

[37] My translation from Manzoni, "Victimale (Spiritualité)," 535, 538.

[38] Denis, *La Spiritualité Victimale En France*, 292.

[39] Thérèse de Lisieux, *Story of a Soul*, 277.

occurring a few days after she made the Oblation. Mother Agnes wrote that on July 7, 1897, Thérèse spoke about what had happened that day in June 1895:

> Well, I was beginning the Way of the Cross; suddenly, I was seized with such a violent love for God that I can't explain it except by saying it felt as though I were totally plunged into fire. Oh! What fire and what sweetness at one and the same time! I was on fire with love, and I felt that one minute more, one second more, and I wouldn't be able to sustain this ardor without dying. I understood, then, what the saints were saying about those states which they experienced so often. As for me, I experienced it only once and for one single instant, falling back immediately into my habitual state of dryness.[40]

Fernand Ouellette considers this to have been an instance of the "wound of love . . . a form of the transverberation, remaining always alive, where the fire of heaven, which strikes her without consuming her, maintains Thérèse unceasingly in the field of God as a chosen holocaust."[41] According to this interpretation, which was originally proposed by the Carmelite expert Marie-Eugène of the Child Jesus,[42] this is the moment when Thérèse's act of self-abandonment was definitively accepted by God and made into a permanent state.[43] From then on she has moved out of the realm of human act and aspiration, and into the realm of being totally an instrument of the divine on Earth.

Thérèse's Mature Teaching

If this was a "permanent state," however, it would not turn out to be one of joy and serenity. Ten months later, on April 5, 1896, Thérèse entered into the "night of faith" that would continue until her death in September 1897. During this time she not only lost all consoling awareness of the

---

[40] Thérèse de Lisieux, *Her Last Conversations* (Washington, DC: Institute of Carmelite Studies, 1977), 77.

[41] My translation from Ouellette, *Autres Trajets Avec Thérèse de Lisieux*, 107–8. He notes also that Francis de Sales describes this phenomenon in *Treatise*, Book VI, chap. 14.

[42] Reported in Guy Gaucher, *John and Thérèse: Flames of Love: The Influence of St. John of the Cross in the Life and Writings of St. Thérèse of Lisieux*, trans. Alexandra Plettenberg-Serban (Alba House, 1999), 123–24.

[43] On abandonment as a "state," see De Meester, *The Power of Confidence*, 306.

presence of God, but also endured excruciating temptations against faith. To complete the grim picture, it was a time of terrible and increasing physical suffering as she went through the last stages of death from tuberculosis.[44] Yet her proclamation of her commitment to abandonment continued to grow in clarity and force. In June 1896 she presented her poem, "My Heaven," which included the lines "Total abandon, that is my only law!/ To sleep on his Heart, so close to his Face—/ This is my Heaven!"[45]

Thérèse's most complete and inspired articulation of her matured insight into abandonment and spiritual childhood, however, comes in the letter that became Manuscript B, chapter IX of *Story of a Soul*. On September 8, 1896, while on retreat, Thérèse delivered this letter to her sister Marie (also a Carmelite in Lisieux), who had requested that she recount her "little doctrine."[46] The introduction begins with the assertion that the way to the "Divine Furnace" of love is "the *surrender* [*abandon*] of the little child who sleeps without fear in its Father's arms." She then quotes the Scriptures about "littleness" gleaned from Céline's notebook (as well as others) and summarizes: "Jesus does not demand great actions from us but simply *surrender* and *gratitude*."[47]

The main part of the letter is written as a direct address to Jesus. It includes a soaring meditation on her vast desires, her recognition of utter powerlessness, and her discovery that it is in accepting weakness, littleness, and powerlessness that God's love is freed to pour out unhindered. She writes:

> I am only a child, powerless and weak, and yet it is my weakness that gives me the boldness of offering myself as *VICTIM of Your Love, O Jesus!* . . . Love has chosen me as a holocaust, me, a weak and imperfect creature. Is not this choice worthy of *Love*? Yes, in order that Love be fully satisfied, it is necessary that It lower Itself, and that It lower Itself to nothingness and transform that nothingness into *fire*.[48]

---

[44] On this period of Thérèse's life, see Frederick L. Miller, *The Trial of Faith of St. Therese of Lisieux* (New York: Alba House, 1998); Jean F. Six, *Light of the Night: The Last Eighteen Months of the Life of Thérèse of Lisieux* (London: SCM, 1996); Mary Frohlich, "Desolation and Doctrine in Thérèse of Lisieux," *Theological Studies* 61, no. 2 (June 1, 2000): 261–79.

[45] Thérèse de Lisieux, *Poetry*, PN 32.

[46] Thérèse de Lisieux, *Story of a Soul*, 189.

[47] Ibid., 188.

[48] Ibid., 195.

The last part of Manuscript B is a meditation on the "weak little bird" whose "bold surrender" (*audacieux abandon*) enables it to receive "an even greater fullness of love" than the great eagles whose bigness prevents them from having "the boldness to appear in Your presence, *to fall asleep in front of You.*"[49] Even though Thérèse will not actually use the phrase "little way"[50] until June 1897 when she wrote Manuscript C (chapters X and XI of *Story of a Soul*), its essential ideas are all summed up in this earlier document. Conrad de Meester summarizes them as follows: "the folly of mercy and confidence without limits; the distance from the 'eagles' who do 'great things'; and the confidence of being accepted as a victim and being raised by God even to the point of being united in Love."[51]

While many other texts could be referenced—especially two poems of May 1897 that cry out from the midst of her physical and spiritual despoilation with even more radical testimonies to absolute abandonment[52]—those we have reviewed are sufficient for our purposes.

Deepening the Insight: Roots in John of the Cross

As a Carmelite, Thérèse understood herself as a daughter of Teresa of Avila. She was also a fervent devotee of John of the Cross, whose writings she quoted at least one hundred times (not counting many other conscious and/or unconscious allusions).[53] As already explicated, her lived familial and community contexts bore strong marks of Salesian and Bérullien influence. Yet on the level of literary resourcing and conscious reflection, it was the teachings of John of the Cross that Thérèse chose as her primary spiritual guidance.

In his book on the relation between Thérèse and John of the Cross, Guy Gaucher discusses three points of influence that are particularly helpful in deepening our insight into Thérèse's approach to "abandonment."[54] These are: 1) the relation between hope, desire, emptiness, and "spiritual childhood"; 2) the image of consuming and transforming fire; 3) the aspiration to "die of love."

---

[49] Ibid., 198–99.
[50] Ibid., 207.
[51] De Meester, *The Power of Confidence*, 202.
[52] Thérèse de Lisieux, *Poetry*, PN 51 and PN 52.
[53] Gaucher, *John and Thérèse: Flames of Love*, 155–56.
[54] Ibid., 99–143.

1) In the notebook that Céline brought to Carmel in 1894, Thérèse read this quotation from John of the Cross: "The more God wants to give us, the more He increases our desires, even making the soul empty so that He can refill it with His goods."[55] She would echo it in her *Oblation* a few months later, writing: "I am certain, then, that you will grant my desires; I know, O my God, that *the more you want to give, the more you make us desire.*"[56] Thérèse follows John in celebrating the centrality of desire, as well as in making the link between radical hope and radical privation. For both Carmelites, hope in God's infinite mercy and power, expressed in burning desire, rises to greater and greater intensity as the soul feels itself completely stripped of its own power and understanding.

2) Thérèse also shared with John of the Cross the attraction to the image of the "living flame" as the supreme expression of encounter with God. John's poem "the Living Flame of Love" describes the consummation of the encounter of flame and soul primarily in tender nuptial terms, within which woundedness and death are integral consequences.[57] Thérèse shifts the balance, placing the image strongly within the *victimale* framework of the holocaust of the victim sacrificed for love. We can see this in each of the three major quotations included in the preceding pages, as well as at other key points in her writing. To review, in the *Oblation* Thérèse wrote, "I OFFER MYSELF AS A VICTIM OF HOLOCAUST TO YOUR MERCIFUL LOVE, asking you to consume me incessantly"; describing the subsequent "transverberation" experience she stated, "Suddenly, I was seized with such a violent love for God that I can't explain it except by saying it felt as though I were totally plunged into fire. Oh! What fire and what sweetness at one and the same time! I was on fire with love"; and in Manuscript B she concluded, "Yes, in order that Love be fully satisfied, it is necessary that it lower Itself, and that It lower Itself to nothingness and transform that nothingness into *fire.*"

One additional quotation, drawn from the end of Manuscript C (only a few months before Thérèse's death), will illuminate the connection

---

[55] Ibid., 99ff. Gaucher indicates that this is John of the Cross's "Maxim 45," but this does not match my version of John's writings. Very similar phrasing is repeated in John's Letter 14 to Madre Leonor de San Gabriel.

[56] Thérèse de Lisieux, *Story of a Soul*, 276.

[57] John of the Cross, *Living Flame of Love*, trans. Kieran Kavanaugh and Otilio Rodriguez, rev. ed., *Collected Works of Saint John of the Cross* (Washington, DC: Institute of Carmelite Studies, 1991).

of this image of "fire" with our themes of abandonment and apostolic service:

> If fire and iron had the use of reason, and if the latter said to the other: "Draw me," would it not prove that it desires to be identified with the fire in such a way that the fire penetrate and drink it up with its burning substance and seem to become one with it? Dear Mother, this is my prayer. I ask Jesus to draw me into the flames of His love, to unite me so closely to Him that He live and act in me. I feel that the more the fire of love burns within my heart, the more I shall say: "Draw me," the more also the souls who will approach me (poor little piece of iron, useless if I withdraw from the divine furnace), the more these souls will run swiftly in the odor of the ointments of their Beloved.[58]

In this image perhaps even more than elsewhere, we can see clearly how Thérèse hybridized Bérullien, Carmelite, and nineteenth-century *victimale* spirituality to articulate her experience of the transforming encounter with God and its apostolic impact. As she abandons herself to consumed in the divine furnace, her union with the flame of God attracts and gives energy to others following her along the same path. Like a candle lighting many others, one person's total self-giving leads to the expansive spread of the fire of divine life.[59]

3) The image of the consuming fire of sacrificial holocaust flows directly into the Carmelite tradition of "dying for love."[60] In several places, including her poem "Living on Love," Thérèse expressed this desire explicitly. She wrote:

> Flame of Love, consume me unceasingly. . . .
> Divine Jesus, make my dream come true:
> To die of Love!
> Dying of Love is what I hope for. . . .
> I want to be set on fire with his Love.[61]

---

[58] Thérèse de Lisieux, *Story of a Soul*, 257.

[59] Thérèse de Lisieux, *Her Last Conversations*, 99. July 15, 1897, no. 5.

[60] See Emmanuel Renault, "Le Désire de Mourir Chez Thérèse d'Avila," in *Sainte Thérèse d'Avila* (Colloque Notre-Dame de Vie, 1982), 183–93; Gaucher, *John and Thérèse: Flames of Love*, 131–43.

[61] Thérèse de Lisieux, *Poetry*, 92.

As she lay on her deathbed, Thérèse had a copy of John of the Cross's *Living Flame of Love* by her bedside. She had marked with pencil several passages referring to "dying of love."[62] One of these passages says that the death of holy souls "is accompanied by a sweetness and a marvelous mellowness." As Thérèse lived her last months of agony without any such sweetness, Gaucher suggests that "she distanced herself from the texts of *The Living Flame*" that seemed to suggest that a holy death would be beautiful and sweet.[63] Instead, she identified herself more and more with Jesus on the Cross. In doing this she turned to other parts of John of the Cross's writings, as well as to the story of John's own agonizing death, in which union with Jesus means literally sharing in his pain, abandonment, and annihilation on the cross.

Finally, this is how Thérèse understood her "little way." When her sisters proposed that it would be "beautiful" if she died immediately after receiving communion on the feast of Our Lady of Mount Carmel, she is said to have replied, "Oh, that wouldn't resemble my little way. Would you want me to leave this little way, then, in order to die?"[64] Thérèse's "little way," then, is not at all a promotion of effete and ethereal piety. Rather, it is the determined practice of solidarity with those most physically and spiritually abandoned, accompanied by the conviction that God is preferentially present among them. While Thérèse no doubt originally approached "abandonment" primarily as a practice of the most radical spiritual poverty, in the end she learned that it converges with a spirituality of solidarity with the poorest of the poor.

Dorothy Day's Appropriation of Thérèse's "Little Way"

Dorothy Day was one of the first to recognize this connection between Thérèse's way and a committed life among the poor. When she was young and on fire for social activism, Day disdained Thérèse as insipid, passive, and apolitical. As she matured, however, her view changed. She took note that both in the Pranzini incident and in her encounter with Pope Leo XIII, young Thérèse followed her own firm interior convictions rather

---

[62] Gaucher, *John and Thérèse: Flames of Love*, 134–35.
[63] Ibid., 139.
[64] Thérèse de Lisieux, *Her Last Conversations*, 98.

than the direct orders of male authority figures.[65] Day saw that when Thérèse chose Pranzini as her "child" and remained committed to him to the end, she already began to take risks to stand alongside the "poorest of the poor" as she understood this within her limited social reality.[66]

More importantly, though, Day came to understand Thérèse's Little Way as the spirituality needed by her Catholic Workers, whose calling is different from that of others who work on behalf of the poor. To "serve the poor" often means providing things needed by the poor while oneself remaining in a comfortable and controlling position. The ideal of the Catholic Worker, however, is to surrender comfort and control in order to live as equals with the most degraded of the poor. Day came to understand that the poor, just as they are—many of them broken beyond repair by trauma, illness, or substance abuse—are the present, living face of Christ. They must simply be loved in very mundane, repetitive, seemingly nonheroic acts such as welcoming, listening, feeding, and forgiving.

Living this way sounds simple and yet is actually very difficult because most often nothing changes. Another day, or week, or year, or decade, and the same annoying needs, insoluble crises, and nasty incidents will just keep piling up, relentlessly revealing one's inability to make a difference. Over the long haul the Catholic Worker can only bear this by surrendering his or her own powerlessness to God. Then, as Thérèse discovered, one's smallness can actually become a venue of God's redeeming love. Day said that far from being futile, such "insignificant" acts are a "sacrament of the present moment—of the little way."[67] Hooper sums up Day's view as asserting that in these actions "we participate in God's action to redeem all human beings. In the very action of working, but also of praying, we work with that God of action."[68]

It was important to Day that the Little Way was a community-building practice equally available to everyone, weak or strong, poor or rich, broken or whole. From Day's point of view, Peter Casarella says, Thérèse "fulfilled Peter Maurin's mandate to 'make a society where it is easier for men to be good.'"[69] Bauerschmidt argues that in this way Day is able to

---

[65] Day, *Therese*, 119–20.

[66] These points are discussed in Hooper, "Dorothy Day's Transposition of Thérèse's 'Little Way.'"

[67] Ibid., 85.

[68] Ibid., 86.

[69] Casarella, "Sisters in Doing the Truth," 479.

discover in Thérèse "not an evasion of the political but an alternative politics." The Little Way appears apolitical, he says, because it does not conform to the "violence of statecraft" by which modernity defines politics.[70] In Day's view, the modern state promises a pain-free utopia while actually waging constant war on the poor.[71] When politics is thus defined as the art of violently imposing one's way on those weaker than oneself, Thérèse is indeed apolitical; but if politics means the art of building a community where all—and especially the poorest—can flourish, then Thérèse can be considered a supreme politician.

Conclusion

Casarella sees both Day and Therese presenting the first act of this alternative and radically inclusive politics as "to overcome weariness and discouragement by surrendering control to Christ, the King who reigns from the Cross."[72] It is important to say clearly, however, that this language of "surrender" could be quite problematic if it were applied crudely to human relations (interpersonal and/or political) instead of strictly to the relation with God. To tell the oppressed that the way of holiness is to surrender to those who have more power would be to collude in keeping them locked into the relation of oppression. Thérèse's focus, however, is elsewhere. Her astonishment at the power of surrender into acknowledgement of one's utter poverty is exactly because this move is so counterintuitive. Observing human relations, we learn to expect that the weak are likely to be further abused and that surrender to superior power is destructive of one's human dignity. She discovers, however, that God's way of relating is the opposite of the human norm: God hurries to lovingly accompany the poor and meets surrender with the gift of a share in God's own power. Viewed thus, Therese's spirituality of abandonment is indeed a "little" but empowering way for the poor and for those committed to walk in solidarity with them.

---

[70] Bauerschmidt, "The Politics of the Little Way," 87–88.
[71] Ibid., 90.
[72] Ibid., 89.

Further Reading

Allaire, James. "Dorothy Day and Thérèse of Lisieux." *Spiritual Life* 43 (1997): 195–200.

Bauerschmidt, Frederic C. "The Politics of the Little Way: Dorothy Day Reads Thérèse of Lisieux." In Sandra Yocum Mize and William L Portier. *American Catholic Traditions: Resources for Renewal*, 77–95. Maryknoll, NY: Orbis, 1997.

Carmel of Tours. *Trésor Du Carmel, Ou, Souvenirs de L'ancien Carmel de France*. 2nd ed. 2 vols. Tours: Paul Bouserez, 1879.

Casarella, Peter J. "Sisters in Doing the Truth: Dorothy Day and St. Thérèse of Lisieux." *Communio* 24 (September 1997), 468–98.

Chowning, Daniel J. "The Spirituality of Francis de Sales and Thérèse of Lisieux." *Spiritual Life* 34 (1988), 91–108.

Dahill, Lisa E. "Reading from the Underside of Selfhood: Dietrich Bonhoeffer and Spiritual Formation." *Spiritus* 1, no. 2 (September 1, 2001): 186–203.

Day, Dorothy. *Therese*, Notre Dame, IN: Fides, 1960.

Conrad de Meester. *The Power of Confidence: Genesis and Structure of the Way of Spiritual Childhood of St. Thérèse of Lisieux*. Translated by Susan Conroy. New York: Alba House, 1998.

Denis, Marcel. *La Spiritualité Victimale En France*. Rome: Centre d'Études Génerale, 1981.

de Sales, François. *The Love of God: A Treatise*. Translated by Vincent Kerns. Westminster, MD: Newman, 1962.

Frohlich, Mary. "Desolation and Doctrine in Thérèse of Lisieux." *Theological Studies* 61, no. 2 (June 1, 2000): 261–79.

Gaucher, Guy. *John and Thérèse: Flames of Love: The Influence of St. John of the Cross in the Life and Writings of St. Thérèse of Lisieux*. Translated by Alexandra Plettenberg-Serban. Alba House, 1999.

Hooper, J. Leon. "Dorothy Day's Transposition of Thérèse's 'Little Way.'" *Theological Studies* 63, no. 1 (March 2002), 68–86.

John of the Cross. *Living Flame of Love*. Translated by Kieran Kavanaugh and Otilio Rodriguez. Revised Edition Collected Works of Saint John of the Cross. Washington, DC: Institute of Carmelite Studies, 1991.

Kane, Paula. "'She Offered Herself Up': The Victim Soul and Victim Spirituality in Catholicism." *Church History* 71 (2002): 80–119.

Krumenacker, Yves. *L'école Française de spiritualité: Des mystiques, des fondateurs, des courants et leurs interprètes*. Paris: Cerf, 1998.

Manzoni, Giuseppe. "Victimale Spiritualité." In *Dictionnaire de spiritualité ascétique et mystique, doctrine et histoire*, 17:531–45. Paris: G. Beauschesne, 1932.

Miller, Frederick L. *The Trial of Faith of St. Therese of Lisieux*. New York: Alba House, 1998.

Morgain, Stéphane-Marie. *Pierre de Bérulle et les Carmelites de France: La querelle du gouvernement 1583-1629*. Paris: Cerf, 1995.

———. "Pierre de Bérulle et Madeleine de Saint-Joseph: Une communion au service du Carmel de France." *Teresianum* 40 (1989): 45–85.

Ouellette, Fernand. *Autres trajets avec Thérèse de Lisieux*. Québec: Fides, 2001.

Parisot, Roger, ed. *L'expérience de Dieu avec Bérulle*. Fides, 1999.

Piat, Stéphane-Joseph. *Histoire d'une famille: Une ecole de sainteté, le foyer où s'épanoit Sainte Thérèse de l'Enfant Jésus*. 4th ed. Office Central de Lisieux, 1946.

Renault, Emmanuel. "Le désire de mourir cChez Thérèse d'Avila." In *Sainte Thérèse d'Avila*, 183–93. Colloque Notre-Dame de Vie, 1982.

Renda, Frances, ed. *A Call to Deeper Love: The Family Correspondence of Saint Thérèse of the Child Jesus, 1863-1885: Blessed Zélie and Louis Martin*. Translated by Ann Connors Hess. Staten Island, NY: St. Pauls, 2011.

Six, Jean F. *Light of the Night: The Last Eighteen Months of the Life of Thérèse of Lisieux*. London: SCM, 1996.

Thérèse de Lisieux. *Her Last Conversations*. Washington, DC: Institute of Carmelite Studies, 1977.

———. *Letters of Saint Thérèse of Lisieux, Volume 2, 1890-1897*. Translated by John Clarke. Institute of Carmelite Studies, 1988.

———. *The Poetry of Saint Thérèse of Lisieux*. Translated by Donald Kinney. Washington, DC: Institute of Carmelite Studies, 1996.

———. *Story of a Soul: The Autobiography of Saint Thérèse of Lisieux*. Translated by John Clarke. 3rd ed-. Washington, DC: ICS Publications, 1996.

Wright, Wendy M. "A Salesian Pentecost: Thérèse of Lisieux, Léonie Aviat, and Salesian Tradition." *Studies in Spirituality* 12 (2002): 156–77.

CHAPTER TEN

Our Perennial Fascination with Thérèse of Lisieux

Ronald Rolheiser, OMI

I am done with great things and big plans, great institutions and big
success. I am for those tiny, invisible loving human forces that work
from individual to individual, creeping through the crannies of the
world like so many rootlets, or like the capillary oozing of water,
which, if given time, will rend the hardest monument of pride.

—William James

Jesus has not given me an indifferent heart!

—Thérèse of Lisieux, *Story of a Soul*

Thérèse's Capacity to Intrigue

Few persons, in recent centuries, have fascinated the religious mind
as has Thérèse of Lisieux. Saints, generally speaking, are not very popular
today. Yet her popularity continues. What is interesting too about her
popularity is that it cuts across many lines, appealing to persons of all
ages, every kind of religious persuasion, and every kind of academic
background. What accounts for this astonishing phenomenon? What is
there about Thérèse and her writings that so captivates and intrigues?

The question of Thérèse's capacity to intrigue all genres of persons is
important because, in trying to answer it, we will, I believe, uncover the
heart of what she was all about, both in her person and in her teaching.
If we can name more clearly what about her captures the heart so strongly,
we will, I believe, be in a better position to articulate her spirituality.

What does make her so intriguing? There have been younger saints, gentler saints, and more heroic saints, but never more popular ones, at least not in recent centuries. What makes Thérèse so special? Thérèse of Lisieux fascinates us and has a rare power to truly and healthily fire both our religious and our romantic imaginations, for three interpenetrating reasons. First, she is a child mystic, the Anne Frank of the spiritual life. Second, she is a woman of extraordinary paradox and complexity. And, third, she has that rare power to touch the previously-touched part inside of us. What is curious is that, most often, we consciously relate to Thérèse only through the first of these three, the child mystic. However, even then, unconsciously, what ultimately captivates us is her other two dimensions, her extraordinary complexity and her power to touch what is deepest in us. All of this, however, needs further explication.

What Is So Special about Thérèse?

1) She is the Anne Frank of the spiritual life. Someone once said that if you want to understand the real tragedy of the Second World War you can read a thousand books on it—or you can read *The Diary of Anne Frank* where you will see, indeed feel, what war does to the human soul. The same might be said about Thérèse of Lisieux and the spiritual life. You can read a thousand books about how precious a human soul is before God and how, because of this, a soul should respond—or you can read Thérèse's *Story of a Soul.*

Thérèse of Lisieux might be called the Anne Frank of the spiritual life. In both Anne Frank and Thérèse you get to drink from a clear, pure spring. You get to see, and feel, deep realities through the prism of a child's innocence, a child's dreams, a child's simplicity, a child's still uncursed enthusiasm, and a child's purity. Few things have the power to touch the heart as deeply as that, and to trigger piety, both good and bad.[1]

---

[1] Because Thérèse died so young and because her diaries express so much the purity and the innocence of a child (and, in her case, all of this coupled with the tragic loss of her mother), it is no accident that a piety has grown up around her that has unfortunately, but effectively, frightened off many persons. For too many people, devotion to Thérèse of Lisieux is understood to be a drink from a cup of sugar—sickening in its sweetness. That is a tragedy for many reasons, but, in a manner of speaking, it comes with the turf. Her life is ideal putty to the pious imagination. Hence serious studies of her must always do a certain hermeneutic of "de-encrustment." On the other hand, however, her capacity

Both Anne Frank and Thérèse of Lisieux have that rare power to inflame the romantic imagination. In them, we get the child-mystic, the Christ-child, instructing the elders in the temple. We are always intrigued by this. It triggers an archetype, though not always a mature one, within us.[2] However, we would do no justice to either Thérèse or Anne Frank if we, naively, thought that what makes their diaries so powerful is their simple innocence. Many children are innocent, have a deep experience of God and of love, and yet their writings or crude drawings inspire no one, save their own mothers. What sets Thérèse and Anne Frank apart? What gives their diaries the power to fire the imagination of millions?

First, they are both great artists. In both of them, we see, not just a child's purity but also an artist's complexity and an artist's talent for aesthetic and transparent expression. Both of their diaries are rare works of art.[3] Many of us keep diaries, and all of us have deep experiences, but few of us are great artists. Thérèse and Anne Frank are among those few and it is for this reason, as much as for their innocence and depth, that their writing so powerfully triggers certain things within us. That is what good art does.

---

to fire piety has its upside. A number of religious analysts, including Karl Rahner, Eric Mascall, and Ernst Käsemann, have, looking at the crisis of belief in our culture and the agnosticism of our daily consciousness, suggested that the churches which have a devotional life, piety, will have the best chance of survival. As Rahner once put it: the day will soon be here when we will either be a mystic or an unbeliever. Piety is the "poor man's" mysticism.

[2] Scholars who study archetypal symbols and energy tell us that we have four basic archetypal energies, viz. King/Queen, Warrior, Magus, Lover. And we have both a healthy and an unhealthy (adolescent) intrigue with the adolescent expressions of these. Hence there is a perennial intrigue with the child prodigy, the hero, the trickster, and the romantic, i.e., the adolescent expressions of mature energy (the adolescent King/Queen = the Christ Child; the adolescent Warrior = the hero; the adolescent Magus = the Trickster; and the adolescent Lover = the Romantic). Thus it is natural to have a certain (immature) intrigue with the Christ-child prodigy who is instructing the elders.

[3] The philosopher Louis Dupré, in his classic work on religious symbol, *The Other Dimension*, normatively defines what makes for true religious art. For him, something is a work of religious art (a book, a piece of music, a statue) if it brings together two things: (i) it has its origins in a true and a profound religious experience, and (ii) it has been given real aesthetic expression. Thérèse's writings, especially *Story of a Soul*, fit this description admirably; indeed *Story of a Soul* can serve as a paradigm. She had a profound religious experience (of preciousness before God) and she was a great artist (she gave rare aesthetic expression to this experience).

However, beyond the truth of that, Thérèse is more than the Anne Frank of the spiritual life. We are, admittedly, intrigued by her innocence, but we are, I submit, even more intrigued by her complexity. There are more dimensions in Thérèse than there are in the young Anne Frank. She is a rare combination of paradoxes and opposites and it is this intriguing near-schizophrenia that lays the real kindling to the fires of the heart.

2) She is a rare combination of opposites. Thérèse is so fascinating because, in her, you get something beyond the child-mystic—namely, that rare combination of paradoxes and opposites seen only in great souls.[4]

As we will try to show, hers was a soul formed by great love and great loss, great simplicity and great complexity, great restlessness and great single-mindedness. It is impossible to understand Thérèse in her person, in her message, and in her appeal to people, without grasping this combination of opposites, this radical paradox, within her. Equally, we also need to understand this to extricate Thérèse from a certain encrusting within an unhealthy piety. She was no mere child saint, the little girl, the "puella," throwing kisses to a hardened, cynical world, as her popular persona unfortunately often makes her out to be. She is a rare mentor of the soul. However, to understand that, we must also understand that combination of opposites that constellated within her.

When you talk about Thérèse of Lisieux, everything must be continually qualified with the phrase, "on the one hand—on the other hand." This is because, while her way might be called "the little way" and exhibits a radical simplicity, she herself was not very simple at all. Her writings and her person always manifest a certain double persona. A richness, a near-contradiction, and a series of paradoxes touch us from various angles and do not let us categorize her too quickly. The mature Thérèse had a rare combination of opposites. Understanding this can help us understand why Thérèse is so intriguing to us. We might begin to describe her as follows.

---

[4] You see this, for example, in people like Socrates, Aristotle, and St. Augustine and, as a prime analogate of course, in Jesus. Great souls are large enough to hold, in tension, near opposites and that is why their disciples are usually not up to the task of faithfully following them and, instead, invariably oversimplify and distort their master's teachings. That is also why someone once coined the expression: Consistency is the product of small minds. That is an exaggeration, of course, but it can help us understand the paradox that lies so deeply in great souls, including that of Thérèse of Lisieux.

The doted-on child . . . who had the tragic childhood. First, to understand the adult Thérèse you must understand her unique childhood. As a child she was, at one and the same time, the doted-on child who also had a tragic childhood. On the one hand, few children have ever been loved as purely, and valued as much, as Thérèse was as a child. Her family literally doted on her. She was their little "Queen" and she was always treated as such. Her every joy, fear, tear, and dream was noticed, valued, chronicled, and often even photographed. She was a very attractive child, physically and psychologically, and this also helped. Her family so loved her and cared for her that at age eleven she was unable to comb her own hair—everything had always been done for her. Also, her family both recognized and acknowledged her specialness from the very beginning. She was her father's favorite and her mother regularly wrote to her relatives about little Thérèse's exceptional character.

Added to all this love is the fact that her family itself was exceptional. Both her father and mother are being considered for canonization—as three or four of her sisters and a couple of her cousins might also be. On this score, she certainly did not draw a short straw.

In essence, Thérèse was the opposite of the abused child. Few persons, in childhood, were ever as loved and valued as purely and affectionately as was Thérèse. This left her with an exceptionally strong self-image and an exceptionally healthy concept of God as loving and valuing us. It helped form an outstanding soul who could later write: "I knew then that if I was loved on earth, I was also loved in heaven."[5] She would remain always the princess, the little girl, the "puella"—knowing that she was loveable and loved.

However, on the other hand, her childhood was marked by exceptional tragedy. She was, in effect, three times orphaned and this so hurt her that, at age nine, she went into a clinical depression from which she almost died.

When Thérèse was born, her mother already had breast cancer and was unable to nurse her. She was a sickly child and the family, fearing she might die, gave her, two months after her birth, over to a wet nurse, a peasant woman who nursed little Thérèse with milk, love, and a very healthy family environment. Thérèse bonded with her as she would with her mother. However, at the age of fourteen months, she was returned to

---

[5] Thérèse of Lisieux, *Story of a Soul*, 93.

her own mother and family. Much has been written about how traumatic this must have been, a child of fourteen months switching families, despite the fact that her own family was so loving and gifted. She was, in effect, orphaned at fourteen months.

However, she soon bonded to Zelie, her real mother, and began to blossom in that extraordinary love that her family showered upon her. But this too was not to last. When she was four-and-one-half years old, and again secure in a network of loving relationships, her mother died. She then bonded to her older sister, Pauline, then sixteen, as a daughter to a mother. This too was to be fractured. When Thérèse was nine, Pauline left the Martin home to enter the Carmelite monastery. This literally shattered Thérèse. Within a couple of months of Pauline's leaving, Thérèse fell into a severe depression—within which she hyperventilated, lay at the edges of a massive nervous breakdown, and fell physically ill to the point where everyone, doctors and her family alike, resigned themselves to the fact that she would die.

These events, among others, helped form a soul that was oversensitive and old before its time. Hence, despite all the love and affection she was showered with, as a child, Thérèse found it difficult to do the normal things of a child—make friends, play games, tease, be carefree. Reflecting back, seeing herself at age ten, she writes:

> My friends were too worldly; they knew too well how to ally the joys of this earth to the service of God. They didn't think about death enough, and yet death had paid its visit to a great number of those whom I knew, the young, the rich, the happy.[6]

These are quite some thoughts for a ten-year-old, as are the ones she recounts in the famous exchange with one of her teachers. Around age seven or eight, one of her teachers asked her what she did every Thursday afternoon, an afternoon on which there were no classes. Thérèse replied: "I think." Her teacher asked her: "And what do you think about?" Thérèse replied: "I think about God, about life, about ETERNITY. . . . *I think!*"[7]

Thérèse had a childhood of exceptional love and exceptional tragedy. These formed her soul in such a way that she became a woman of deep

---

[6] Ibid., 73.
[7] Ibid., 74. The emphases are her own.

sensitivity and exceptional complexity. She would, throughout her whole life, exhibit both that love and that tragedy and, for this reason, she always remained a unique combination of the fairy-princess, Tinkerbell, and the archetypal wisdom woman, Sophia.

The archetypal child, Tinkerbell . . . but who is Sophia, the crone, the wise, white-haired, old woman. Second, to understand her, Thérèse always remained the child who would end every letter she wrote with the words, "I kiss you with my whole heart",[8] even as she was ever the white-haired, adult, crone, Sophia, who could tell us things like:

> It's not death that will come in search of me, it's God.[9] I think we have to be very careful not to seek ourselves; for we can get a broken heart that way.[10]

> I felt it more valuable to speak to God rather than to speak about Him, for there is so much self-love intermingled with spiritual conversations.[11]

> There are no miracles, no raptures, no ecstasies—only service.[12]

Thérèse was always the archetypal child, Tinkerbell, protesting her youth and littleness, even as she left no doubt that she had already made friends with her mortality and that her hair had whitened through an aging that is born of pain. Given her childhood, it is not surprising that Tinkerbell and Sophia were so married inside her and that everything she says bears the mark of both.

The peasant . . . but who is the artist. Third, Thérèse had little formal education. As a child, she had been too sensitive to stay for long in normal school and her father had, at a point, hired a tutor for her. This was a bit of a hit-and-miss affair and, although she was obviously very bright, she did not have consistent, sustained classes. Moreover, she left home and school for the Carmelite convent at age fifteen. Hence, in terms of formal

---

[8] She uses this expression, and other similar ones, countless times, but for just one example, see her letter to Pauline of March 1, 1884: *General Correspondence*, vol. 1 (Washington, DC: ICS Publications, 1982 ed.), 191.

[9] Thérèse of Lisieux, *Last Conversations* (Washington, DC: ICS Publications, 1977 ed.), 41.

[10] Ibid., 111.

[11] Ibid., 87.

[12] Ibid., 235.

education, she had the rough equivalent to what we would today call an elementary school education. And this shows. Among other things, she had trouble spelling correctly. More important than the lack of much formal education, however, is the fact that she had, in a manner of speaking, a peasant's heart. By temperament she was innocent, pious, nonintellectual, always childlike, and radiated a simplicity bordering on naiveté.

But, as always with Thérèse, there is "on the other hand." Within all that simplicity and inside that peasant's heart, she was, at the same time, a natural artist, with all the complexity, insight, and torment of personality that this brings. She was an exceptionally gifted writer, faulty spelling notwithstanding. Her language and construction exhibit remarkable color, verve, and transparency. Her diary is, first of all, a work of beauty. It does a whole lot more than communicate a bunch of biographical data. It inflames the heart, as does all good art, and, understood (as all good art should be) within the forms of its time, it is also devoid of the sentimentality and saccharine quality that it is often accused of and which lesser works fall into. *Story of a Soul* is not an oversweet holy card, either in content or in style. There is in it the simplicity of the peasant but also the tortured complexity of the artist. Thérèse was both, peasant and artist. Maybe that helps explain why, today, she has been named a Doctor of the Church.

The martyr who is detached from the world . . . but who has an excessive love for her family and the beauty of this world. Fourth, Thérèse manifests a similar paradox to that of Pierre Teilhard de Chardin. In his spiritual masterpiece, *Le Milieu Divin*, Teilhard describes himself as waking up in this world on fire with two great loves, love of God and love of the world. He experiences each as an incurable wound. For Teilhard, a sense of God can take your breath away—but so too can the beauty and power of this world.

Thérèse has the same great paradox within her makeup. On the one hand, she is clearly the detached, religious ascetic whose own needs always take second place to the higher demands of faith. From the time she is a very young child until the day she dies, her perspective is always colored, indeed it is dominated, by her sense of God and the next life. She has no major regrets about leaving her home, giving up all dreams of husband and children, giving up all worldly ambitions, and ultimately even in dying at age twenty-four. She lives, and happily so, in this world within a certain holy detachment. God is central and everything else, including all personal desires and ambitions, must take a back seat to that.

However, Thérèse does not exactly radiate the lack of energy and joyless indifference of someone clinically depressed, nor indeed the negative attitude toward the joys of this life that is sometimes seen in unbalanced religious figures. She is more like Teilhard. The beauty of this world, and the love that this world offers, also took her breath away (even if it never managed to fully derail her). Thus, for all her detachment at one level, she was excessively attached to her family, needing almost daily letters and gifts to sustain herself. She also loved the beautiful things of this earth, and made no apologies for that fact. She loved anything pretty—flowers, objects, clothing—and she loved herself to look pretty, albeit she never lost a proper perspective on this concern.

In this matter, detachment and attachment, Thérèse was, like in everything else, a mixture of opposites. Reading her will help you see the preciousness of everything human, especially of human love, even as it also helps you see its relativity.

The congenital loner . . . but who is ultimately able to embrace the whole world. Fifth, Thérèse was, by nature, a very lonely person. People familiar with her have pointed this out, not only because it is evident in her biography and letters, but also by studying photographs of her. We have many such photos and always, in every one of them, even when she is with her family or community, Thérèse is, in some deep way, profoundly alone. There was a congenital loneliness within her that all the affection in the world could never really penetrate.

Thérèse's loneliness had a particular quality to it. Where Thérèse was lonely was not so much because she lived, celibate and single, in a monastery within which there were long periods of silence and where the rules forbade most kinds of intimacy and contact. Her loneliness was more of a moral nature. She suffered from moral loneliness.

What is this moral loneliness? Inside of each of us there is a part of our being that might be called our moral soul. It is that place where we feel most strongly about the right and wrong of things and where all that is most precious to us is cherished, guarded, and held. It is also the place that feels violated when it is not sufficiently honored and respected. It is in this deep inner place that we, ultimately, feel most alone. More deeply than our longing for a sexual partner, we long for moral affinity—that is, for someone to visit us in that deep part of ourselves where all that is most precious to us is cherished and guarded. Our deepest longing is for someone to "sleep with" morally. This is particularly true for very sensitive souls.

From the time that Thérèse was a little girl she was out of place on the playground, different from her peers, and spent her leisure hours thinking about "God and eternity." Thus, Thérèse was fiercely lonely, morally lonely, a pilgrim in every sense of that word. This quality of loneliness is everywhere present in her person and in her writings, and is clearly one of the reasons why her *Story of a Soul* speaks so deeply to many millions of people.

Yet, and this is a paradox that borders on contradiction, Thérèse was a person who also embraced everyone who ever had contact with her and, in a more abstract yet real way, everyone in the whole world. Thérèse was always alone and yet she was intensely in community. She stood apart from others and yet was envied by others for the way she was present inside of the group. This was true for each three of her families—her blood family, the Martins; her faith family, the Carmelites; and her universal family, the world. In each of these families, she was somehow distant and alone, and yet she was the paradigm for community within each. Thus, for example, her relationship to the "world family" manifests this. Thérèse was tucked away in a remote monastery and when she died she was probably known by less than two hundred people. Yet, even before she died, as she slept alone on her celibate cot, the world lay at the center of her heart and her heart lay at the center of the world's heart. Today, of course, she is a household name, known and loved by millions of persons, and she is the patron of world missions. Thérèse was the loner who ultimately embraced the world. Both aspects, her loneliness and her intimacy with everything and everybody, color every page of her writings.

The restless, driven spirit . . . but who does, as does the saint, will-the-one-thing. Sixth, Thérèse was by nature not just lonely, she was also deeply restless. When you have a heart the size of the Grand Canyon, not many things in this life will satisfy you. Thérèse was, like all restless people, tormented by constant yearning. She wanted everything, as a famous incident in her childhood so well illustrates. One day her older sister, Leonie, came into the room where Thérèse and her other sister, Celine, were playing. Leonie was carrying a basket filled with colorful balls of string and pretty pieces of cloth. She asked each of her younger sisters to choose one item that they could keep. Celine chose a ball of wool. As for

Thérèse . . . well, she just took the whole basket and walked off with the words: "I choose all!"[13] That was typical of her temperament. She was a person so driven by restlessness that the world was never enough for her. Yet, in the end, Thérèse could make an obscure monastery be enough.

Søren Kierkegaard once defined a saint by saying that a saint is someone who can will the one thing—God. Thérèse, despite the torment of a restless heart, was able to do that and to sustain it. She felt within herself, as soon as she came to consciousness (as she honestly acknowledges), the sense that she was destined for glory. Yet, she could live life in a way where she could be satisfied to say: "My glory is to remain a hidden glory and Carmel is the place where God has chosen to hide me."[14]

Tangential to this, Thérèse had another remarkable paradox within her. She could, as theologian Hans Urs von Balthasar once phrased it, consciously self-canonize and yet never become a narcissist.[15] For all her seeking for glory, she could in all truth say on her deathbed: "I'm no egoist; it's God whom I love, not myself!"[16]

Thérèse of Lisieux is a study in contrasts. What makes her so intriguing is the rare complexity that is only found in great souls.

3) She is attuned to the preciousness of the human soul before God and has, concomitantly, the capacity to touch that previously-touched part inside of us. Thérèse is the Anne Frank of the spiritual life, a true artist, and a woman of extraordinary complexity. However, at the end of the day, that is not the real reason why she has the power to touch hearts so deeply. What ultimately makes her writings so powerful and rightly makes her a Doctor of the Church?

Thérèse is powerful because her writings touch that part of us that has previously been touched. That is obviously a very curious expression. What is meant by it? Inside each of us, beyond what we can name, each of us has a dark memory of having once been touched and caressed by hands far gentler than our own. That caress has left a permanent mark— the imprint of a love so tender and good that its memory becomes a prism

---

[13] Thérèse of Lisieux, *Story of a Soul*, 27.

[14] Ibid., 58 and 72 (for her sense of being born for and destined for glory).

[15] See Raymond Gawronski, *Word and Silence—Hans Urs Von Balthasar and the Spiritual Encounter Between East and West* (Grand Rapids, MI: Eerdmans, 1995), 206.

[16] Thérèse of Lisieux, *Last Conversations*, 114.

through which we see everything else. This brand lies beyond conscious memory but forms the center of the heart and soul.

This is not an easy concept to explain without sounding sentimental. Perhaps the old myths and legends capture it best when they say that, before being born, each soul is kissed by God and then goes through life always, in some dark way, remembering that kiss and measuring everything it experiences in relation to that original sweetness. To be in touch with your heart is to be in touch with this primordial kiss, with both its preciousness and its meaning.

What exactly is being said here? Within each of us, at that place where all that is most precious takes its root, there is an inchoate sense of having once been touched, caressed, loved, and valued in a way that is beyond anything we have ever consciously experienced. In fact, all the goodness, love, value, and tenderness we experience in life fall short precisely because we already know something deeper. When we feel frustrated, angry, betrayed, violated, or enraged it is, in fact, because our outside experience is so different from what we already hold dear inside.

We all have this place, a place in the heart, where we hold all that is most precious and sacred to us. From that place our own kisses issue forth, as do our tears. It is the place we carefully guard from others, yet the place where we would most want others to come. It is the place where we are the most deeply alone and yet the place of intimacy. It is the place of innocence and yet the place where we are violated. It is the place of our compassion and the place of our rage. In that place we are holy. There we are temples of God, sacred spaces of truth and love. It is there too that we bear God's image.

However, this must be understood: The image of God within us is not to be thought of as some beautiful icon stamped inside of the soul. No. The image of God in us is energy, fire, memory—especially the memory of a touch so tender and loving that its goodness and truth become the energy and prism through which we see everything. Thus we recognize goodness and truth outside of us precisely because they resonate with something that is already inside of us. Things "touch our hearts" when they touch us here. It is because we have already been touched and caressed that we seek for a soulmate, for someone to join us in this tender space.

We measure everything in life by how it touches this place. Why do certain experiences touch us so deeply? Do not our hearts burn within us in the presence of any truth, love, goodness, or tenderness that is genuine and deep? Is not all knowledge simply a waking up to something we already know? Is not all love simply a question of being respected for something we already are? Are not the touch and tenderness that bring ecstasy nothing other than the stirring of deep memory? Are not the ideals that inspire hope only the reminder of words somebody has already spoken to us? Does not our desire for innocence (and innocent means "not wounded") mirror some primal unwounded place deep within us? And when we feel violated, is it not because someone has irreverently entered the sacred inside us?

When we are in touch with this memory and respect its sensitivities, then we are feeling our souls. At those times, faith, hope, and love will spring up in us, and both joy and tears will flow through us pretty freely. We will be constantly stabbed by the innocence and beauty of children, and pain and gratitude will, alternately, bring us to our knees. That is what it means to be recollected, to inchoately remember, to feel the memory of God in us. That memory is what both fires our energy and provides us with a prism through which to see and understand.

Thérèse of Lisieux, in her person and in her writings, is powerful because she touches that previously-touched part of us. What her life and her writings do is help us remember that primordial kiss of God and in that memory we know how unique, precious, and loved we are. Reading Thérèse softens our hearts (without softening our heads, as happens with saccharine piety) and helps melt the cynicism, bitterness, and callousness that accrues with age and deadens the memory of once having been caressed by hands more gentle than our own.

What Thérèse brings us can be understood too by comparing it to its opposite, the life of someone who has never been valued or, worse, has been positively abused. Imagine someone who is conceived and born without being wanted, who lives in a home where he is considered only a burden and another mouth to feed, and who is constantly told in word and in attitude that he is worthless. During his youth and as an adult, he never once is loved and valued for who he is and never once experiences what Jesus felt when he saw the heavens open and heard the voice of his Father say: "This is my beloved child in whom I take delight!" Never once in all his life does anyone touch that previously-touched area within him where God once kissed his soul. His whole life is experienced as an unwanted accident, as something unimportant, as something useless, and as just one unnoticed, passing phenomenon among one hundred billion others. That would be the antithesis of Thérèse of Lisieux.

This would be the case with someone who, as a young girl, had suffered the ravages of sexual abuse. What has happened in the abuse is that this person has been radically violated (rather than kissed again) in that deep previously-touched spot. That action has told her categorically that what is most important to her is not important and that she is disposable.

This too is the antithesis of Thérèse of Lisieux. Her life was the opposite. Despite being painfully orphaned and falling into clinical depression because of loss, Thérèse, like Jesus, heard very clearly, and pretty constantly, the words: "You are my beloved child in whom I take delight!" Again and again, that previously-touched part of her was gently kissed and she was made to know that she was precious, loved, valued, and unique among a hundred million.

The net result of being loved so specially was not that this made her an egoist (which is the result of improper, not excess, love). It had the opposite effect. It attuned her to the preciousness of the human soul and gave what she wrote about life and about her own life its great medicinal power. Thérèse has power to touch us deeply because she was herself deeply touched. She has such great power to point out to us our own preciousness because she knew herself to be precious. She shows us our uniqueness because her own experience of being so uniquely valued made it evident to her how unique each person is before God. Indeed, this is also what makes her a doctor of the soul. The stirring of that dark memory inside of us heals as nothing else can.

Ultimately, Thérèse's appeal comes from this and it is on this that scholars and theologians might well turn to her for some help. She understood how precious is the human soul and, being an artist, she was able to give rare articulation to this.

Equally, being loved so uniquely as a child did not, as is the common supposition in these things, create a spoiled child. On the contrary, being so loved and valued, Thérèse realized, very early, what was then asked of her in return in terms of response—namely, fidelity, self-sacrifice, and boldness before God.

Moreover, and this is of critical importance for understanding her spirituality, Thérèse's experience of being loved so specially, lies at the basis of her "little way." Looking at her life, Thérèse was able to conclude that, being so loved on earth, she was also obviously loved by God in heaven. Her experience helped her to know the truth of Jesus' statement that no hair falls from one's head or tear from one's eye, except that it is noticed by God.

However, from the time of her "conversion", at the age of thirteen, when she overcame her hypersensitivity in her Christmas experience, leaving, as she put it, her childhood behind her, she began more and more to notice that what was true for her was less true for others. Their joys, pains, and dreams were not being noticed. Her mission then became that of "noticing the unnoticed drops of blood flowing out of the wounds of Christ".

Thus, in the essential metaphor that undergirds her "little way", she writes:

> One Sunday, looking at a picture of Our Lord on the Cross, I was struck by the blood flowing from one of his divine hands. I felt a pang of great sorrow when thinking this blood was falling on the ground without anyone's hastening to gather it up. I was resolved to remain in spirit at the foot of the Cross and to receive its dew.[17]
>
> Oh, I don't want this precious blood to be lost. I shall spend my life gathering it up for the good of souls.[18]
>
> To live from love is to dry Your Face.[19]

What Thérèse means by this metaphor is quite complex, and is more fully explored in the chapter by Mary Frohlich. However, suffice to say here that the core of Thérèse's spirituality is not so much doing little hidden things for Christ as it is noticing the unnoticed drops of blood within the body of Christ. That is, it is noticing and valuing fully the unique and precious quality of other people's stories, tears, pains, and joys.

Conclusion

Thérèse intrigues for many reasons. She is the Anne Frank of the spiritual life and she manifests a rare and a most fascinating complexity. That alone would suffice to explain her popularity. But it would not explain

---

[17] Thérèse of Lisieux, *Journey of a Soul*, 99.
[18] Thérèse of Lisieux, *Last Conversations*, 126.
[19] Ibid., 190.

why her person, her story, and her writings are so powerful and so healing. Thérèse is powerful because her person, her story, and her writings touch us in that previously-touched place inside of us. Thérèse helps stir God's kiss.

EPILOGUE

Fragments of Our Conversation—
Some Poignant Echoes

Ronald Rolheiser, OMI

After Jesus' disciples had fed the crowd with the five loaves and two fish, Jesus asked them to gather up the fragments that were left scattered on the ground, so that nothing should be lost. They gathered up twelve baskets of fragments.

At the end of a conference within which many rich loaves and fishes were shared, what fragments need to be picked up and highlighted?

What follows is a collage of pithy sayings that left echoes long after the speakers' actual voices had faded.

Echoes of Eugène de Mazenod

- Comfort a suffering church.
- Everything that honors Mary must honor Jesus.
- We must lead people to become *human*, then *Christian*, then *saints*.
- Live with the pain of the church, like a mother with her children.
- See the world through the eyes of the Crucified Savior.
- My advice is to read every day a chapter of Francis de Sales's *Introduction to the Devout Life*."

Echoes of François de Sales

- Spirituality needs a turn toward gentleness.

197

- Don't obsess about heresy and sin.
- Loose morals among Catholics are not the cause of Protestantism.
- Do not practice hatred for the body.
- *The Song of Songs* reveals God's desire to be in intimacy with us.
- God is love and consequently is found in places of concord.
- We should not be shocked by the impurities of the world.
- God's mercy is infinitely stronger than all the sins of the world.
- Not all kinds of zeal are born equal!
- Our bodies need gentleness, like Balaam's donkey.
- Spirituality needs to be framed in the language of the heart.
- The exchange of hearts takes place through the practice of the little virtues: gentleness, littleness, hiddenness, humility.

Echoes of Cardinal Pierre de Bérulle

- In the incarnation, God is adored in a new adoration.
- The heart of the Virgin is the first altar.
- Don't ever think that your sins are so great that God's mercy cannot purify them.

Echoes of Jean-Jacques Olier

- Lord, clothe us with yourself so that we may be nothing in ourselves.

Echoes of Jean Eudes

- May never a day go by without my suffering something for love of you.

Echoes of Jean-Pierre de Caussade

- It is only your heart that must be changed.
- Holiness consists in willing all that God wills for us.

Echoes of Thérèse of Lisieux

- Charity is my only star.

- It is more valuable to speak to God than to speak about God.

- Sanctity does not consist in this or that practice, but in making ourselves humble and hidden in God's arms.

Echoes of Charles de Foucauld

- Lord, I put myself into your hands with infinite confidence.

- Contemplate the divine presence hidden in the other, the foreigner, the stranger, the forgotten, the abandoned one.

Echoes of Vincent de Paul

- Honor the times of weariness in the life of Jesus.

- God is equally served by both sexes.

- In taking our faith to the streets: *For a monastery, use the houses of the sick; for an enclosure, use obedience; for a grate, use fear of God; for a veil, use modesty; and for profession, use continual confidence.*

- We must not flatter ourselves by the warmth of our imaginations. God asks for concrete deeds.

Some Final Echoes from Our Speakers

- This is the best of times and this is the worst of times.

- How do we preach self-renunciation to a generation intrigued with "selfies"?

- Is there a fragile coexistence between breakdown and breakthrough?

- For transformation we first need a dismantling.

- In our worst crises of division and despondency, driven to our knees, we need to ask God: What is love now?

- Don't be soft on doctrine, but be pastoral within that truth.

- It's our baptismal identity that counts.

- Each syllable of Scripture is a particle of the Body of Christ.

- Mary's womb is a tabernacle.
- This is not so much a school or a theory, but *a way.*
- I wish you many crosses in your life!

- And twelve key words summarize the French School of Spirituality: *incarnation, adoration, service, self-renunciation, abandonment, surrender, mission, gentleness, littleness, hiddenness, the poor, Mary.*

INDEX